Praise for *Appalachia Bare*

To embark upon reading the book *Appalachia Bare* is to take the first step in a journey through Appalachian literature, folkways, and folklore, through the language, loves, and habits of a region and its people, a culture still holding to its European heritage, especially the ways of European Highlanders with their fierce pride and determination. The collection features the prose—fiction and scholarly nonfiction—and poetry of *Appalachian Bare Online Magazine* co-founders Edward Francisco and Delonda Shown Anderson. Francisco brings firsthand accounts of conversations with such well-known Appalachian literary figures as George Brosi and George Scarbrough, along with the results of his research into other prominent writers such as Jesse Stuart and James Still. Anderson's essay on "What We Don't Do Anymore" reminisces on family dinners where scrumptious food vies with robust storytelling around crowded family dinner tables. The reader's romp continues through such treats as a history of a much-loved ballad and a story of a "sin-eater." *Appalachia Bare* is a book that both delights and informs.

Connie Jordan Green
Author of *Nameless as the Minnows* and other works

In this wide-ranging collection, Ed Francisco and Delonda Anderson find the pulse of the hills and hidden hollows of Appalachian life, past and present. Through interviews, reminiscences, reviews, poems, and stories, Anderson and Francisco highlight the regional nuance and rich personal histories that set Appalachia apart, honoring the people and place in a way that's both engaging and thoughtful. Celebrating bootleggers and sin eaters but destroying hillbilly stereotypes along the way, the authors weave voices as diverse as a Hip Hop poet and a Cherokee Chieftainess into their tapestry. Full of sharp insights and generous compassion, this is a miscellany that renders the world of Appalachia both familiar and newly strange.

Robert Vaughan

Co-author of *The South in Perspective: An Anthology of Southern Literature* with a forthcoming book about Allen Tate.

Appalachia Bare

EDWARD FRANCISCO
and
DELONDA SHOWN ANDERSON
Editors of Appalachia Bare Online Magazine

Purple Breeze
PRESS

Purple Breeze Press, LLC

purplebreezepress.com

Appalachia Bare
© 2026 Delonda Shown Anderson

Library of Congress Cataloguing in Publication Data Names: Francisco, Edward and Anderson, Delonda Shown, authors
Title: Appalachia Bare
Description: First edition. | Purple Breeze Press, 2026

Library of Congress Control Number: 2025922819
ISBN Paperback: 979-8-9918895-6-8

Book designed by Streetlight Graphics

Table of Contents

For Linda
—Edward Francisco

For my beautiful sons, Tré and Gabriel
—Delonda Shown Anderson

For all our people in Appalachia

PREFACE

T RENCH POETRY? TRENCH LITERATURE? WHAT about a 'Pathos Style'? I have often searched for a collective name for the writing in Appalachia. Our writing isn't quite Southern Literature (probably because we aren't really Southern). And we certainly aren't privy to the everyday lives and traditions of our neighbors Up North. We're highlanders living in a mountainous region that runs from Alabama/ Mississippi all the way up through Canada. And, as people who live in the Appalachian Mountains, we have experiences and histories that are sometimes, shall we say, a little out of the norm. As such, our creativity (in all genres and forms) is influenced and shaped by personal encounters and an oral history that dates back centuries. With that in mind, it makes sense to assume that only a person who is born or transplanted in these mountains understands our everyday lives. So, when a young or a seasoned Appalachian writer sends work outside our region, it is likely *pshaw*ed and ends up in a sad little file until it's purged from the Recycle Bin. Of course, a few of our writers here and there make it out of the trenches. So what does all this have to do with the book?

Appalachia Bare is a compilation of articles, stories, and poetry written by the editors and co-founders of *Appalachia Bare Online Magazine*: acclaimed writer Edward Francisco and me. In order to properly discuss the book, I feel it pertinent to talk about the magazine—how it came to be, why it came to be, and what it has become.

The first James Agee Conference I attended at Pellissippi State Community College in Knoxville, Tennessee, taught me a lot about how Appalachians (me included) view our*selves*. During one discussion, for example, someone lamented that everybody (i.e., the rest of the nation) thinks we have a drug problem, but this person believed it wasn't as bad as what's reported. Then he regaled the group with a few light-hearted stories about his "meth head" neighbors who lived in a shabby trailer down the road. Another person said we should 'talk right' because 'nobody understands us without an interpreter.' Another discussion surrounded our murderous history, what with feuds and all. (It ain't just Appalachia that has a murderous history in this country. Chicago's underworld, for example, has bloodied the streets on several occasions throughout history. It's all the same, except one is photographed with spats and three-piece-suits while the other is portrayed as barefoot, haggard, and draped with rifles.) Still another discussion revolved around poverty porn and how that plight is exaggerated in the region.

I took all those stories home, stewed for a while, and asked myself two questions: Why aren't people here proud of where they were born and raised? Why are they so negative about it all? And the answers kept pinging. We have never been taught a collective history about us and these mountains. Just pieces here and there. We have not been taught about why we speak differently, or that we speak an ancient dialect of which we should be proud, or that these mountains are one of the oldest (particularly the Blue Ridge Mountains) ranges in the world, or that it's okay to have ancestors with a colorful past because it made us who we are: a beautiful people full of creativity, intelligence, and ingenuity.

I took my concerns to friend and mentor Edward Francisco, and we tossed around solutions. What exactly did we want to accomplish? We wanted a place free from ads that focused on our region's unique histories, stories, pedigrees, and accomplishments—for Appalachian audiences *and* national audiences. We wanted a place to tell *our own* stories, instead of continuing to allow others outside the region that privilege. We wanted to design a space that featured creative Appalachians or stories *about* Appalachia, particularly since venues outside the region have often misunderstood our culture or style and have perhaps been less willing to publish good works by mountain people. What materialized from our discussion was *Appalachia Bare*, a nonprofit online magazine that has been publishing Appalachian stories in every genre for over five years (and growing). More good news and exciting opportunities were around the corner.

A number of months ago, Purple Breeze Press had read the editors' works on *Appalachia Bare* and graciously offered Ed and me a book deal that featured our personal works from the site. The opportunity was such an amazing surprise.

For this project, Ed and I have endeavored to choose works that offer a fairly well-rounded view of what Appalachians highly regard: family, people, region, culture. Our thoughts have been that this book will help promote our magazine, give it more credence, and reach a wider audience. Our hope is that this book is just the beginning and that it opens more opportunities to showcase Appalachian contributors and further spread our humble intentions.

Delonda Shown Anderson
Chief Editor/ Co-founder, *Appalachia Bare*

MOUNTAIN FAMILY

1
Stroll

(For Henry)

by Edward Francisco

The sidewalk, his nursery.
The stroller, his crib.
Together my grandson
and I cruise the Low Country
bejeweled in dew after
last night's downpour.
Our gentle jostle over humpbacked
pavement signals our arrival.
We attract a following: first,
a neighbor woman rushing
across the street to catch
a glimpse of him: "He's
beautiful—too pretty to be
a boy."

Then a trio of ravens
stately strutting under
a canopy of Magnolias
casting wide arcs of shade.
At nine months he won't

recall how we winced and weaved
to avoid direct exposure
or how this morning roses
shivered, voluptuous pears
bobbed on their branches,
and the sky leaked a palate
of colors in the east.

My wife laments
we might not live
to see him graduate
eighteen years from now.
I say we have to live
as if we won't.
The wheels of the stroller
record oscillations of time
spent, sped, and slowing

Invoking seventy-two names
of God found in the Kabala,
I plead with angelic presences
to surround him with an aura,
a force field, a penumbra
of protection when I'm gone.

But today he's safe,
and I'm his chauffeur,
careful to glance left,
then right, then left again,
a mantra I say aloud
for a time when he grasps

the need to pause to hear
voices whispering in switchgrass
encroaching to obscure his
view.

Crisscrossing a matrix
of side streets, we roll
upon another stroller
rattling around a corner
toward us. The little
girl's mother and I check
on each other's progress
in getting the babies to nap.
I wonder if they visit
in dreams of whatever
sort babies have?

Once more we set sail,
skirting puddles, navigating
to archipelagos of dry
surface soaked by sun.
Ahead our destination:
In the side yard, a copse
of bushes with a wren and her
nestlings tucked safely inside.
I assure him we too are
birds of a feather soaring
at dizzying heights until
drifting on pillows
of wind we rock our
gentle cradle at last
coming home to roost.

2
Eating Appalachia, 1975

by Delonda Shown Anderson

He presses down the pedal as he hastens through the holler,
screeching around swerving curves before *They*
take the Valiant like they took the old Fury
and the houses on Job Street, on Love Street, and Food Street.
Daddy yaks Valiant and Vietnam. Mama answers so and so.

Little Brother and I assemble at attention, edgy and rigid,
sweat-sliding across backseat vinyl to the zigzag curves.
Daddy talks of *needing*—guns, knives, cars, clothes, boats, bars—
And he'd have them too, Ey God, if it wasn't for Vietnam and…
A heavy, squinted eye flashes in the rearview.
Mama bellows so and so and so.

My belly growls through the backseat like hungry vomit.
Curves keep coming. Out the window, I glimpse the jagged
ledges of rock walls, peer up and catch the billow-clouded sky.
On Brother's side, trailers bombard old mountain boroughs in
aluminum
shanty towns, and holler churches sermonize the Bible on the
front signs.

Jesus Loves the Little Children.

I look at brother and ponder.

He and I played mud monsters in the rain
before the sun cavalry came and dried our lives.
He and I scuttled furtively like Natives in the forest,
without splitting a twig, to sneak and smoke rabbit backer.
He and I sat silent outside, stunned and solid as a Jesus prayer,
Waiting for the Lord to quell fist bombs and uttered guns.

He looks at me, wide blue eyes, and I hear his stomach rumble.
I grin at him, grab the window roller, motion for his own.
We roll, frantic as Mama's factory bobbin,
poke our noggins out the windows, open wide our mouths,
Laugh, and eat Appalachia.

3
Potato Soup with a Side of Poverty

by Delonda Shown Anderson

I HAVE WRITTEN A LITTLE BIT about my love for these mountains, about my fond—and not so fond—memories living deep in the holler. The place where I grew up was an offshoot of an area in East Tennessee called Demory Hollow. At one point in time, Demory was a community all its own, with a church, school, grocer, and lodge. The small borough was a hop, skip, and a jump from another little town called Agee. Not many people know this, but the town was named after the writer James Agee's great grandfather, James Harris Agee. My people and his people lived next door to one another. In fact, I am kin to the Agees through my maternal McNeeley line. In 1936, the TVA flooded the area, and if anything is left of Agee, it's buried underwater. The remaining area was renamed Grantsboro, after its founder, Revolutionary War soldier and surveyor, James Grant. Norris Lake was less than five minutes away in all directions from Demory. My father took us camping and fishing in his favorite hidey holes. He once told me that a small amphitheater was near that lake back in the day, and plays were performed there. Now, my father's favorite hidden places and the entire area is smothered with real estate and big, fine lakeside homes.

Some mornings, mist and fog funneled through the veins of Demory Hollow and settled down like a blanket. The morning sun pierced through the haze and its rays glistened like God's light was among us. We lived down one of the hollers on a hillside there, where hills and mountains hugged our road from both sides. People might call it a bit claustrophobic. We lived among the most diverse flora in the nation, if not the world. And critters were so close they were like family. One time, I even saw a black mountain lion slinking along a hillside. Some people believe me; many people don't. If it wasn't a mountain lion, it was a Maine Coon, because it was huge. The old folks called these cats "painters," or *panthers*.

The author's father, Benny Franklin Shown, Sr.
with a mess of rockfish, ca. 1980s.

Food. Food was always an issue. The forest was aplenty with edibles: paw paws, mayapples, crabapples, walnuts, huckleberries, mulberries, wild raspberries and blackberries and strawberries, poke salet, edible grasses, etc. My father worked various jobs back then, here and there, being unsettled after less than a decade home from his tour in the Vietnam War. After work, he fished or frog-gigged and brought home a string or a mess of food. We had chickens and eggs. We had two slaughter hogs once. When my dad came back from the slaughterhouse, his face was as pale as a sheet of paper. He said he never wanted to see that again. He said he could still hear them. "They scream like a person," he said. I guess the experience brought the war back in his mind. From then on, any pigs on the property were pets. Food was still scarce, but we survived and were grateful. On Sundays and holidays, we visited my great-grandparents or great-aunts and enjoyed big dinners. People kept coming—dozens of them. And food was plentiful.

The problem for my family was winter. And winters were long back in the holler. Every winter we were "snowed in" and had to wait weeks for the roads to thaw enough to get out and go to the store. My father used tire chains. Four-wheel-drives were *way* beyond our grasp. The trip to town was normally between twenty to thirty minutes (depending on how fast you took the curves). Snow and ice made the trip an excruciating, knuckle-whitening hour or more ordeal.

> *Please bear with me for a soapbox moment. I don't know how many times I hear people who weren't born, raised, or reared here laugh about how school was canceled for just "a little bit of snow," when snow where they once lived was sometimes five feet tall. I dare anyone of them to say that after they take a little journey in the wintertime up to East Tennessee's White Oak or Caryville Mountain or Duff or Jellico Mountain or way back in any holler where the sun doesn't shine and the snow doesn't melt for months and salt trucks are a pipedream. See if it's possible to leave when it snows, or especially when it ices or sleets. Determine then if it's safe for kids to go to school. (Of course, these times were before face-time and Zoom classes were a thing.)*

But enough of my digression and back to food. Did we prepare for a dearth of food in winter? Sure. As best we could. We couldn't afford a pressure canner, but my mother did can in a water bath, mostly jelly, fruits, tomatoes, pickles, or ketchup. We froze what we could. To be sure, my father hunted. But hunting is a gamble—win some, lose some. Suffice it to say, we ate *A LOT* of potatoes: fried, baked, raw, and soup. It seemed like we had either potato soup or cornbread and milk about every other day. We had potato soup so often, I foundered on it for life.

As I said before, winters were long back in the holler. The season started around November, and the mountains weren't completely thawed until about April or even May. Did I mention we had no running water in winter? When the water pipes were installed all down the holler, they weren't deep enough or insulated well. So, they froze from November or December until the thaw. We saved water all year for cooking and washing. From time to time, we trekked to a springhouse for water. We used melted snow to flush the toilet. Chamber pots were also a thing. Our situation improved when I was about twelve years old. My father found a steady job as a policeman. My mother worked at a textile factory. My parents had a well dug for water. Eventually, the waterline was fixed and improved. Of course, winter never changed. But we were better prepared every year.

The author's mother, Pamela Joy *Brooks* Shown
eating cornbread and milk, 1979.

I am by no means complaining. No, not that. I'm proud of who I am and from where I came. Though we were dirt poor and sometimes stuck and stir crazy, I look back on those days with an odd fondness. Sure, we were at each other's throats with cabin fever. Snowball fights were one cure. Sledding was another. For me, it was reading and writing. At times we were hungry, but we never starved. My experiences made me scrappy. I don't know if that's a good thing or a bad thing. What I *have* learned is that poverty makes a person humble. Hunger makes a person grateful. Being Appalachian makes a person resourceful. Ingenuity is in our blood.

4
Christmas Eve 2017

by Edward Francisco

A clock tick away
from thirty
my grandson lowers
onto a chair beside me
where we stare
at the curious
chiaroscuro of Christmas
lights blinking in a
pattern as undetectable
as the reasons for his
diagnosis.

He sips air
with the feeblest exertion
of swamp-diseased lungs.
Some days he compares it
to inhaling gauze, others to
swallowing fish hooks.
Either way, the cosmic
prankster of mirth and misery
won't let him forget that
"shit can get real in a hurry."

What he says he'll miss most
is the chance to make
mistakes he won't live
to regret.
To him
being dead
is knowing this
is his last Christmas
with familiar strangers
who can't love him enough
to save him.

He thanks me for
not praying for a miracle
and secures a promise
I'll deliver his eulogy
when he slides out of focus
in time.

In the half-dark
between us
he drinks to my health.

A corridor
narrows to a point
like a lesson in perspective,
then vanishes

He won't survive the spring.
His short story ends in past

tense, leaving his whereabouts
a matter of mute speculation.
All that's certain is
he entered the space-time
continuum prematurely
and left the same way.

He's an actuarial accident.

In the absence
of life-time accomplishments,
I say to those
gathered for his service
that he was nothing
if not authentic.

What I can't say
is whether he regretted
surviving an uneasy birth
just to occupy an organism
flawed in design
and programmed for untimely
obsolescence.

A riot
at the cellular level
triggered a chain reaction
manifesting
in his brain's discovery
its knowledge was insufficient
for the task at hand

and subsequent disappointment
it was never any other
way.

5
Elegy to a Grandson

by Edward Francisco

Grief undulates
like an inchworm
and just as slowly.
It forces one to use
the conditional tense:

He would have been…
if he hadn't…

Or tugging the knot
of time:

He would have been…
if he had…

Died or lived.

Flip a coin.
Settle the issue
once and for all.
Wear the result

like a raincoat,
too snug,
constricting the shoulders,
like a straitjacket,
strangling the odd breath.
His was a false start.
Slotted into the space-time continuum
too soon,
he left the same way.
What to make of
the in-between?
The eyelid's blink
before the leopard
pounces on its shadow
in a wading pool?
He sang the lyrics
not knowing how the tune
would end:

"… remind me
of a warm safe
place
where as a child
I'd hide
and pray for the thunder
and the rain
to quietly
pass me by."

In the event of (you know),
do not resuscitate:

instructions of
a young man
encrypted in genetic code
inscrutable
as a roll of the dice.
Then snake eyes.

If only a woman
would marry him
for a few minutes.
Fists thunder
toward Heaven's throne
where sits gloating
the craftiest trickster
of them all.

And we are left to
muse at the not-ness
and never-will-be
of our own exquisite
efforts
to avoid using
the past tense.

6

Before They Took Him

by Delonda Shown Anderson

They waited for me before they took him.
I closed the car door, slogged past family,
noted the numbed, distant faces
and swollen, zoned eyes;
passed the old country roses,
sweet and sundry;
passed his hand-crafted shed
that smelled of fresh cedar,
heard the bustle of birds all around, aflutter.

I am here, now.

I make measured steps to the backdoor, lightly
opened.
Daddy reclines on the couch, a sheet cloaked
across,
shrouded half-way, like Jesus.

Mom says they waited for me before they took
him,
keeps asking,
Do you want to see him?

I shake my head endless and say it will raze
me.

She lowers her head and I hear:
The old women say if you don't look,
you'll not believe it and go mad.

Murmurs occur about the service.
Hospice hugs and prays but cannot stay.
Weeping seeps from nieces
once the body bag squeaks in.
The big-boned mortician twists toward me
with a cold-boned smile, and asks,
Do you want to see him before we take him?

Mom said they waited for me.
I don't want to go mad.
So, I do as I am bid,
tenderly unfold the blanket,
and see.

7

Grandfather Raised a Little Cane

by Edward Francisco

FOR GENERATIONS, MY MOTHER'S FAMILY were bootleggers all the way down to my great grandfather, a grizzled old man with a withered arm who constantly chewed tobacco and who was always licking the little reservoirs of brown tobacco juice that gathered at the corners of his mouth.

Despite his appearance, he was the most popular man in three counties since he managed to make the best sour mash around. According to my grandmother, it was a matter of great pride to him, and he never sold a single quart without first testing it himself.

"It's a sorry sumbitch that won't drink his own likker," he used to say.

Such pronouncements were rare for the old man though because he had a peculiar reverence for language that didn't permit him to talk to people who talked much. Instead, he preferred to sit quietly in an old wicker bottom rocking chair on the edge of the porch and spit tobacco juice into the grass. He would time each of his spits to the forward rocking of the chair.

For all his reticence, though, the old man didn't mind sitting and listening to other people swap stories and gossip. But the only times he ever interrupted were when somebody challenged his conviction that a Baptist was a bootlegger's best friend or when his nephew Hiram came around. Hiram got under the old man's skin like a blister. And the old man whittled himself a birch cane and laid it beside the rocker just in case Hiram ever irritated him enough and the old man wanted to crack Hiram's skull.

I remember my grandmother telling me how one day Hiram came over and was teasing my great grandfather about his arm which he had to lay across his lap whenever he was rocking. Almost everybody knew the story about the arm, how it had been shattered by a Minié ball at the Battle of Chickamauga, and how the surgeons, rather than amputating it, had removed the shards of bone and attached a banjo string from my great grandfather's elbow to his wrist. By some miracle he did not contract gangrene, and the string never bothered him unless Hiram was around.

"Why donchee pull out that banjer string and pick us a tune?" Hiram teased.

The old man's face reddened.

"That ain't real funny, Hiram."

"Whatsa matter, cain't ye do it? I didn't figure ye could."

"It's a little pile of shit I care what you figure, Hiram."

Hiram began hooting as the old man reached down for his cane, and, with a single motion, swung it in a wide arc at Hiram's head. He cracked Hiram's jaw with it.

"Goddammit," Hiram cried, "you done broke my jaw!"

The old man spat once in the yard and resumed rocking. Then he said,

"Y'know, Hiram, I'm figurin' you'll be needin a string to wire them teeth together. Maybe I got one you can borry."

The old man pointed to his arm and grinned, his rusty old mouth showing pieces of tobacco.

"You crazy old sumbitch. I ought to kill you!" Hiram screamed.

But already the left side of Hiram's face was beginning to swell and tears were streaming down his cheeks. All my great grandfather had to do was hold up the cane.

As a matter of fact, Hiram never did anything to pay the old man in kind. And according to my grandmother, he even tolerated rather stoically all the bad jokes about how all my great grandfather had to do to get Hiram to shut up was "raise a little cane."

8

The Ballad of Barbara Allen

by Delonda Shown Anderson

M<small>Y MATERNAL GREAT-GRANDMOTHER, CORA (MCNEELEY)</small> Goins, lived a good deal of her adult life in a coal camp, just down the road from Kentucky, in Westbourne, Tennessee. So many of my people lived in that camp, including my grandmother and my mother. As the coal boom slowed and the company's profits waned, the coal barons abandoned Westbourne, leaving the remaining residents to find alternate housing before the area was razed. So, the Goins family moved to surrounding regions. My mother was *very* close to her grandmother, and she often brought my brother and I to visit her.

I was eleven years old when Old Mamaw Goins passed on and consider myself incredibly fortunate to have spent time with her. (Yes, that's what some of us Appalachians call our great grandparents—Old Mamaw, Old Papaw. The word "Mamaw" is believed to be from the Scottish Lowlands and means "my mother." If we further break down the word Mamaw, *Ma* refers to a person's mother. *Maw* refers to a mother's mother. Old Mamaw would then be the older mother of my mother's mother.)

Though I do remember her, my memories are formed with childhood swatches that never formed into a cohesive pattern: I remember her smile and her demeanor. I remember her voice sounded gritty and wise. And I loved to touch her because her skin was as soft as a bread bun. She and I often sat outside under the shade tree eating Ritz crackers and enjoying one another's company. I remember riding with my mother to take Old Mamaw on errands. And I was usually around when she and my mom sat on lawn chairs in the front yard, talking and laughing.

The author's great grandmother, Cora Lee *McNeeley* Goins,
atop her steps in LaFollette, Tennessee, ca. 1970s.

She was and remains so much to me. Her story, her perseverance, her resilience, her spunk is stitched tightly within my own make up and carries me through just about anything. Whenever I've encountered tragedy or seemingly unsurmountable obstacles, her face comes to mind, and I am comforted. She had immense internal strength and her presence—all four feet eleven inches and about 90 pounds—commanded respect.

I still hang onto my mother's stories about her. In particular for this writing, my mom told me Old Mamaw sang the old ballads, mostly "Barbara Allen." Old Mamaw's mother sang it to her when she was a child in the late 1800s. She knew it by heart, which tells me she heard it quite often. I happened upon stanzas my mom copied of "Barbry Allen" (the title my old mamaw used), with notes along the margins of how my great-grandmother sang it. Finding it sparked a desire to write about it.

Versions of "Barbara Allen" derive from Great Britain, Ireland, and the United States, a great swath of which are found in the Appalachian Mountains. The popular belief is that the ballad came from Scotland. The title has several different spellings from "Barbara Allen" to "Barbara Allan," "Barbry Allen," to "Bawbie Allen," etc. The male character seems to switch between "Sweet William" and "Sir John Græme." This narrative song is arguably the most popular ballad of all time.

The earliest written reference to "Barbara Allen" is in Samuel Pepys's diary entry dated January 2, 1665/66: "… but above all, my dear Mrs. Knipp, with whom I sang, and in perfect pleasure was I to hear her sing, and especially her little Scotch song of 'Barbary Allen'…"

Other early references are found in England's broadside ballads. For around four hundred years, from the 1400s to the 1800s, various ballads were printed on broadsides using presses or printing presses, and peddled by street vendors, especially where crowds gathered. Dates for the broadside "Barbara Allen's Cruelty, or, The Young Man's Tragedy," are speculative, ranging anywhere from 1675 to 1750. The University of Glasgow has a few broadsides of "Barbara Allen" as late as 1855.

Authors and folklorists have documented the ballad. Scottish writer and publisher Allan Ramsay, who published the 1740 *The Tea-table Miscellany: or, a Collection of Choice Songs, Scots and English*, lists the ballad as "Bonny Barbara Allan." Oliver Goldsmith also refers to it in *The Vicar of Wakefield*, published in 1766. In chapter four, he writes: "These harmless people had several ways of being good company, while one played, the other would sing some soothing ballad, Johnny Armstrong's last good night, or the cruelty of Barbara Allen." Goldsmith must have been quite moved by the ballad because he once said: "the music of the finest singer is dissonance compared to when an old dairymaid sung me into tears with 'Johnny Armstrong's Last Goodnight' or 'The Cruelty of Barbara Allen.'"

Written in 1812, Bishop Thomas Percy's posthumous *Reliques of Ancient English Poetry: Consisting of Old Heroic Ballads, Songs, and Other Pieces of Our Earlier Poets* contains two variations of the ballad. The first (Roman Numeral V) is titled, "Barbara Allen's Cruelty," and the second (Roman Numeral VII) is "Sir John Grehme and Barbara Allen."

Perhaps the most well-known ballad collector is American scholar and folklorist Francis J. Child. Child realized the importance of recording the old ballads for posterity. His extensive volumes, *The English and Scottish Popular Ballads*, were dedicated to collecting and preserving the "history of the words and themes" in old ballads. Instead of copying "ballads sung by local bards, Child built his collection from the study of printed sources," of which I'm pretty certain the aforementioned sources were used. "Barbara Allen" is listed at #84 in his selection, as "Bonny Barbara Allan." He notes three variations—A, B, and C—and the differences are recognizable by the first line:

A. "It was in and about the Martinmas time…"

B. "In Scarlet Town, where I was bound…"

C. "It fell about the Lammas time…"

So, how is it that so many versions (some say over one hundred) of "Barbara Allen" exist? Ballads were passed down by oral tradition. A word was changed here, a sentence there. Elements may have been added to express certain situations or quandaries. Plus, many of these narratives were (and still are) delivered as whimsical or even as political humor. If a person wanted to play a joke on someone, the joker simply replaced the name on the ballad to suit the recipient.

Regardless of dates, intent, or variations, "Barbara Allen" is a well-known ballad that has been sung for over four hundred years (at least). My Old Mamaw's rendition, via my mom's memory on paper, is transcribed below. I like to think of her singing it to my mom on their many walks together, along paths where blackberries are plentiful, where country roses in bedraggled beauty greet them on both sides, where swaying grasses sing their windy ovations, and cool moss grows soft and plush along the way; and they are both smiling and happy.

"Barbry Allan"

It was in and about the Martinmas time,
When the green leaves were a-fallin',
That Sir John Graham in the West Country
Fell in love with Barbry Allan.

He sent his man down through the town
To the place where she was dwellin':
"O hast and come to my master dear,
If ye be Barbry Allan."

O slowly, slowly rose she up,
To the place where he was lyin',
And when she drew the curtain by, said:
"Young man, I think you're dyin'."

"O yes I'm sick and very, very sick,
And 'tis all for Barbry Allan."
"O the better for me ye shall never be,
Though your heart's blood were a-spillin'."

"Don't you recall, young man, said she
"When ye the cups were fillin',
That ye made the toasts go round and round,
And slighted Barbry Allan?"

He turned his face unto the wall,
And death with him was dealin':

"Farewell, farewell, my dear friends all,
And be kind to Barbry Allan."

And slowly, slowly, rose she up.
And slowly, slowly left him,
And sighing said she could not stay,
Since life was taken from him.

She had not gone a mile but two
When she heard the death-bell knellin',
And every stroke that death-bell made
Cried "Woe to Barbry Allan!"

"O Mother, Mother, make my bed,
O make it soft and narrow:
Since my love died for me today,
I'll die for him a'morrow."

9
Untamed Hours

by Delonda Shown Anderson

Capturing a misty Blue Ridge morning,
we scuttled uphill, down dale, taking up trails,
traipsing through dew-covered fields,
and slipped off, passing untamed hours of existence.

We rested near calm lakes
roused by walleye's sporadic splash,
or bluegill's breath bubbles or striders atop the water
or dew-dripped sprinkles pit-patting a cappella.

We walked by wild honeysuckle's sweet, fragrant flowers
or white pine's fresh-scented resin,
and trod upon the old dirt
thoroughfares unearthed by agrarian ancestors;

passed underneath tree-covered darkness
into the cool backwoods blessed with clear,
trickling creeks and streams so pure
we cupped our hands to sip and swig;

meandered through hollers among the oddly hospitable
who fed us what they had
before they teetered atop narrow bridges
and hung so tight to lottery miracles, the wind turned back.

We journeyed home, our brains self-storages
of nature's brilliance, and begged for *more* untamed hours,
for just some eek of Mother Nature's radiance,
to tide us all over into days.

MOUNTAIN PEOPLE

10

Florence Reece: Champion of Appalachia

by Edward Francisco

M Y STAGE PLAY, *WHICH SIDE Are You On: The Florence Reece Story* debuted at Pellissippi State Community College on April 15, 2016. The play recounts episodes in the life of Florence Reece, an American social activist, poet, and folk song writer—and veteran of the bloody Harlan County, Kentucky, coal wars of the 1930s that pitted coal miners and union organizers on one side against the coal companies, hired thugs, and law enforcement on the other. The war included strikes, skirmishes, bombings, executions, and the occupation of Harlan County by both state and federal troops for more than a decade. The daughter and wife of coal miners, Reece penned the song "Which Side Are You On?" that became a social justice anthem after Pete Seeger recorded it in 1940.

One of the challenges of writing the play was the paucity of biographical information about Florence Reece. I knew some of the broad strokes of her life but was forced to imagine particulars supplied by research and interviews. Fortunately, I recalled stories told to me by my grandmother about her father, my great-grandfather, a coal miner named William, aka "Kildee," Thomas, who mined coal in southeastern Tennessee during the decades spanning the play. Consequently, I conflated both stories, my grandmother's and Florence's, as a way to depict the hardscrabble lives of miners and their families in the coal country of southern Appalachia.

To my thinking, three scenes best characterize Florence's tenacious pluck and un-redoubtable determination. The first occurs when gun thugs riddle her home with gunfire after Florence anticipates their arrival and orders her six children to hide under the bed. Miraculously, no one was injured. In the aftermath, she tore a page from a wall calendar and scribbled lyrics of the now-famous protest song.

The second episode occurs at the Highlander Folk School, a social justice leadership training center founded in Monteagle Mountain, Tennessee, by Myles Horton and Don West in 1932. There Florence and her husband, Sam, encountered activist notables Reverend Will Campbell and Dr. Martin Luther King in September of 1957. Influenced by Mahatma Gandhi's philosophy of non-violent, civil resistance, King provides his own version of Gandhi's teaching with which Florence takes issue at once:

FLORENCE REECE: Martin, this Gandhi feller—I read a newspaper piece that he said he was a lawyer with a first-class ticket on a train in India. But a station policeman ordered him back to third class. Just like Rosa [Parks].

MARTIN LUTHER KING JR: Yes.

FLORENCE: But Gandhi refused and was arrested.

MLK: That's right.

FLORENCE: So Gandhi arranged a—peaceful protest, what you called—

MLK: Non-violent resistance.

FLORENCE: Us miners would call it a strike. Only Gandhi asked people in India to lay down on the railroad tracks to stop the train.

MLK: Yes.

FLORENCE: And the trains stopped.

MLK: Yes.

FLORENCE: The way I see it, Mr. Gandhi was pretty sure of the outcome before he got it. He counted on the British people to be civilized. Civilized people don't run over people laying on the railroad tracks. But if you're a striking miner in Eastern Kentucky and lay down in the road, you can count on some scab to run you over with his car.

The play's climax takes place at the hospital bedside of Florence's husband Sam, succumbing to the final stages of Black Lung disease. What follows is an imagined snippet of their final conversation:

SAM: Now what's wrong, Florence?

FLORENCE: What do you mean, what's wrong?

SAM: Are you in a twitch because I'm dying?

FLORENCE: What do you think?

SAM: You knew it would come to this.

FLORENCE: Of course, I knew it would come to this. Just not this way.

SAM: What way then?

FLORENCE: Did you ever think that all we did warn't enough? That what we tried to do came to nought?

Sam Reece died in 1978 from the scourge of Black Lung. After a lifetime of advocating for social justice, Florence Reece died of a heart attack in 1986 at the age of 86 in Knoxville, Tennessee. However, Florence Reece's "Which Side Are You On?" lives on in many renditions.

11
Interview with George Brosi

by Edward Francisco

G EORGE BROSI MOVED WITH HIS mother and sister to join his father in Oak Ridge, Tennessee, in January 1944 when the Army Corps of Engineers finished building their house. He graduated from Oak Ridge High School in 1960, Carleton College in 1965, and earned an M.A. Ed. From Western Carolina University in 1991. He is the co-editor of *Jesse Stuart, The Man and His Books* for the Jesse Stuart Foundation, *No Lonesome Road: The Prose and Poetry of Don West* for the University of Illinois Press, and *Appalachian Gateway: An Anthology of Contemporary Stories and Poetry* for the University of Tennessee press. He founded Appalachian Mountain Books in 1982. It is a book business specializing exclusively in books about the Appalachian South that serves academic libraries, brings a display of books to various regional conferences and festivals, and continually updates the website, ApMtBooks.com. He has received awards for promoting Appalachian Literature from the Appalachian Studies Association, the Appalachian Writers Association, the Mountain Heritage Literary Festival, and the Hindman Settlement School. In the 1990s, he taught students in humble circumstances in a prison and in off-campus centers at shopping plazas on reclaimed strip mines, as well as at Kentucky's "flagship" university. In the 2000s, he edited *Appalachian Heritage Magazine* for Berea College in Kentucky. In his younger days, George worked full time for civil rights, peace, economic justice, and environmental organizations. Subsequently, he has continued to do volunteer work for progressive electoral candidates and for non-profits concerned with these issues.

Interview

EDWARD FRANCISCO: Connie Green, Marilou Awiakta, and you grew up in Oak Ridge, Tennessee. Because I've always been fascinated with the intersectionality of writing and place, would you share some of your experiences as a boy growing up in the "Secret City?"

GEORGE BROSI: I'm a big fan of both Connie Green and Marilou Awiakta, although I do not recall ever talking with either specifically about Oak Ridge. During the fifties when I was a secondary student there, I attended lectures in Oak Ridge by both Eleanor Roosevelt and Margaret Mead. During the question period, Margaret Mead chided Oak Ridgers for being aloof and unconcerned about the surrounding Appalachian area. And integration happened in Oak Ridge when I was in high school. I participated in the Civil Rights Movement in Oak Ridge in the summer between my freshman and sophomore years in college, 1961. Issues of war and peace were inescapable in Oak Ridge. Civil liberties, too, was there. In high school, I somehow came across a leftist magazine and innocently wrote them a letter to the editor. My father was super freaked out because he had security clearance. None of this resulted in most Oak Ridgers becoming involved in these issues, but it did for me.

EF: Wordsworth wrote that "The child is father of the man." Did you receive any intimations in childhood hinting that you would become an activist, editor, and author?

GB: I was always a rebel. I don't know why. When it was my turn to read the Bible verse at the start of my public elementary school day, I would often read, "Jesus wept," knowing I'd be paddled for not reading a longer verse, yet not fully understanding the irony at the time. In high school, I wrote a letter to the editor protesting the fact that our basketball coach only played our African American player when the other team agreed, but the player was conveniently declared academically ineligible before my letter could be printed. I was the only boy in Ms. Baird's junior English class to get an A from her; perhaps she felt that her rebellious student might have promise as a writer.

EF: For a time, you attended college in the Deep North (i.e., Minnesota) where you were exposed to the Civil Rights Movement and the Student Non-Violent Coordinating Committee (SNCC). Later, you joined the Students for a Democratic Society (SDS) organization and were assigned to the Ann Arbor, Michigan, office. Obviously, these experiences contributed to your increasing awareness of toxic inequalities in American society. I wonder, though. Was it necessary to travel to far-flung places in order to learn strategies of nonviolent resistance? I pose this question because you've indicated more than once that the arrangement wasn't always reciprocated and that many activists from outside the region entering Appalachia in the 1960s adopted a paternalistic attitude and behaved obnoxiously.

GB: I'm strongly for people experiencing life beyond their own back yard. I'm thankful that I have had the good fortune of living up north and in California, but I always saw that as temporary and made a point of moving back as soon as I could. I'm also glad I have lived, for a summer or more in Appalachian North Carolina, West Virginia, and Kentucky, as well as Tennessee, in terms of my understanding of Appalachia. Sure, newcomers can be obnoxious—in fact that is the reputation that Oak Ridgers have in Northern Anderson County. The North Carolina mountains have their Florida people, and some of the young people who came to Appalachia in the 60s and beyond lacked sensitivity. But in every case, I think they have provided the youth, especially, with a sense that differences are not inherently threatening. Of course, it must be a two-way street of mutual respect and openness. East Tennessee certainly has its share of great writers and activists, but traveling and living in different places certainly broadened my outlook.

EF: Langston Hughes said that a writer had to be both "of the tribe" and "a bearer of the light within the tribe." Wendell Berry, too, speaks of his family's estrangement from him during the years he opposed the war in Vietnam. My question to you: What was your experience of being an activist—some might say *radical*—while living and working at home in Appalachia? You don't seem to have been afforded the buffer of distance during one of the most tumultuous periods in recent American history.

GB: Yes, I *am* a radical. I agree with Langston Hughes, that writers almost always tend to be people who have experienced more than one culture and can get out of themselves in order to have the perspective necessary for good writing. When I was protesting the Vietnam War, I had a cousin who was career military and a cousin who worked for Dow Chemical, the makers of napalm. In 1965, my partner in Nashville was African American, and I've also recently had an African American partner here in Berea, Kentucky. So, I have experienced micro and macro aggressions, both in terms of race and politics. It is a small price to pay for being able to feel like I am having at least a little impact to make life better for the most vulnerable. I am well aware that others have paid much greater prices, including the ultimate price.

EF: When I hear the word *Appalachia*, George Brosi springs to mind. However, I can't think of you without thinking of your lovely wife, Connie, who was so kind and gracious to me on occasions when you visited Pellissippi State. I know you've said that one thing of which you're proudest was your marriage to Connie. Share with us how you met and how your love and partnership flowered over the years.

GB: Connie and I met at a party after the Rally Against Repression in Nashville, a gathering in support of the Knoxville 22 who unfurled anti-Vietnam War banners at a Richard Nixon/ Billy Graham event in Knoxville and were jailed. Connie had not seen me before, so she asked a friend who I was. The answer was melodramatic: "What? You mean you don't know George Brosi? He is one of the ten most wanted revolutionaries in America." Gross hyperbole, but it sure eased my path into her heart. Before we met, she had taught at Pine Mountain Settlement School, way back in the mountains, and at an all-Black school in Nashville. Our first home was a small farm in the Sequatchie Valley. She loved kids, and we have seven of them. Our farm and garden work, our kids, and our shared commitment to Appalachia, to better race relations, and to peace was a pretty solid foundation. Her death of cancer in 2015 has been difficult for all eight of us, but it has also brought us together.

EF: For the longest time, Appalachian writers and literature were underrepresented or, at best, considered a subset of "Southern Literature." When you and Connie established Appalachian Mountain Books in 1982, was part of your motivation to give exposure to regional writers overlooked or ignored by mainstream publishers and critics? What else did you hope to do?

GB: Yes, when we first started displaying our Appalachian books, it was common for people to exclaim, "I didn't know there were so many books about our region!" A degree of pride in one's own heritage and self-confidence allows people to not be threatened and to feel comfortable with those from different backgrounds. Of course, there is a fine line between this kind of positive pride and the dangers of chauvinism. But books do often allow people to realize that there is bad as well as good in their own traditions and to make a point of trying to overcome the bad while embracing the good.

EF: Since its establishment in 1973, *Appalachian Heritage Magazine* has been an important venue for new and established voices in Southern Appalachia. Your editorship of the magazine followed stints by Sidney Saylor Farr and Jim Gage. Obviously, you had a particular vision for *Appalachian Heritage*. In which direction did you wish the magazine to go? What innovations did you adopt to achieve the goals you had in mind?

GB: Yes, Al Stewart and Sidney and Jim set the magazine on a strong foundation. I agreed with them—and not the current editor, sadly—that we needed to only carry the work of regional writers and to provide a mix of distinguished people of letters along with fresh new voices. I guess I was a demon for punishment because I instituted a featured author and a featured artist or photographer for each issue—again, something that has been discontinued—and we invited each featured author to the Berea College campus. Like any other category of people, there are in-groups among Appalachian authors. One of my commitments as editor of *Appalachian Heritage* and for my current website (https://apmtbooks.com/) is to be scrupulously inclusive, both in terms of under-represented groups and all kinds of "outsiders." For example, my website includes over 100 books about Black Appalachians. The issue of the magazine that I'm most proud of was our Cherokee issue. It has some pages with the Cherokee syllabary opposite English, and almost all the authors were enrolled members of the Eastern Band. We celebrated the issue at the Museum of the Cherokee People in Cherokee, North Carolina, and the Principal Chief was our master of ceremonies.

EF: Let's hearken back to some Appalachian writers born in the early twentieth century: Jesse Stuart (about whom you wrote a book), James Still, and George Scarbrough. I'm loathe to consider the challenges these men faced in simply obtaining an education. All three attended Lincoln Memorial University and all experienced interruptions in their education because they lacked funds for sustained attendance. At times, I'm amazed they persisted. Would you discuss some of the challenges Appalachian writers have always faced given the anti-intellectual atmosphere of the region and cultural values often at odds with learning?

GB: There has been a strain of anti-intellectualism in society for a long time. Apparently, in the Garden of Eden, the Tree of

Knowledge was viewed as the greatest threat to the patriarchy. Unfortunately, the last four years have seen a rise in anti-intellectual feeling that I hope will be short-lived. Earlier, our writers persevered through difficulties to move into an intellectual arena. Our region is blessed with what can be considered three different kinds of authors, in the past and even now: the well-educated ones, like Thomas Wolfe and James Agee, who both went to Harvard; those with little formal education and an almost backwoods background like Byron Herbert Reece and Forrest Carter; and those who have stepped out into a wider world, like Robert Morgan, who grew up in a rural family without a car but has taught most of his professional life at Cornell, an Ivy League University. The backgrounds of regional writers—how privileged or challenged—have not been an important determinant of how brilliant or accomplished any of them have become. Impediments to receiving a good education have been reduced considerably since the 1960s due to diligent efforts by many, both inside and outside educational administration, but we still have a long way to go.

EF: Appalachian writer David C. Hsiung notes that the word Appalachia evokes in the modern imagination a "host of images and stereotypes involving feuds, individualism, moonshine, subsistence farming, quilting bees, illiteracy, dueling banjos, and many other things." Hsiung made that statement twenty years ago. Have we talked back enough to the stereotypes that Hsiung mentions, and, if we haven't, how should we proceed?

GB: I'm a big fan of David Hsiung. I think his book *Two Worlds in the Tennessee Mountains* tells an important story—I know it is a scholarly book, not a tale, but it *does* tell a story. His thesis is essentially that stereotypes of mountain people have mostly originated *within* our region, although sometimes reinforced from outside. It was and is often county seat power structures who most disdain the people who live in the hills beyond. I actually think we *have* talked back those stereotypes enough. Today, do women, do African Americans, do Latinx people, do native people put lots of energy into arguing against their stereotypes? No, their energy goes into showing that they are worthy. Why call attention to the lies and thereby reinforce them?

EF: You had to anticipate this final question. What is your assessment of J.D. Vance's *Hillbilly Elegy*? Did you know Ron Howard is making a movie inspired by Vance's memoir?

GB: I have had two encounters with J.D. Vance. In the first, I showed him my very negative review of his book on my iPhone. His response was most gracious. I gave him a hug next time I saw him. The language of his book suggests that he thinks he is the only one who has overcome a challenging background. Of course, that is ridiculous. The people I know who were not offended by the book are the people who *have* overcome a challenging background and *felt* sometimes like they *were* the only ones, so they hardly notice Vance's language in that regard. His language also may lead readers to think that everybody in the region has some of the negative qualities of his kinfolks, and that is their own fault. I disagree, but I still think we need to stop writing about stereotypes. If you feel J.D. Vance's experiences, writing, or opinions do not represent you, please do not call attention to them by complaining about them. Write your own story!

12
Joyous Freedom

An Interview with
Knoxville, Tennessee's Fourth Poet Laureate
Joseph "Black Atticus" Woods
by Delonda Shown Anderson

Joseph 'Black Atticus' Woods—
Knoxville, Tennessee's 4th Poet Laureate.

N EAR THE TAIL END OF 2023, I had the great honor of interviewing Knoxville, Tennessee's fourth Poet Laureate, Joseph Woods,
aka Black Atticus. The esteemed Woods is a hip-hop artist and spoken
word poet who weaves words into a tapestry of storytelling and poetry.
In 2013, he co-founded Good Guy Collective, a community that encourages and inspires artists to create music through hip-hop. Joseph founded
PoBoys and Poets, "a monthly open mic featuring guest spoken word
artist storytellers & songwriters."

He once imparted, "Word is fire," to young writers at a Young Creative Writers Workshop, hosted by Pellissippi State Community College. Merriam-Webster Dictionary says the word "fire" is:

burning passion; liveliness of imagination; brilliance, luminosity; a rapidly delivered series (as of remarks); to give life and spirit to; to fill with passion or enthusiasm; to light up as if by fire; to propel.

Joseph embodies the very words used to define 'fire' through his awareness, mastery, skill, and passion for wordsmithery. His writing is poignant, and his spoken word poetry is powerful. I am so pleased to present the following excerpts of an interview with such a creative, phonological bard.

For the complete interview, including the audio, visit: https://www.appalachiabare.com/joyous-freedom-joseph-black-atticus-woods/.

Interview (excerpt)

DELONDA ANDERSON: So, the questions that I have, you've probably been asked a thousand times. But I tried to choose things that were about poetry and spoken word. What is your opinion—what do you think the purpose of poetry is?

BLACK ATTICUS: Oooh, the purpose of poetry. Oh, gosh. I've never been asked that question. I'm sure that it's many definitions on this one. I feel like it's a way to enhance the frequency of language. I feel like it's a, it's a dance, right?

I mean, because you just say it and then thus it's a sentence. I think for me, that's the purpose of it, right? 'Cause when I study it beyond like emotionally what it does, I do feel like poetry helps you connect with yourself, connect with healing, connect through things or express yourself. I mean all those things we already know, but I think practically, as far as function-wise, I think it just helps increase the frequency.

DA: What do you think is the most important element of a good poem?

BA: Oh, um, it's 'set up and spike,' right? Like, how do you get me to understanding? So, of course, clarity, enough clarity to be understood or enough clarity, uh, even if it's vague. Give me good words to interpret with, you know what I mean? So, the way the words are used to bring the reader or the listener to understanding. The journey of it is a good thing. And I call it 'set up and spike.' Yeah, that's my thing.

DA: Do you consider yourself more of a spoken word poet?

BA: Oh, absolutely. Absolutely. I mean, you know, I went from rapper, then poet, right? And now writer, like for me, it was in that order. And I feel like, just like with hip-hop, usually with the lyricists, you either start off freestyling, or you start off writing. And the goal is to get to where we can't tell which one you're doing. Like, did they write that down or make it off the top of the head? Finding that blend. And [it's] the same thing, I think, with poetry, at least with the introduction of spoken word, I think a lot of us were emphasizing the performance.

Emphasizing like saying it aloud and not so much concerned about how it read. Because a lot of slam poetry doesn't work on paper. At all. Just like a lot of page poetry does not work on stage, right? If they can't *read* what you're doing, they're going to miss some of the nuances. So, I feel like mastery is getting to that middle point. That's my goal. I want you to be able to almost see it. See it as I say it out loud. But for me, I started off out loud before actual writing.

I'm just *now* at the point where I feel like this is ready to be on page. And printed. That's how much I revere actual written word.

DA: What inspired you to write poetry from the beginning? I know you said you were a rap artist in the beginning.

BA: Yes, rhyming. Yes, rhymes. For me, it just started off with hip-hop, so the beat, the culture, the cool. I remember, you know, growing up in the South, during the 90s, during hip-hop, like late 80s, early 90s.

For me, it would have been early 90s, right? Coming out of the whole 80s era, loving Phil Collins, Prince. You know, the eighties were great. Hip-hop really took off around 90, 92, 93, really took off during what they call the golden era.

So, I was fascinated with it, but all the voices were either from the West coast or up North. Most of them were from up North. So, it wasn't until the South finally started having something to say, artists out of Memphis like Playa Fly, and then you had, of course, Master P and No Limit. The South finally had something they were saying. I wasn't necessarily crazy about it, but I was glad to go, 'Okay, we got something.' And then when Outkast was on, oh, it was over.

So, I think for me, when I got my hands on—I laugh to say it now, but, uh, Biggie Smalls' first album—and then also a group called Black Star, which had Mos Def and Talib Kweli. When I got my hands on those, something about hearing young men, you know, maybe ten, twelve years older than me at the time, and hearing them speak so intelligently and making it sound cool, like being nerdy was cool. So, I was like, 'Oh snap.' 'Cause I was a comic book reading super geek. I was like, yeah, this is great.

It caught me at a time when I was already drawing comic books and making storylines. And the comic books I was reading, that's what got me into language in the first place. My uncle Ronnie had given me all his comic books from his childhood. So, these are printed before I was even born, but man, the writing was so much more dense.

The writers at that time, we're talking 60s, 70s, maybe late 50s, just had a more extensive vocabulary. I was always looking up words anyway, because I wanted to understand what Conan was going through. And so that had me fascinated.

Then I remember hearing Talib Kweli on a song where he said, "Are you stopping us? It's preposterous, like an androgynous misogynist." And I was just like, what did he say? What? So that was the first time spoken word had actually got me to want to go back to the dictionary. Usually, it had been comic books.

And so, I said, dude done said some stuff. And I was like, okay, cool. So we can do these things. And I think it was a way of tapping into the genius.

Then of course, when I heard Biggie Smalls—uh, no pun intended—he was "notorious" for saying more with less. It was the first time I'd ever heard like over half the dudes in my neighborhood broken down into a fragment sentence. He was so good at that. I was like, oh man, he just summed up everybody in my neighborhood. How'd he do that? I thought it was powerful, so I got addicted to it. I wanted to learn how to do that.

DA: Can you share an experience where you felt particularly rewarded or satisfied as a poet?

BA: I mean beyond the city of Knoxville voting me as Poet Laureate, that's one for sure. That's a road I didn't know I was on. Yeah, I was blown away with that one. And then to find out that they've wanted me to be this like years ago, they were wanting this to happen.

I feel like it took Rhea's term for them to really get an idea what they were really asking for. Rhea [Carmon] was a great blend because she's also on page *and* she hits the stage. She's both. And I feel like them going, 'Oh, you know what? Spoken word's pretty powerful. Let's go ahead and get *him*.' I think that was a great handoff.

DA: I think everything's a challenge, really, if you think about it.

BA: It is. I have writers, though, that blow my mind with how brazen they are. How vulnerable they are. And, I've been really good at tapping into emotion, and I can tap into frequencies that people resonate with, but I've still kept extremely private. Certain topics I've never talked about. I've never talked about my sex life. I've never talked about my traumas, at least not at length. I usually use a character, which is really what took off mainly, when I had characters like Langston Washington Carver, a poem based on a pompous professor and a college owner that I had when I was going to Nossi College of Art in Nashville.

I got Sergeant Six Weeks. Everybody loves the sergeant, the drill sergeant, but it was through these characters I was actually able to talk about the things that I actually wanted to speak on. I just couldn't think of a more clever way to do it.

But the next work I'm putting out I'm going to be telling the story of growing up in Park City, and I'm going to be addressing some traumas that I've never talked about. So that's going to be probably the most difficult thing I've ever done. And I was inspired by my cousin Bush, his last project and working through *Shape-Up*, with him. Actually, all these albums we've been working together on.

And then Rhea. Rhea just did her one-woman show, *When a Teacher Breaks Free*, so watching those two kind of put the stamp in it. I'm already two albums ahead, so the next one I'm going to do is really going to be like a reconnection. Just a reconnection with the audience for a minute. But I've never talked about things that happen behind the scenes, off the mic. And a lot of pushback that I get. Just like anybody else does. I mean, sometimes if you got family, it ain't always perfect. And it ain't always as supportive as you think it's gonna be.

DA: Do you prefer to write by hand or on your smartphone or on your computer?

BA: Right now, I prefer typing because it is closer to the speed of my thought. I love to write by hand, but, man, my mind goes, and I'd be feeling kind of like I'm dragging like, "aaaah"… cramps in the hands. Don't get me wrong, in situations with the pen, okay, I can put it like this. It depends on the scenario, right? If I'm on a bus or a plane, or if I'm a passenger, I'm pen and paper. But if it's a scenario where I got all my stuff and there's a plug, I'm going to type it, throw some headphones on, or whatever.

For some odd reason, I really like writing in high elevations. So, whether I'm in a really tall building, or whether I'm on a mountain, or whatever. High elevation. For some reason, I write like crazy. Give me a good view. I'm out.

One of my best friends, Carlton Star Relaford, took me to Kingsport for his family reunion. We get up there and they're having the barbecue and, uh, I hope they didn't think I was being rude, but I couldn't help it. The view and the elevation. I just grabbed a pen and paper, sat back, and started writing. That's the first time I realized it. I was like, there's something about being elevated. Yeah. Really does it for me.

DA: How do you resolve creating art for self-expression versus creating it for an audience?

BA: I think, for me, rule number one is if you're going to share it, you got to answer your *why*. And you should consider your audience. *If* it's to be shared, and if it's not going to be shared… If it happens to work out for other people, great. If not, cool. It's a hard balance because I do wish for myself and all creators to get where my brother Philip is right now. Like he's been here for years. I don't know how he got there. He's a videographer, but he's at the perfect quan of like, you know, put something out and go, 'Hey, I like it.' Okay. 'I don't like it.' Okay. Like he's totally neutral.

Me, however? I don't like dodging that. If the aim is to connect, then it needs to connect. So, I consider that with anything I know I'm going to share. Now, I have gotten to the point where, I don't feel as though I truly did the piece justice if it doesn't change me. That's how I make sure I'm still involved. If it doesn't affect me, then how do I expect it to affect you, right? Some of my funnier pieces, when I wrote it, had me cracking up. I was laughing my ass off when everybody else heard it.

So, that's how I know it has a higher chance of connecting. Yeah, the last one I did like that, they definitely laughed at the parts that cracked me up the most. I think it's similar with any artist or anybody creating something…

DA: If your entire body of work could only impart one message to readers or listeners, what would you want it to be?

BA: That's probably the *best* question. Seriously. Uh, I'm leaning toward… 'joyous freedom.'

And getting back to it is the most important thing we can do in this life. Which lends to what I haven't addressed in my work is that, I actually had to have a friend point out to me that I've been through more traumas than I've ever bothered to acknowledge.

Then I have realized that it's been a while since I've been nervous to approach a page. Because there's so much room on a blank page, and you know what you got to say. And so, it's like, I think for me, like going to an open mic, which is my, which is my aim.

I want to get open mics on every side of town. And I want them to have their own autonomy. I want them to grow in their own way, you know, be their own animal. So that I can come in as a poet and… it has its own feel, got its own culture.

You know, the common ground is the word. I love going to open mics, and I love seeing the new poet. It doesn't matter their age. It's their first time sharing something they've kept private for so long, and there's something about hearing that tremble in their voice or seeing that paper shaking.

It reminds me, 'Oh yeah, this is important,' because I think that's a plight with anyone who's been at practice with their discipline for so long. We plateau and we start getting kind of stagnant. And sometimes it's good to reconnect with that moment, like, why are you so nervous? Because this *matters*. And so, this is pushing me to what makes *me* nervous. A lot of this doesn't. Doesn't at all. I can get in front of a crowd of 2,000 and just do some stuff I know and be happy. No problem. But getting to what I don't talk about or pushing toward what I haven't, now *that* makes me nervous.

DA: Do you, whenever you write, like, let's say you have a notebook full of little writings here and there. Do you ever look back on your work and piece together, like, this poem, I like this line, and this poem, I like this line and this works? Do you do that?

BA: Mmm. I call it playing Tetris. Yeah, I play Tetris sometimes at work. One of my favorite rappers, MF Doom, and I heard this from Oriana Lee, who was married to Count Bass D at the time.

Count Bass D is one of the few artists that MF Doom has ever collaborated with and actually said their name. MF Doom would do a lot of features and never say the person's name. So, him and Count Bass had a real connection. The point is that MF Doom used to write lines on sticky notes, and he had a room full of sticky notes. And he would just pull verses together that way. These are lines he already agreed on a long time ago. And if you listen to his rhyme style, it does sound like, why is it so random? But it's great. It's really great.

So, yeah, I definitely play Tetris. I wish I could do it at that level, but I don't know. I keep notes now of just one or two lines. It doesn't have to be the whole poem, but if it's a good line, it's a good line. It'll find a home later. I'm real good on that, more so with songs. I got tons of songs.

DA: Can you share more about your projects that you're working on?

BA: The first one I'm tentatively calling it RAP—rhythm assisted poetry. Rhythm assisted poetry. I'm actually going to be dropping the first single that I've dropped in a while. What I want to do with it is really, it's all about reconnecting. I think I've come to a place in my life, stepping into the storyteller. And I do feel like that's a goal. Let's go back to Robbie, my liaison.

We used to think the whole point of the rhyme was that you've got to be effective. And, you know, hip-hop is extremely competitive. I think that's why I gravitated so well to slam culture because slam is also very competitive. We literally give five random people scorecards and we're brazenly judging art. What sucks and what doesn't. So, I loved it.

But hip-hop. I think we set the bar at a realistic level. Imagine writing a rhyme and saying a rhyme that's so interesting, that you could say it live at a barbecue. That's gotta be a good rhyme, man, to make somebody stop long enough to ignore the potato salad. You know what I mean? You're saying something that actually holds my attention? Live, at the barbecue like Nas. That's saying a lot. So yeah, holding people's attention. It's all about the effect. And I want to reconnect with that. I want to reconnect with what got me into this in the first place. What was my initial love for the way words move and how they can move, right? The first one is kind of like reintroduction, reconnect with not just the audience, but also with my love for the art.

And then the second one [working project] is going to be telling the story. That's going to be Park City Pedestrian. And I've already connected on all these projects. I'm working with visual artists. I'm working with Beth Meadows. And she made this wood sculpture piece… And I'm hoping to work with, um, Drake.

Beautiful, uh, wonderful painter. Wonderful painter here in town. Vincent Drake. We're gonna do a collaboration, because I think over the last few years working with Good Guy Collective and helping everybody pretty much produce their projects, I was having a problem for years seeing it visually. How does it look in video? Because I came from the age of you just heard the rap song on the radio. You know, before video killed the radio star. I think that's why I love Doom so much. He wore the mask because he wasn't worried about what he looked like… I'm working with them because I feel like the years I've spent helping people doing graphics or whatever, helping people with their business plans and making logos and making t-shirts and stuff like that, there's something that happens to people once it crystallizes into reality.

13

The Brilliant but Troubled
Anna Catherine Wiley

by Delonda Shown Anderson

A FEW YEARS AGO, I VISITED the Coal Creek Miners Museum in Rocky Top (formerly Lake City, formerly Coal Creek), Anderson County, Tennessee. The facility provides a historical glimpse into the lives of coal miners in the Fraterville and Briceville mines, particularly from the late 1800s to the 1930s. The museum houses a vintage variety of miner equipment such as tools, uniforms, miner hats (including open flame), lunch buckets, etc. The walls are covered with an array of historical information. On a far end, amidst all the mining material, a small section is devoted to a lone woman, an artist named Anna Catherine Wiley.

Anna Catherine Wiley was born in Coal Creek, Tennessee, on January 9, 1879, to Edwin Floyd Wiley and Mary Catherine *McAdoo* Wiley. Coal Creek was a booming town with coal deposits several layers deep inside adjacent mountains. The coal there was of the highest quality and purchased by cities across the Southeast. So, what does coal have to do with Catherine Wiley the artist? Well, her connection to the fossil fuel began with her paternal grandfather, Henry Howard Wiley. He was a pretty crafty civil engineer and businessman. He partnered with lawyer William McEwen "for the purpose of acquiring and clearing the titles to several 5000-acre tracts of coal-bearing lands." He ran his first coal mine in 1847 and later formed the Coal Creek Mining and Manufacturing Company, which, after some dealings with Knoxville and "New York financiers," provided land for the operations. Catherine's father, Edwin, followed in Henry's footsteps and later formed the Wiley Coal Company, which "was active from July 1881 to March 13, 1909."

Catherine attended public schools as a young girl. In 1895, at just sixteen years old, she enrolled at the University of Tennessee, Knoxville (UTK), making her one of the first female students to attend the college. She drew illustrations for the university's yearbook, which brought her notice. Yet Catherine didn't want the same old mundane art training that prepared women, for the most part, to work as illustrators. In 1903, she packed her bags and went to New York to study at the Art Students League. She often painted interior art and women going about everyday life. Her style had a "new impressionist quality" and was considered to be the "American adaptation of Monet's Impressionism." Her successes and art advocacy brought acceptance and appreciation to southern women artists.

She returned to Knoxville in 1905 and taught art at UTK for fourteen years. The art program was (oddly) within the School of Home Economics at the time. Catherine remolded the university's art education and transformed the department into "one of the best in the South." Upon her return to Knoxville, Catherine received additional training from noted portrait and outdoor artist Lloyd Branson, "the first Knoxvillian who made an entire career of art." Also during this time, she penned art reviews for the Knoxville newspaper.

Catherine flourished. She was a key figure in the Nicholson Art League in Knoxville, a group well known for their artistic talents. She won Most Meritorious Collection at the Appalachian Exposition in Knoxville, 1910, and she was awarded the Best Southern Artist at the 1917 Southwestern Fair in Atlanta, Georgia. Her goal was always to portray the "inner life" of her models, as Wiley herself says:

> Only when paintings make us realize more acutely the poetry that lies within us all, the romance that we ourselves feel, the power of our own spirit, the "externalisation" [sic] of our own soul, as it were—only then it has meaning.

She gained attention for women artists throughout Appalachia and the South, chairing the Fine Arts Department for National Conservation

Exposition, and exhibiting paintings at various sites across the United States.

Just when Catherine's artwork received recognition and praise, she plummeted—hard. In 1926, she had "a 'mental breakdown'" and was hospitalized. She remained hospitalized until she died in 1958. Her mental decline was evident some time before the hospitalization. Her artwork took on "darker tones" moving toward Expressionism that "manifested in the form of urgent brushwork and hollow-eyed figures." As far as anyone knows, she never painted again after entering the hospital.

The most obvious question is... *What happened*? Sources vary on the reasons and that makes it quite the mystery. Some sources write that Catherine and the aforementioned Lloyd Branson were lovers. Neither of them ever married and one source hints that a particular painting, *The Nude* (1911), within which an unknown woman lies sparsely covered, breasts exposed, her left arm draped across her face, is the image of Catherine. Certainly, if they weren't lovers, they were devoted friends. Sources say the deaths of her father (d. 1919) and Branson (d. 1925) drove her to madness. Personally, I would add a bit more information (not that anyone can discern her rationale). I think the reason may have been a *totality* of deaths. Her brother, librarian and English professor, Edwin M. Wiley, died in 1924. And her mother died in 1926, the year Catherine was hospitalized. So, in six years, from age forty to forty-seven, she lost her mother, father, brother, and intimate friend. If anyone has experienced the deaths of several close persons—one right after another—in such a short time period, that person knows a soul-crushing suffering.

Anna Catherine Wiley died May 16, 1958, in Philadelphia County, Pennsylvania, and she's buried at the Old Gray Cemetery in Knoxville, Tennessee. She was a renowned Appalachian impressionist whose paintings and sketches have recently gained popularity and value. As recently as 2012, her untitled painting of a mother and child sitting in a meadow was purchased by the Knoxville Museum of Art for $107,000. Catherine Wiley has a historical marker located in downtown Knoxville on the corner of Union Avenue and South Gay Street. I'll end here with a quote Catherine once wrote about art:

... we cannot fail to broaden our horizon; to find new beauties all around us, and to gain a deeper sympathy with the various aspects of life. We all need this enlargement of vision, America needs art to help her above materialism; and we, the women of America, in many ways the arbiters of taste of our nation, need it not only for its practical help in our homes, but in that larger sense of personal culture...

14
Appalachia's Sons: A Triptych of Talent

by Edward Francisco

Their similarities were keen enough to define an archetype of the Appalachian writer at mid-20th century. Their differences were such as to make each a singular talent. Jesse Stuart, James Still, and George Scarbrough knew one another and admired each other's work. All possessed shared experiences of growing up on hard-scrabble farms, all struggled to get an education, and all hailed from families they unequivocally described as "colorful."

Jesse Stuart

JESSE STUART, KENTUCKY POET LAUREATE and chronicler of the state's mountain life, was born on August 8, 1907, in a log cabin in W-Hollow, Kentucky. His father, Mitchell, was a farmer, coal miner, and railroad section hand. Stuart once wrote that "My father's family was Scotch. In Kentucky the Stuarts have been feudists, boozers, country preachers, Republicans, and soldiers." Stuart was the first in his family to graduate from high school. Afterwards, he worked for eleven months of "pure hell" in a steel mill and then enrolled at Lincoln Memorial University (LMU). After LMU, Stuart taught high school in Greenup, Kentucky. At age twenty-four, he was asked to be superintendent of Greenup County schools. Stuart's first book of poems, *Man with a Bull-Tongue Plow*, was published in 1934 and provided the impetus for his receiving a Guggenheim Fellowship.

Stuart described how he was plowing in the field one day when he stopped and wrote the first line of a sonnet: "I am a farmer singing at the plow." It was a propitious beginning as his first volume of verse featured 703 sonnets. His mastery of the form is seen in the following:

"Prayer for My Father"

Be with him, Time, extend his stay some longer,
He fights to live more than oaks fight to grow;
Be with him, Time, and make his body stronger
And give his heart more strength to make blood flow.
He's cheated Death for forty years and more
To walk upon the crust of earth he's known;
Give him more years before you close the door.
Be kind to him—his better days were sown
With pick and shovel deep in dark coal mine
And laying railroad steel to earn us bread
To carry home upon his back to nine.
Be with him, Time, delay the hour of dread.
Give him the extra time you have to spare
To plod upon his little mountain farm;
He'll love some leisure days without a care
Before Death takes him gently by the arm.

Stuart went on to write sixty books, excelling in the genres of poetry, short stories, and novels. He died in 1984 at age 77.

James Still

J AMES STILL WAS NO PROVINCIAL writer, despite his humble origins. Born on July 16, 1906, in Lafayette, Alabama, Still lived most of his life in Hindman, Kentucky. Like Stuart and Scarbrough, he attended Lincoln Memorial University (LMU). At the beginning of his junior year, he had no money to continue college. A professor found a sponsor, who paid for Still's education at LMU, where he received his B.A. in 1929, and also at Vanderbilt University, where he received his M.A. in 1930.

After completing his education, Still went to Knott County, Kentucky, in 1932 to search for a job during the Great Depression. He settled into working as a librarian at the Hindman Settlement School where he began to write his first novel, *River of Earth*, published in 1940, for which he received the Southern Author's Award. A little-known factoid about Still was the extent of his correspondence with other major American writers, including Elizabeth Maddox Roberts, Robert Penn Warren, and Robert Frost.

Perhaps his most influential correspondence was his exchange with Frost. Frost's existentially chilling sonnet "Design," published in 1922, was an obvious influence for Still's sonnet "Pattern for Death," published more than a decade after Frost's poem. Both poems feature a spider, Frost's "fat and white," Still's "clever, fastidious, and intricate." Both spiders hint at something dark and ominous, creating in the reader a sense of fear and dread. The fundamental question posed by each lyric is whether life's designs are benevolent, malevolent, or random. The similarities of subject and style are seen below:

"Design"

I found a dimpled spider, fat and white,
On a white heal-all, holding up a moth
Like a white piece of rigid satin cloth—
Assorted characters of death and blight
Mixed ready to begin the morning right,

Like the ingredients of a witches' broth—
A snow-drop spider, a flower like a froth,
And dead wings carried like a paper kite.

What had that flower to do with being white,
The wayside blue and innocent heal-all?
What brought the kindred spider to that height,
Then steered the white moth thither in the night?
What but design of darkness to appall?—
If design govern in a thing so small.

– Robert Frost

"Pattern for Death"

The spider puzzles his legs and rests his web
On aftergrass. No winds stir here to break
The quiet design, nothing protests the weaving
Of taut threads in a ladder of silk:
He is clever, he is fastidious, and intricate;
He is skilled with his cords of hate.

Who can escape through the grass: The crane-fly
Quivers its body in paralytic sleep;
The giant moths shed their golden dust
From fettered wings, and the spider speeds his lust.

Who reads the language of direction? Where may we pass
Through the immense pattern sheer as glass?

– James Still

What's worse than a God or gods killing us for their sport? Answer: no god at all. All is a random configuration of molecules colliding. Frost and Still viewed life through the same lens. Too, their poems display striking similarities in diction, tone, and treatment of complex metaphysical themes.

Apart from writing books, Still traveled extensively throughout his life, exploring at least twenty-six different countries in Europe and Central America. Despite his global travels, Still always returned to his log cabin in Knott County, living there until his death at age 94 in 2001.

George Scarbrough

BORN IN PATTY, TENNESSEE, IN 1915, George Scarbrough lamented for much of his life the lack of critical attention his work received. Certainly, Scarbrough never garnered the recognition of the poets who endorsed his books, luminaries such as Allen Tate, Andrew Lytle, and James Dickey. One reason for his omission from this elite cadre was his failure to embrace modernism and its attendant free verse experiments. Scarbrough complained about being "self-taught" early in his career, and it is accurate to say that he wrote almost exclusively in traditional forms. Only with the publication of *Invitation to Kim* in 1989, and its subsequent nomination for the Pulitzer Prize in 1990, do we witness a stylistic transformation characterized by innovation and eclecticism. Two poems demonstrate this progression, the first a classic rhyming poem, the second an example of short-lined free verse:

"Death is a Short Word"
Like a sparrow sitting in a wide walk,
I myself grew small and precise inside
In exact proportion to how much he died;
And it was thus it affected my talk

For if he sank and wrestled in a sound,
I said immaculately thrifty words,
The beautiful, voweled speeches of birds
That love short sound,

As if in the projection of clean speech,
The bright impossible face of death
Was set backward by my careful breath,
Him I retrieved, restored. But let him reach

Pertness again, be lively, learn to smile
In some way I remembered, order died
And my amazing tongue became untied
And roar arose and lingered for a while,

Till he subsided into pale and pallid,
Closing his shining eyes: then I perceived
The catastrophic tongue again believed
Only the monosyllable finally valid.

"Tenantry"
(Polk County, Tennessee)

Always in transit
we were always temporarily
in exile
each new place seeming
after a while
and for a while
our home.

Because no matter
how far we traveled
on the edge of strangeness
in a small country,
the earth ran before us
down red clay roads
blurred with summer dust,
banked with winter mud.

It was the measurable,
pleasurable earth
that was home.
Nobody who loved it
could ever be really alien.
Its tough clay, deep loam,
hill rocks, small flowers
were always the signs
of a homecoming.

We wound down through them
to them,
and the house we came to,
whispering with dead hollyhocks
or once in spring
sill-high in daisies,
was unimportant.
Wherever it stood,
it stood in earth,
and the earth welcomed us,
open, gateless,
one place as another.
And each place seemed
after a while
and for a while
our home:
because the country
was only a mansion
kind of dwelling
in which there were many
rooms.

We only moved from one
room to another,
getting acquainted
with the whole house.

And always the earth
was the new floor under us,
the blue pinewoods the walls
rising around us,
the windows the openings
in the blue trees
through which we glimpsed,
always further on,
sometimes beyond the river,
the real wall of the mountain,
in whose shadow
for a little while
we assumed ourselves safe,
secure and comfortable
as happy animals
in an unvisited lair:

which is why perhaps
no house we ever lived in
stood behind a fence,
no door we ever opened
had a key.

It was beautiful like that
For a little while.

The love of George Scarbrough's life was his mother, Louise Anabel McDowell Scarbrough, who taught her son to read before he entered grammar school. His father, William Oscar Scarbrough, a rough-hewn tenant farmer, was a source of embarrassment to the poet, and vice versa. "He never understood my peculiar ways," Scarbrough once imparted.

Authors George Scarbrough and Edward Francisco
in Oak Ridge, Tennessee, ca. 1990s.

I was fortunate enough to know Still and Scarbrough, and Stuart tangentially, through Scarbrough's recollection of him. George was my friend for almost thirty years. He was a brilliant poet at his best but also a first-rate prankster. Those visiting him at his home on 100 Darwin Lane in Oak Ridge, Tennessee, will recall the rubber snakes he placed strategically around the yard and on the porch. He also never learned to drive, making him dependent on friends to take him to the grocery store and post office. "All the manuscripts I've sent out," he complained, "and I've never so much as made my postage back." As for being unable to drive, George dramatically recited Tennessee Williams' Blanche Dubois to me as I took him to do errands: "I have always depended on the kindness of strangers."

I recall the afternoon George Scarbrough introduced his friend James Still to me at a literary conference we were attending. After readings and presentations, we three sat and had a fine, long discussion about poets, Appalachia, and the world beyond. At one point I realized I was sitting amid Titans whose genius we wouldn't likely encounter again. George ensured my connection with Stuart by giving me a pair of cuff links Stuart had given him: silver dolphins with studded rubies. "You're the only person I know who'll wear them," he said. After Scarbrough's death in 2008 at age 93, I learned that Jesse Stuart's niece was the mother of Pellissippi State's dean Mike North. We had a proper ceremony at the college, during which I returned the cuff links to the Stuart family. Our marketing people didn't want to cover the event, saying that no one knew who Jesse Stuart was.

That's one reason I'm writing this piece—so that a triptych of Appalachian talent doesn't die a second, more final, time. Fortunately, these sons of the region haunt me from time to time, leaving small hints of their presence. Recently, while helping my son Gabriel move into a new home in Charleston, South Carolina, I discovered a copy of George Scarbrough's only novel, *A Summer Ago*. A copy can be found in the rare book room of the East Tennessee Historical Society in Knoxville.

Rarer for me was the inscription on the inside cover:

> *Gabriel:*
> *This book is for you—*
> *A gift from one boy to another.*
> *Keep it in remembrance.*
> *I love you, Buddy.*
> *—George Scarbrough, Christmas 1994*

15

On the Other Side of Agee

by Delonda Shown Anderson

W HEN I WAS ABOUT FIVE years old (right before we moved to the holler), my family and I lived in a little green house on a little paved street in Jacksboro, Tennessee. My younger brother and I often felt cramped in our small, grassy yard, so we regularly wandered—but rarely too far—from our mom's sight.

Sometimes, we ventured naughtily onto the street, and that's when ever-vigilant Ms. Agee stood resolutely on her front porch, dressed in her muumuu, and kindly scolded us until we turned and went home. Ms. Agee lived across the street, cattycorner to our house. As my brother and I crept slowly back, chagrined with our heads down, our mother stood on *our* front porch and said a polite "thank you" to Ms. Agee.

I asked my mother once why Ms. Agee was so mean and yelled at us. Though I cannot remember the conversation verbatim, I can piece enough together to tell you it went something like this:

"Hit's dangerous. Ms. Agee was at one time a principal so she cares about kids. She ain't yelling atchunz, she's protectin' ye."

"She was a *principal?*" (I remember being pretty flabbergasted because I longed to attend school but was still too young. Ms. Agee had just become highly esteemed in my twinkling eyes.)

"Yes. She was. Ever since they come to Campbell County, the Agees've pretty much been teachers or business owners or served in high office. Ms. Agee's someway kin to James Agee. He was a famous writer, but I don't thank he liked his people too much. He didn't write too kindly about us here."

From that moment on, I made sure my little brother and I stayed clear of the road. Every time I passed by Ms. Agee's house, I grinned big and waved bigger. But these words lingered in my mind: *James Agee... I don't thank he liked his people too much.* My little girl brain pondered on such heavy words. As an adult, I journeyed to find their truth.

In the Tennessee county of James Agee's lineage, his name and accomplishments have rarely been recognized. He appears too distant, like a swinging rope too far away to grasp. *Why?* The same presumptions about his attitude toward his paternal family or the mountainous region they settled might be a few reasons. For one thing, scholars have washed over the surname side of Agee—the mountain side, the "backward" people. As a result, they have surreptitiously claimed their own version of Agee, thereby making the Appalachian Agee a man in the distance. Perhaps the reason lies in the dichotomy between the misconceptions about mountain people being uneducated, lazy, or poor, and the product of the mountains that was the Exeter or Harvard Agee. Perhaps Poe's 1840s assertion that "uncouth and fierce races of men" populate these *Ragged Mountains* has been standard all along.

It is so unfortunate that literary scholars have neglected the Agee lineage, particularly because the author himself spent most of his life focused on his father. Without diving into his surname, scholars provide an inadequate assessment of James Agee—as a man and as a writer. How is it possible when examining the pivotal point that altered and haunted Agee's life—his father's shocking and untimely death—so little scholarly research into the Agee cognomen exists? Is his father's side nonessential? Are his mountain people considered too uncivilized or dimwitted? Certainly, these are rhetorical questions. But they bring issues to light which scholars have neglected about James Agee and other Appalachian authors and thereby expose a wound. Appalachian writers should be recognized in their fullness, especially when you consider the contributions they and their ancestors bring to the region and the nation.

The Agees were originally a French Huguenot noble class, but when Louis XIV revoked the Edict of Nantes, they and other protestants were forced to flee. I could explore the story of the first Agee to arrive here (James Agee's fifth paternal great-grandfather, Mathieu) and how he landed in the Colony of Virginia around 1700, obtained a substantial five-thousand acres, and became the forebear who spawned all the Agees in the U.S. But that juicy information digresses from the more pressing need to edify his backwoods ancestors. I shall begin in the place where Agee's ancestors and mine met, talked, and shared community: in Campbell County, Tennessee.

The first of James Rufus Agee's ancestors to live in Tennessee was his third great-grandfather, Isaac Godwin Agee. He was said to be a Tennessee pioneer who married Mary Smith, a woman with possible family connections to Captain John Smith, distinguished husband of Pocahantas. In 1813, Isaac Agee was a court appointed road overseer. Men were needed to manage particular stretches of road. The Great Wagon road was a heavily traveled thoroughfare for settlers and stretched from Pennsylvania to Maryland, from Tennessee to Cumberland Gap, on into South Carolina.

Isaac's son, James Agee (**Many** given names were *James* in Agee's family.) was James Rufus Agee's great-great grandfather. He also settled in Campbell County, Tennessee, and worked as a farmer. He fought in the War of 1812, listed as a "Musician/U.S. Rifler" and later served in the Tennessee Legislature in its infancy.

This James Agee's son, James Harris Agee, was arguably the most significant figure for Campbell County in the mid-1800s. He was an educated man who worked as a farmer while he simultaneously studied medicine. He became a doctor in 1853. During the Civil War, James Harris moved with his family to Indiana and worked as a farmer and teacher until he joined the Union's Indiana regiment "of which he was orderly sergeant and served guard duty…" After the war, he and his family returned to Campbell County, where he farmed and practiced medicine. Not only was James Harris Agee a farmer, a doctor, and a war hero, he was also elected three times to the house of legislature to represent Campbell County. He was subsequently elected state senator to represent Campbell, Claiborne, Grainger, Scott, and Union counties. After one senate term, he chose to work in the legal field and was appointed to the office of clerk and master of the chancery court of Campbell County. He was "naturally aggressive" and "a wide-awake, public spirited man" who was "of noble character and high standing," and whose public service was "characterized by ability, integrity and justice."

The town of Agee was named in honor of James Harris Agee, but has since been renamed Grantsboro. James Harris's son, James William, was elected Cambell County sheriff and was also a U.S. Commissioner. Another son, John, followed his father's career choice and became a doctor. Son, Joseph, worked for the county's Board of Education. Still another son, Henry Clay, was a farmer who became James Rufus Agee's grandfather.

In the 1880 census, Henry Clay Agee's occupation was listed as "boot maker." From 1890 onward, records show he was a farmer. He married Moss "Mossie" Agee and had eight children. Henry's son, Alfred Franklin Agee lived in the town of LaFollette, Campbell County. He was postmaster and later served as city commissioner. He was heavily involved in politics and election campaigns. He was also a prominent business owner, establishing a furniture and undertaking business (an odd but popular combination in the old days). Henry's son, Hugh James "Jay" Agee was James Rufus Agee's father.

Hugh James "Jay" Agee was born and raised in Campbell County, Tennessee. He continued his education and became a Postal Clerk. His postal service record says he resided at "Clinch Street" in Knoxville, Tennessee, at least in the earlier part of 1905. He found a postal position in Panama and worked there from 1905-1908. He met and fell in love with a young girl who was originally from Kalamazoo, Michigan, named Laura Whitman Tyler. They married and had two children: James Rufus Agee and Emma Ferrand Agee.

James Agee is slowly being resurrected in Tennessee and Appalachia. Sholars and biographers are changing somewhat. Paul F. Brown, in his recent book, *Rufus: James Agee in Tennessee*, presents a fantastic, well-researched account of James Agee's Tennessee and Appalachian roots.

Some say the reason James Agee is rarely recognized as a local literary figure is due to several character portrayals in his posthumously awarded Pulitzer Prize winning novel, *A Death in the Family*. Some of those depictions may be accurate; others may not. But, in my quest to find truth, I realized something. The fact that the characters are *there*, the fact that the book exists at all, tells me he thought often (and for *decades*) about his Agee side, and that he longed for just another portion of their goodness.

16

Faulkner in Knoxville

by Edward Francisco

A LL AFICIONADOS OF SOUTHERN LITERATURE know that William Faulkner's literary landscape was the alluvial soil of the Mississippi Delta, the author's "little postage stamp of native soil," in his own memorable phrase. However, Faulkner's biographers often overlook or downplay his connections to Tennessee. For instance, Faulkner's great-grandfather and namesake, William Clark Falkner, was a Tennessean and Confederate war hero. The Nobel Laureate's fondness for Memphis, his city to the north, is well-documented, too. His characters, especially in *The Reivers*, find Memphis a place of excitement and escape. In 1927, the writer made frequent trips to Bluff City, as Memphis is known to locals, where he was introduced to a madam named Bella Rivers, who offered him a job as landlord in her brothel, a satisfying arrangement because, in Faulkner's words, it was "the perfect milieu for an artist to work in." Memphis also was essential in helping Faulkner determine the geographical boundaries of his native South: The South "begins in the lobby of the Peabody Hotel in Memphis and extends down to the Gulf of Mexico."

However, few scholars know or realize the amount of time William Faulkner traveled or stayed in the eastern part of the state, in particular, in or near Knoxville. Faulkner's treks began in 1954 when his daughter Jill married Paul Summers, a West Point cadet. The couple chose Charlottesville, Virginia, home to the University of Virginia, as their place of residence. (In 1957 and 1958, Faulkner gave a famous lecture series at U. Va.) As Faulkner and his wife Estelle sought to visit their daughter when possible, the author plotted their course from Oxford,

Mississippi, to Jill's Virginia home, by traveling "backroads" and state highways, given Faulkner's antipathy to the burgeoning and soon-to-be ubiquitous interstate system. On the first journey, the Mississippian discovered the midpoint to be Knoxville. In the late 1950s and early 1960s, a Holiday Inn sat at the corner of 17th Street and Grand Avenue.

When Faulkner attempted to procure a room for the night, hotel staff declined to assign him one, pointing to a "No Pets Allowed" sign in the window. As an avid hunter, Faulkner apparently traveled with his two hounds whenever he took a road trip. Maybe oblivious, but the hotel management had just turned away the Nobel Laureate of the United States. Faulkner drove into the black night, he and Estelle staring at their headlights' reflection on the surface of Andrew Johnson Highway. Eight miles north of Knoxville, the couple spotted a glaring neon sign advertising the eight-unit Arrow Motel. Its marquis promised a phone and (black and white) TV in every room. Joseph Blotner's two-volume biography of Faulkner states that the Faulkners stopped there regularly on their trips to see Jill but doesn't record any of the circumstances that took place there. The story would have ended as a footnote were it not for a student in my American literature class twenty years ago.

My student, a young man named Warren, approached me excitedly one day after class. We'd just spent the period discussing William Faulkner's short story "A Rose for Emily." Warren explained that he had a direct link to William Faulkner via his grandfather who'd once owned the Arrow Motel. Warren averred that his grandfather and Faulkner befriended each other. Together they'd sit in aluminum chairs on the lawn outside the office of the motor inn, swapping tales about their shared interests that included hunting, cat fishing, and Jack Daniel's whisky, of which the two men shared generous libations. Faulkner claimed to know Lem Motlow, founder of Jack Daniel's Distillery in Lynchburg, Tennessee. Warren's grandfather never inquired about Faulkner's work, having read somewhere about the author's penchant for privacy. One day a reporter for the *Knoxville Journal*, who'd heard that Faulkner was staying at the Arrow, attempted to get an interview but was shooed off the premises by Warren's grandfather who chastised him, saying,

"You didn't want him in Knoxville when he tried to check into the Holiday Inn. You sure as hell aren't going to bother him here."

Toward the end of our conversation, Warren said he had a gift for me. From his pocket he produced what appeared to be a postcard.

"It's a sign-in card signed by William Faulkner the last time he stayed at the Arrow Motel. I want you to have it."

Turning it over in my hand, I inspected the card. Faulkner had been assigned unit three at the motel. He was driving a 1961 Nash Rambler. The date on the card was May 5, 1962—almost two months to the day before Faulkner died of a heart attack. In the bottom right corner was William Faulkner's inimitable scrawl. At that instant, I realized I held in my hand a living artifact.

"This is quite a trophy, Warren. Are you sure you want me to have it?"

"I'm sure," he said. "I wanted to give it to someone who'd appreciate it."

I thanked him profusely. Some time passed. Knowing that Faulkner's admirers appreciate any new small scrap of information about him, I wrote a piece describing how the sign-in card passed into my possession. Editors at the Faulkner Review published the submission and a photocopy of the card.

Not long after, I received a call from a man identifying himself as the chief archivist of the William Faulkner Collection at the University of Mississippi.

"We read your article in the Faulkner Review," he said, "and double checked the Blotner biography. Sure enough, Faulkner was at the Arrow Motel when you said he was."

We weren't off on a good foot. Was he challenging my scholarly integrity?

"The reason I'm calling, Professor Francisco, is that the Faulkner Archives here at Ole Miss has expanded beyond trade and limited editions to include manuscript materials and ephemeral items. What I'm saying, Professor, is that we'd like to have your sign-in card here in the archives."

"Would you now?" I said, liking him less by the minute.

"Be reasonable, Professor. Faulkner was a native Mississippian."

"Hold on," I interrupted. "Lest I be remiss in reminding you: Faulkner's great-grandfather was from Tennessee. Faulkner traveled extensively in Tennessee, and he set his Pulitzer Prize winning novel, *The Reivers*, in Memphis. He was in Tennessee when he signed the motel card."

"What could you possibly want with that scrap of paper? It belongs to us!" he huffed.

"No, it doesn't. It belongs to me. But here's what I'll do. The next time you come to Knoxville, drop by. For a nominal fee, I'll let you view my little treasure before tucking it back safely in the catacombs of the Francisco Archives."

A click on the phone signaled an end to our negotiations. To this day, I'm still the proud owner of a small piece of Faulkner's legacy.

From time to time, I drive past the Arrow Motel, undoubtedly gaudier and shabbier now than it was when Faulkner stayed there. Still, I imagine him sitting on the lawn in a folding chair, puffing his ubiquitous pipe, sipping Jack Daniel's whisky, and whiling away the time by recounting the story of a Mississippi-sized catfish that got away. As a literary fantasy, it doesn't get much better than that.

17

Richard Marius' *Reading Faulkner,* A Book Review

By Edward Francisco

A S A GRADUATE STUDENT IN the 1970s and college English instructor in the 1980s, I could scarcely ignore the tempestuous currents spawned by the literary and cultural movement known as Deconstruction. The brainchild of contemporary French philosopher Jacque Derrida, Deconstruction challenged decades of academia's approach to understanding literature. Deconstructionists argued that culture itself was a text. As such, the movement's adherents assumed that all discourse, even historical narrative, is essentially disguised as self-revelatory messages. Being subjective, the text is indeterminate, having no fixed meaning, so when we read, we're prone to misread (because nothing is as it seems). Despite an absence of textual meaning, Deconstructionists were somehow able to ferret out the subterranean motives and undisclosed agendas of some of the most recognized writers in the Western canon. In a short time, readers were cautioned not to lionize writers whose work was tainted by privilege and whose "truth" was as elusive as will-o-the-wisp. Unable to acknowledge the shadowy aspects of their literary output, authors required the assistance of Deconstructionists to peel away the onion, exposing layers of classism, racism, and misogyny lurking among the pages.

One particular author posthumously positioned in the crosshairs of this movement was Mississippi novelist and Nobel Laureate William Faulkner whose disparagement seemed justified on several grounds. Overnight, Faulkner became a pariah and a litmus test of one's sensibility. To be an apologist for the author was tantamount to committing academic suicide. Ph.D. students were no longer encouraged to write dissertations about his work. College literature anthologies deliberately omitted selections from the Faulkner canon. Perception is persuasion in literary studies, and the perception of earlier readers who'd failed to notice the unsavory signifiers in Faulkner's fiction only underscored the urgent need to eradiate the author's noxious influence. Thus, no one actually needed to read Faulkner to pronounce judgment on him. Ready-made categories supplied that purpose, nor was the irony lost on some readers that the apostles of indeterminacy had determined Faulkner's fate as a litterateur unworthy of attention based on the indeterminacy of his language amid accusations of racism.

Soon Faulkner became an embarrassment—especially to Southern students aspiring to teach literature in high school or college. Even as writers of color were praising Faulkner for his nuanced depiction of race relations in his native Mississippi, my peers and I were urged to feel shame for our effusive admiration for the author.

By 1990, the ascendency of Deconstruction was in decline but not without consequences. If people thought about Faulkner at all, it was often to ask why Faulkner was important.

It would undoubtedly take someone with nominal similarities to Faulkner to rescue the author from the simulacrum of oblivion. Historian, novelist, and Harvard professor, Richard C. Marius answered the call. An East Tennessean by birth, Marius failed to fulfill his mother's expectation that he become a minister of the gospel, opting instead to pursue academic studies in history at the University of Tennessee, and afterward, at Yale University, where he received a Ph.D., writing his dissertation on the Renaissance and Reformation movements under the direction of Roland Bainton, for forty-two years professor of ecclesiastical history at Yale.

Marius began his college teaching career at Gettysburg College, and later, at the University of Tennessee, the author's alma mater, where he wrote his first novel, *The Coming of Rain*, set in eastern Tennessee. In 1978, he was tapped to be director of Expository Writing at Harvard University. During the academic year 1996-1997, Marius was asked by university officials to prepare a series of lectures about Faulkner's novels for a seminar of undergraduate students. In 1999, Marius succumbed to pancreatic cancer before the lectures could be collected, edited, and published. Friends took on those tasks, submitting a complete manuscript to the University of Tennessee Press in 2006. The end result was *Reading Faulkner*, a collection of lectures on Faulkner's first thirteen novels. Marius understood the need for rationale detailing his purpose in writing such a book:

> Time and again I am asked by people, anxious and even embarrassed, "Why should I read William Faulkner?" or, "What book of Faulkner's should I read first?" a question that carries with it the dreadful implication that the person who asks it has not read Faulkner at all. Both these questions come to me with much the same spirit that someone might ask for a recommendation of a dentist who might do a quick and not too painful root canal.

Aware that literary tastes are faddist and fleeting, Marius moderates his enthusiasm for Faulkner's earliest novels, roughhewn productions for which he had no models to follow, with the possible exception of Sherwood Anderson's *Winesburg, Ohio*. (Anderson offered to get the fledgling writer's first novel, *Soldiers' Pay*, published as long as Anderson didn't have to read it.) Marius could be describing his own history as a smalltown young man with literary aspirations when he describes the arc of Faulkner's career as a paradigm for other Southern writers.

> I should point out here one of the primary qualities of much southern literature. The writer merely by being a writer, being educated well enough to take up the profession of letters, becomes alienated from the society that otherwise holds him in its tight communal grasp. Both sides of this equation are essential. Until the past three decades, the south was a small-town society with the small towns as oases of commerce dependent of the farms lying around them. Both rural and small-town societies from time immemorial exercise sharp or heavy authority on the individual enforcing conformity, tolerating eccentricity only when it seems harmless.

Soldiers' Pay came out in 1926, the same year that Ernest Hemingway published his first novel, *The Sun Also Rises*. Faulkner's book received little notice; Hemingway's *tour de force* was hugely successful. *Soldiers' Pay* attempts to depict the widespread malaise following World War I. Faulkner's tale drips with gloominess. Marius describes the origin and evolution of the book's title:

> *Soldiers' Pay*, the title Faulkner finally chose for his own first novel, is part of the mystique of the "lost generation." He called it "Mayday" at first—the word that ships at sea send when they are sinking and need help fast. *Soldiers' Pay*, as a title, reflects that the soldier's pay is never sufficient to compensate the soldier for what he has suffered.

Marius points out that the book isn't really about the presumed protagonist, Mahon:

> Faulkner never writes a novel where there is one protagonist, one hero on whom the novel focuses throughout. He uses multiple points of view in this novel, writing in the third person, shifting from the minds of his characters in an omniscient way. These multiple points of view will be a feature of most of his fiction, and sometimes as in *The Sound and the Fury*, and *As I Lay Dying* he does multiple points of view in the first person, a technique that *ipso facto* eliminates the omniscient narrator.

Marius adds:

> I want to make a suggestion here that I will come back to, that Faulkner in experimenting with multiple points of view is engaging in something like the striving of the cubist painters a little earlier, the effort to place all the dimensions of reality on a single plane, here the plane of our consciousness.

Marius' description of Faulkner's incipient literary experiments anticipates the novelists' unique introduction of stream of consciousness technique (i.e., recording a character's interior monologue) making Faulkner peerless among American writers of the time. Arguably only Anglo-Irish author James Joyce (*Ulysses*) and British novelist Virginia Woolf (*Mrs. Dalloway*) would ascend to the steep aerie occupied by

Faulkner at the end of his career. (I'm aware, as was certainly Marius, that the 1922 publication of Joyce's *Ulysses* signaled for some readers the death knell for the novel because Joyce had done in that book all a novel could be expected to do (I maintain that Faulkner demonstrated otherwise.).)

Marius spends little time or space discussing Faulkner's second novel, *Mosquitoes*. Marius explains the reason why:

Mosquitoes is generally considered Faulkner's worst novel, and because we have so much to do in this course, I'm not going to spend much time on it. It is a novel where not much happens. A group of people are run aground in a yacht on Lake Pontchartrain outside New Orleans, and they talk a lot. The Semitic man, Julius, in *Mosquitoes*, makes a comment that seems to apply to the [emerging] ideologies of the world:

"After all, it doesn't make any difference what you believe. Man is not only nourished by convictions, he is nourished by any conviction. Whatever you believe, you'll always annoy someone, but you yourself will follow and bleed and die for it in the face of law, hell, or high water. And those who die for causes will perish for any cause, the more tawdry it is, the quicker they flock to it. And be quite happy at it, too. It's a provision of providence to keep their time occupied." He sucked at his cigar but it was dead.

"Do you know who is the happiest man in the world today? Mussolini, of course. And do you know who are next? The poor devils he will get killed with his Caesar illusion. Don't pity them, however; were it not Mussolini and his illusion, it would be someone else and his cause. I believe it is some grand cosmic scheme for fertilizing the earth. And it could be so much worse," he added. "Who knows? They might all migrate to America and fall into the hands of Henry Ford."

The nihilistic passage expresses the temper of the times for many following the Great War in Europe:

I would like to suggest that in the wake of World War I, great masses of people sought something to fill the horrible vacuum left by the collapse of old ideologies in the massacre and meaninglessness of the war. Some turned to communism, some to forms of Statism like Fascism and Naziism, all of them tending to divide the "masses" from the upper middle-classes and that part of the intelligentsia still devoted to Western liberal traditions. To such people, leaders like Mussolini and Hitler seemed absurd, the target of jokes and satire.

After the first two novels, William Faulkner obeyed the mantra: "Go thou and do otherwise." Not only would he focus exclusively on his "little postage stamp of native soil," in and around Oxford, Mississippi, but he grappled with unsavory and taboo subjects, such as suicide, incest, and miscegenation. In a few years, his literary consciousness catapulted into a future of possibilities for prose fiction that Faulkner largely created. For this reason, Marius sees need to insert an interregnum into his analysis before exploring works from Faulkner's most creative period. The title of Marius' chapter is "Faulkner and Blacks: The Endemic Problem of Racism in American Society."

Marius grasps the predicament confronting Faulkner as a Southerner and a writer:

In dealing with the problem in literature we have to deal with the N word, "nigger," very probably the most obscene word in the English language for its cumulative associations of bondage, inferiority, and contempt when uttered by white people against blacks. The word has such terrible connotations that it has had an ironic effect on whites. White southerners believe that they are not prejudiced if they don't use it. So for the writer, the use of the word poses a doubly ironic problem. Not to use it implies that the South and the nation as a whole were better about race than they were, and yet to use it may condemn the writer as racist.

As the inheritor of a skein of feudal complexities, the future Nobel Laureate couldn't skirt the problem of signification conveyed by the N word. Marius, the historian and border South novelist, explains:

I don't think we get much satisfaction in trying to find in Faulkner racial attitudes that would achieve the ideal of democracy where all men—and women—of whatever color and origin are considered equal, or if not considered individually equal are at least considered equal in their opportunities to be thought worthy of respect and capable of morality and intelligence on the same level of any other individual regardless of color.

Faulkner's novels drip with a tainted history, nor is the reader likely to find an egalitarian impulse of the sort literary modernism often imparts. This circumstance shouldn't prove surprising given Faulkner's now famous maxim: "The past is never dead. It's not even past." Despite some critics' observations that the author was fixated on the past, Faulkner was no adherent to the old order but viewed clearly how the rot of racism contaminated every aspect of Southern history and experience. And, as his novels show, racism is the catalyst for the dynastic collapse of aristocratic families whose desperate effort to hold onto a façade of "respectability" ultimately accords them the status of clowns.

The first of these dynastic novels that Marius discusses is *The Sound and the Fury*, the title an allusion to Shakespeare's *Macbeth*, the soliloquy where the murderous king asserts that "Life's but a walking shadow/ a tale/ told by an idiot, full of sound and fury/ signifying nothing." Anyone professing Faulkner's allegiance to the romantic nostalgia for the antebellum South fails to see that the collapse of the Old South created an existential vacuum of which Faulkner was the literary heir. The novel chronicles the decline of the Compson family, once a model of the wealthy, slave-owning Southern aristocracy before the Civil War. The characters aren't so much stereotypes as grotesque caricatures of what they were once expected to be. Faulkner experiments with multiple points of view in the story. Section one is narrated through the sensibilities of thirty-three-year-old Benjy, youngest of the Compson children. Benjy is mentally challenged. Resultingly, his descriptions are literal, simplistic, and sensual. As with his brother Quentin, Benjy fixates on his sister, Caddy, and her emergent sexuality and promiscuity. Quentin is a doomed romantic. He worships a chivalric ideal of womanhood inseparable from virginity. Quentin is evidence that everything to the

Compsons is either/or. Marius describes the inevitable consequences of adhering to this dichotomy:

> … the Compsons is an either/or. If Caddy does not live up to the grand expectations of a southern lady, she is not a member of the family at all. If Benjy is not worthy of being a Bascomb, his name must be changed. And if Quentin cannot possess Caddy and cannot stop thinking of her body and the honor it represents, he must kill himself.

As a student of Harvard, Quentin is questioned by his roommate Shreve who is fascinated by the South and its aura of mystery. Aware of the tensions and contradictions riddling his native region, Quentin is crushed by the burden of defending the Lost Cause. His self-torture is exquisite as he rages against every fiber of his being, shouting about the South, "I don't hate it! I don't hate it!" Completing this chapter of his family's tragedy, he jumps into the Charles River and drowns. The only Compson nominally succeeding is the money-grubbing Jason. His impulses reflect the vulgar actions and intentions of a rising class of the *nouvous riches*. As Marius observes, Jason drives the final nail in the Compson family coffin because he "sees sex entirely as biological release and who never has any intention of having a child to carry on the Compson line."

Faulkner's *As I Lay Dying* is a dark comedy, grotesquely so. The book lacks a conventional plot; instead, the novel is narrated by fifteen characters over fifty-nine chapters. Hence, the reader is the unifying consciousness tasked with discovering a complete story from the sum of its disparate voices. The narrative is about the death of Addie Bundren and her poor rural family's quest to honor her wish to be buried several hundred miles away in her hometown of Jefferson, Mississippi. The arduous nature of the journey shows the extent of Addie's contempt for her family and her desire to punish them. (One critic notes that the name *Bundren* is an anagram of *burden*.)

Marius asserts that

> The most powerful image in *As I Lay Dying* is the stench of Addie's body, the horror that it causes as the coffin-laden wagon moves through the countryside. This is an image from the Middle

Ages, the Renaissance—the *memento mori*—for no matter what glory and grandeur we ascend, we ultimately become food for worms. The novel has as much religion in it as any work of Faulkner's—and religion is impotent against death.

In a *Paris Review* interview, Faulkner described how a good story could be told by pitting characters against the elements: earth, air, fire, and water. Throughout the course of this novel, Faulkner pits the family against all four—to stunning effect. In fact, the reader wonders at a universe so hostile to human aims. This novel guarantees a spot for Faulkner in the annals of absurdist literature.

Southern novelist, poet, essayist, and Pulitzer Prize recipient, Robert Penn Warren, observed once that "the epistemology of the world can be found in the pages of Faulkner's *Absalom, Absalom!*." The reader would be hasty to challenge this claim. Upon its publication in 1936, devotees of Faulkner were dazzled and confused by the novel's experiments with style and viewpoint. As with other of Faulkner's novels, *Absalom, Absalom!* Depicts familial collapse. The title refers to the Biblical story of Absalom, a wayward son of King David, who was killed while fighting against the empire his father built.

Set in Mississippi in the nineteenth century, *Absalom, Absalom!* tells the story of Thomas Sutpen, a poor white man from West Virginia who rebels against his family, especially his alcoholic father, and migrates to Haiti, where he becomes the overseer of a plantation, marries and learns that his wife (and consequently his son, whom he rejects) is of mixed race.

Determined to overcome his lowly origins, Sutpen moves to the Deep South in 1833 where he establishes his own slaveholding empire. His overbalanced sense of racial superiority poisons his relationships so that by the novel's end, his plantation lies in ruins and his only living heir is a mentally deficient great-grandson of mixed blood.

In describing Sutpen, Marius offers the following assessment:

Sutpen is a sort of Nietzschean superman who refuses to accept the condition of his birth. We have already seen that Faulkner has in previous books depicted conventional morality as arbitrary, as conformity to society rather than substantially grounded in divine or human nature. He seems to have adopted for his characters both Darwin and Freud. Our human nature demands that we reproduce our species. In this effort Sutpen becomes one of the most Darwinian of his characters, but also biblical in that the Hebrew Bible offers immortality of a sort only to those who propagate children, especially sons.

Faulkner harbors no sentimentality regarding Sutpen and his struggles. After all, everyone operates under the pressures of family and history. Marius identifies the tipping point in the story:

At a certain moment when he has treated the supreme tragedy of the South in the story of Thomas Sutpen, Faulkner seems to draw back. He has in Absalom, Absalom! given us a South where incest can be excused but where a faint trace of African blood in Bon is enough to cause Henry to shoot him dead. This bleak business, catastrophe indeed, and with how much catharsis? Perhaps the catharsis lies only in our release at having spoken the unspoken truth about the South. Racial issues in the South have always gone on among people in "polite society" as an undercurrent of murmuring, euphemism, jokes, and other forms of elliptical discourse where the bare, blunt meaning of what is said is partly concealed and seldom said in overt and unmistakable language. It is at last a sort of catharsis to have Faulkner say the truth clearly: the morality of the South is such that incest between brother and sister can be accepted, but marriage to a man with one-sixteenth African blood is such a taboo that any man who threatens to violate that taboo can be permissibly killed.

Ever the epistemologist, Faulkner seems consumed with how we know things. Talk is undependable, especially with its reliance on echo, rumor, and innuendo. When Faulkner gave a series of lectures at the University of Virginia in 1957, a student zeroed in on this theme when asking a question about Sutpen:

Q. Mr. Faulkner, in *Absalom, Absalom!* does anyone of the people who talks about Sutpen have the right view, or is it more or less a case of thirteen ways of looking at a blackbird with none of them right?

A. That's it exactly. I think that no one individual can look at truth. It blinds you. You look at it and you see one phase of it. Someone else looks at it and sees a slightly awry phase of it. But taken all together, the truth is in what they saw though nobody saw the truth intact. So these are true as far as Miss Rosa and as Quentin saw it. Quentin's father saw what he believed was truth, that was all he saw. But the old man was himself a little too big for people no greater in stature than Quentin and Miss Rosa and Mr. Compson to see all at once. It would have taken perhaps a wiser or more tolerant or more sensitive or more thoughtful person to see him as he was. It was, as you say, thirteen ways of looking at a blackbird. But the truth, I would like to think, comes out, that when the reader has read all these thirteen different ways of looking at the blackbird, the reader has his own fourteenth image of that blackbird which I would like to think is the truth.

Richard Marius set himself a considerable task in preparing the lectures in *Reading Faulkner* for a class of undergraduate students. I can envision him scratching his head, asking himself, "What do they know? More importantly, what *don't* they know?" Likely he found himself symbolically navigating between the extremes of Scylla and Charybdis—no mean feat. The value of this book lies in Marius' studied analyses of Faulkner's novels during the most creative period of the author's life. Marius brings his considerable talents as a novelist, historian, and biographer to bear on some of the most salient themes in Faulkner's canon. Equally, if not more, important is Professor Marius' reminder that great literature repays our readings of texts on which we might conceivably meditate for eternity.

18

Cormac McCarthy's *Stella Maris*:
A Book Review

By Edward Francisco

Cantor, Gauss, Riemann, Euler. Hilbert.
Poincaré. Noether. Hypatia. Klein, Minkowski,
Turing, von Neumann. Cauchy, Lie, Dedekind,
Brouwer. Boole. Peano. Hamilton, Laplace, Lagrange.

I F YOU'RE UNFAMILIAR WITH THE names and contributions of the theoretical mathematicians in the modern era, then you may find Cormac McCarthy's latest novel *Stella Maris* a challenging read. It doesn't have to be, even if you're one of those people who find it exasperating that 2 is the only even prime number, constituting a set of itself; or that the appearance and pattern of prime numbers aren't predictable, though the set of primes appears to be infinite; or that some infinities are denser than others, meaning there are more real than natural numbers—even though there are infinite sets of both.

Set in 1972 in Black Falls, Wisconsin, the novel opens as Alicia Western, twenty-year-old mathematics prodigy, admits herself to a psychiatric hospital after receiving a diagnosis of paranoid schizophrenia. Told entirely from the transcripts of Alicia's therapy sessions with resident psychiatrist Dr. Cohen, Alicia's story unfolds as a series of evolutions revealing the extent to which her genius is manifestly frightening. Not only is she hypermnesic, gifted with photographic recall, but she also experiences numbers and letters in color, a condition called synesthesia. At one point in their exchange, Dr. Cohen quizzes Alicia about the perceived elegance of equations:

Are the equations themselves beautiful?

Not if you don't know what they mean.

Is $E=mc^2$ a thing of beauty?

You should see it in color.

Alicia has spent three years majoring in mathematics at Princeton and a year as a doctoral candidate at the University of Chicago. Drawn to math for its presumptive promise of predictability, she instead discovers to her disappointment that operations of advanced mathematics are anything but stable and that the elite coterie of theoretical mathematicians orbiting in the highest realms of abstraction often have a tenuous hold on reality. To illustrate her point, she relates to Cohen the longish narrative of David Hilbert and Kurt Gödel. Hilbert, a German mathematician considered one of the greats of the late nineteenth and early twentieth centuries, spent four decades trying to discover an axiom uniting all branches of mathematics. Fellow German Kurt Gödel upended Hilbert's formulations in a paper read in Venice in 1931 now popularly called the Incompleteness Theorem. Gödel's work is best understood in the context of paradox:

Consider the sentence: "This statement is false." Is it true? If so, that would make the statement false. But if it's false, then the statement is true. This sentence creates an unsolvable paradox; if it's not true and it's not false, then what is it?

Where mathematics is concerned, Alicia admits she's at the end of her tether "because you can't mathematize mathematics." In other words, Gödel's theorem means there can be no mathematical theory of everything, no unification of what's provable and what's true. Mathematics exists outside operations of the human mind. The inadequacies of math sadden Alicia, as heard in the following exchange about the insufficiency of numbers that don't add up:

You're skeptical about mathematics?

Yes.

You feel disappointed in the discipline in some way?

I'm not sure how you can be skeptical about the entire subject.

I know.

But it has disappointed you.

That would be one way to put it.

How would it do that?

Well. In this case it was led by a group of evil and aberrant and wholly malicious partial differential equations who had conspired to usurp their own reality from the questionable circuitry of its creator's brain not unlike the rebellion which Milton describes and to fly their colors as an independent nation unaccountable to God or man alike. Something like that.

Alicia makes a convincing case for an indissoluble connection between math and madness, describing the last days of her hero Kurt Gödel:

He wouldn't eat. Thought the food was poisoned. When he died he weighed about seventy pounds. Oppenheimer [nuclear physicist and 'father of the atomic bomb'] was head of IAS [Institute for Advanced Study] at the time and he would go over to see him in the hospital. One day the doctor came in. He didn't know who Gödel was—just some nutty professor from the university—and Oppenheimer told him to take care of Gödel because he was the greatest logician since Aristotle. And the doctor nodded and began to edge toward the door and Oppenheimer realized that he was thinking: Good God, now there's two of them.

McCarthy's novels have a way of circling back to East Tennessee, in this case to provide Alicia's backstory. As part of his therapeutic initiative, Dr. Cohen asks about her upbringing. Alicia discloses she was born in Los Alamos, New Mexico, but spent her childhood in Wartburg, Tennessee, close to Oak Ridge, where her physicist father had worked for Robert Oppenheimer in developing the atomic bomb.

He'd also married a local girl, a beauty contestant and later Alicia's mother, who'd taken pains to conceal her Jewishness. Dr. Cohen asks Alicia what being Jewish is like for her. She replies that "Jews represent two percent of the population and eighty percent of mathematicians. If those numbers were even a little more skewed, we'd be talking about a separate species."

If Jews are copiously represented in mathematics, women are not, despite tallying significant achievements. Alicia takes for granted she will be an outlier in the hyper-cerebral atmosphere of the University of Chicago. With a few exceptions, Alicia is snubbed by colleagues in the traditionally male-dominated field. Being diagnosed as mentally ill augments the complexities she experiences as a mathematician and a woman. She acknowledges the problematic status of smart women opposing the status quo in every age:

Women enjoy a different history of madness. From witchcraft to hysteria we're just bad news. We know that women were condemned as witches because they were mentally unstable but no one has considered the numbers—even few as they might be—of women who were stoned to death for being bright. That I havent wound up chained to a cellar wall or burned at the stake is not a testament to our ascending civility but to our ascending skepticism. If we still believed in witches we'd still be burning them. Hooknosed crones strapped into the electric chair. No one has ever seemed to comment that the stereotypical witch is meant to appear Jewish. I guess the skepticism is okay. If you can stomach what goes with it. I'm happy to be treated well but I don't know that it's an uncertain business. When this world which reason has created is carried off at last it will take reason with it. And it will be a long time coming back.

Perhaps the most interesting detail Alicia reveals is her father's imperviousness to the terrors he and his coterie of scientists unleash on the world. Their lack of imagination regarding the consequences for future generations is troubling. Dr. Cohen asks if Alicia's father ever lost sleep for his participation in the Manhattan Project:

> My father didnt sleep before the bomb and he didnt sleep after. I think most of the scientists didnt give that much thought to what was going to happen. They were just having a good time. They all said the same thing about the Manhattan Project. That they'd never had so much fun in their lives. But anyone who doesnt understand that the Manhattan Project is one of the most significant events in human history hasnt been paying attention. It's up there with fire and language.

McCarthy's *Stella Maris* has an ending but not a conclusion, though Alicia hints at one that never materializes when Dr. Cohen indicates their therapy session is over:

> I think our time is up.
>
> I know. Hold my hand.
>
> Hold your hand?
>
> Yes. I want you to.
>
> All right. Why?
>
> Because that's what people do when they're waiting for the end of something.

Readers shouldn't expect much of a plot either. There are no high moments we've come to expect from narrative. McCarthy isn't the only author to write a plotless novel. James Joyce and his *Finnegan's Wake* come readily to mind. In some ways, *Stella Maris* is as frustrating as

Joyce's sprawling stream-of-consciousness experiment. Like Joyce, too, McCarthy eschews such niceties as punctuation. However, his hardcore readers won't be deterred by the novelist's eccentricities as it's been sixteen years since his novel *The Road* was released. That's been a long dry spell for his readership.

McCarthy's *Stella Maris* delivers particularly with the characterization of Alicia Western who is steadfastly unforgettable, by turns fragile and frightening. McCarthy has successfully deconstructed the rarefied world of advanced mathematics. Those keeping up with him know the author has spent years at the Santa Fe Institute, a think tank billing itself as a place asking "big questions." As the only writer in residence at the institute, McCarthy has been the decades-long beneficiary of conversations with mathematicians and physicists over a long span of time. We can only speculate about his colleagues' influence, but McCarthy's *Stella Maris* illuminates the life of the higher mind with shimmering intelligence and flashes of brilliance uniquely the author's own.

19

Nancy Nanye'hi Ward– Cherokee Warrior for Peace

by Delonda Shown Anderson

W HILE MEANDERING THROUGH THE MUSEUM of Appalachia's treasure trove in Norris, Tennessee, I came across an exhibit encased in glass and was intrigued by the words: "She has been called: The Cherokee Chieftainess. The Pocahontas of the West, One of the Great Women in American History." In another section, I read the big bold name of this incredible, yet somewhat controversial, woman: Nancy Ward.

Join me in discovering her life's journey. I have striven to provide accurate second-hand sources, names, and pronunciations, though I understand some information is uncertain. I will respectfully leave that for the reader to ponder. That being said, let's dive into history.

Nancy Ward's Cherokee name was Nanye'hi (pronounced nahn-YEH-hee), meaning "one who goes about." She was born in Chota, Tennessee, into the Wolf Clan in 1738. One thing to note: The Cherokee bloodline was matrilineal, meaning descendants and kinships were traced through the mother's line. She was purportedly born to Tame Doe of the Wolf Clan, though no historical documents can verify the name. I say "purportedly" because the identity of her parents has been debated. Many sources say Nanye'hi's father was Fivekiller from the Delaware Lenni Lenapé Tribe. She married a Cherokee warrior named Kingfisher (Tsu-la), from the Deer clan. The couple had two children: a daughter, Ka-ti (aka Catherine), and a son, Five Killer (Hi-s-ki-ti-hi).

In 1775, Kingfisher and a reported five-hundred Cherokee warriors went to war against the Muscogee (Creek) Tribe at the Battle of Taliwa in Georgia. Nanye'hi fought alongside her husband, hiding behind a log. She chewed bullets so they would be "more pointed and deadly." Kingfisher was killed before her very eyes. She took up his musket, marched with purpose, mobilized the Cherokee warriors, and helped lead them to victory. And she fought valiantly. The defeated Muscogee left that territory, as far as I could deduce, for good.

Nancy Ward likeness.

Nanye'hi was bestowed with honors for her bravery. By unanimous consent, she was named Ghighau (pronounced Gee-gah-ooo), or, Beloved Woman. The lifetime title was enormously powerful. The Cherokee believed the "Great Spirit spoke through the Beloved woman." As Ghighau, she became head of the Women's Council and could overrule men's decisions. She sat on the Council of Chiefs and had the right to vote on issues. She had pardoning power and could initiate proceedings to remove an unfit Chief. She also prepared the sacred rite of the warrior's "Black Drink," a "life-protecting potion for the warriors as they purified themselves for war."

Several years after Kingfisher's death, she married English trader, Bryant Ward (aka Bryan), who lived with the Cherokee for a time. She subsequently changed her name to the English-speaking "Nancy." She and Bryant had a daughter named Betsy. Many sources claim marriage wasn't a lifelong contract for the Cherokee. Bryant left Nancy and, depending on the source, either moved to South Carolina as a single man, or was already married to a woman there. Nancy and her daughter reportedly visited the Wards in South Carolina several times and were warmly welcomed.

The American Revolution stirred into a frenzy. The Cherokee Tribe was split about who to support during the war. Most Cherokee sided with the British. Nancy Ward sided with the Colonists. She believed peace and co-existence with the settlers was the best way to go. Her cousin Dragging Canoe (Tsiyu Gansini), however, was passionately against peace with the white settlers, saying, "Whole Indian Nations have melted away like snowballs in the sun before the white man's advance..."

Other factors may have determined support for the Colonists. Harold Felton, in his book *Nancy Ward, Cherokee*, says the Tribe desperately needed weapons to drive back the Chickasaw. They met and voted on whether to relinquish more of their land to white settlers in exchange for weapons. Though Dragging Canoe agreed they needed weapons, he opposed giving away more Cherokee land. The transfer occurred, however, and, in 1776, an understandably resentful and angry Dragging Canoe organized warriors to attack white settlers.

Nancy performed the Black Drink rite for Dragging Canoe and the warriors. After the ceremony, she sent clandestine messages to the settlers warning them about an imminent attack. The tip-off gave them time to fend off the assault. Dragging Canoe was injured and thirteen Cherokee warriors were killed. His fury was further stoked and a "full-scale war with the newly formed United States" began. In October 1776, Continental troops fought against the Cherokee and wiped out most of their villages. In every battle, Ward's village was spared, likely because of her Colonist support. The Cherokee paid a high price for Dragging Canoe's actions. In 1777, they signed a peace treaty that gave the United States 5,000,264 acres of their land.

Ward's pardoning powers are well recorded during this time. The Cherokee captured a woman named Lydia Bean. She and her husband were the first permanent settlers in Tennessee. The tribe sentenced her to burn at the stake. The kindling was lit. Nancy Ward "reportedly strode to the mound where Mrs. Bean was tied, kicked out the fires at her feet, and cut the ropes that bound her." Ward allegedly said: "It revolts my soul that Cherokee warriors would stoop so low as to torture a squaw. No woman shall be tortured... while I am 'Ghi-ga-u.'"

Nancy harbored Lydia Bean for several months. Bean taught her weaving and dairying, before she was escorted home by Ward's brother, Longfellow (Tuskeegeeteetee), and son, Five Killer. Nancy was also known to free "Patriot prisoners."

Ward's motives for supporting the United States have been highly debated. Debra Michals' article "Nanyehi (Nancy) Ward" writes the following:

> ... some say she supported the colonists' cause against the British; others believe she was trying to retain friendships with powerful Euro American leaders; and others argue she was pragmatic, recognizing that the outnumbered Cherokee were best served by avoiding further conflicts.

Nancy herself said, "The white men are our brothers. The same house shelters us and the same sky covers us all." Harold Felton wrote that she likely took a gamble: Helping the Revolutionaries would hopefully guarantee Cherokee independence and freedom.

Nancy is considered a hero in American history. She may have even "helped change the course of the Revolutionary War." Angela Minor's *Smoky Mountain Living Magazine* article about Nancy indicates that "Ward and George Washington may have saved each other's lives." Ward's letter to Washington was found in Thomas Jefferson's documents.

Conversely, her motives have been criticized and questioned by many in the Cherokee Nation. According to the New York Historical Society's article, "Life Story: Nanyehi Nancy Ward (1738-1822)," Nancy

> ... played a critical role in moving the Cherokee Nation away from their traditions and toward a more Westernized way of life... her attitude of acceptance toward white settlers gave them the ability to encroach on Cherokee territory. Today some Cherokees consider her a traitor, while Tsiyu Gansini is considered a hero for advocating armed resistance.

The Revolutionary War ended, and Britain surrendered all lands across the Mississippi River—including Cherokee territory—to the newly-formed United States. Of course, the Tribe was altogether left out of the deal. The white population exploded. The settlers disregarded *any* deals made between the Cherokee Tribe and the U.S. government, and the land grab was on. The appropriation and takeover ensured further clashes between Cherokee and settlers.

After years of conflict, the settlers urged for peace. Discussions were held circa 1781. Ward represented the Cherokee, saying, in part:

> … we are your mothers; you are our sons. Our cry is all for peace; let it continue. This peace must last forever. Let your women's sons be ours; let our sons be yours. Let your women hear our words.

Her speech was well-received; the Cherokee kept some of their lands; and a peace deal was signed. The treaty was broken less than ten years later, after a Cherokee Chief was allegedly murdered by white men.

Colonist takeovers were relentless. In 1817, several Cherokee Chiefs negotiated a treaty (Hiwassee Purchase of 1819), ceding land to the U.S. Federal government. Nancy Ward was almost eighty years old and could not travel to attend the negotiations. She sent a written appeal for the Cherokee Chiefs to leave the Tribe's land alone. Her advice was rejected. The treaty went forward, opening the flood gates for white settlers. Nancy was forced to move near the Ocoee River, where she ran an inn. She also took care of orphans, earning the nickname "Granny Ward."

By this time, the Cherokee Nation had become more patriarchal and Westernized, and the Beloved Woman no longer had a voice or power. The "Westernized grip" on women in Cherokee society had just begun. About seven years after the Hiwassee Purchase, rules for women were drastically changed. Cherokee women no longer had the right to vote, and they were prohibited from participating in government. The changes were "officially recognized in the Cherokee Constitution."

Nanye'hi "Nancy" Ward died in 1822, and sources claim "a light rose from her body, fluttered around the room like a bird, left through an open door, and disappeared toward Chota." She is buried in the Nancy Ward

Cemetery in Polk County, Tennessee, near her brother, Longfellow. She was described as "queenly and commanding in appearance and manner and… a winsome and resourceful woman." Renowned botanist Thomas Nuttall compiled an oral description of her as "tall, erect, and beautiful, with a prominent nose, regular features, clear complexion, long, silken black hair, large piercing black eyes, and an imperious air." Her sixth great-granddaughter, Terri Randolph, said "She was born with great character and maturity. But also possessed humility with others."

Nancy Ward statue.

A little bit of a mystery surrounds Nancy Ward, or, well, her likeness. James Abraham Walker sculpted a statue of her in around 1876, intending for it to be placed at her gravesite. For some odd reason, the figure was in a *Grainger County*, Tennessee, cemetery for more than seventy years. The statue disappeared from there in the 1980s, then reappeared in an antique show in New York City. The likeness is now allegedly in the possession of an antiques dealer in Maine.

Nancy Ward, for good or bad, was arguably the most influential woman in the Cherokee Nation's history. She not only introduced dairy farming to the tribe, she also helped transform the government "to a republic." She was a peacemaker and go-between at a time when political and colonialist powder kegs were packed, shaken, and set ablaze. Expansion was shocking and especially brutal. Perhaps she truly did see the writing on the wall. Thousands of white faces with a surplus of weaponry had settled in Cherokee territory, with more to come. Or, perhaps the Great Spirit truly did speak through her. At the crux of the Cherokee spirituality is a philosophy of balance and harmony. As Beloved Woman, she spent almost seventy years striving for peace and harmony—for the Cherokee Nation and for *all* peoples.

20
Danita Dodson's *The Medicine Woods,* A Book Review

By Delonda Shown Anderson

D ANITA DODSON'S THIRD BOOK OF poetry is called *The Medicine Woods*. Her poems speak so easily to my heart, so I wanted to write the review for her new collection. In *The Medicine Woods*, her poems conjure longings for Appalachian soil and ancestors. Her poems tug gently and encourage me to see beautiful memories of the past that I buried so long ago due to time and circumstances. They remind me about place and Earth and elements and ancestors.

I could evaluate the poetic elements and mechanics of Dodson's poetry—how she combines stunning imagery and perfect diction, how the poetic elements are masterfully and precisely polished. I could write about these things only. However, what I'd like to do is share with the reader my perceptions and, later, how the poems move me. So, we'll follow Danita Dodson as she weaves and walks a moving journey through *The Medicine Woods*.

The collection is divided into four sections: "Snapshots of Woodland Well-Being," "Voices and Vestiges in Earth," "Meditations for Healing," and "Keepers." Inside these sections, Dodson guides the reader deep into mystical places. We see Earth's beauty and hear her tongues. We seek to heal our Earth, even as we accept her curatives and restoratives; and we maintain her as our ancestors did.

Everything in these mountains—from flora to fauna, detritus to lichen, human to woodland creature—everything works in harmony. Dodson's poems present a stunning visual and aural orchestra that presses us to realize we are all connected, and humankind is just one part of the grand symphony.

Dodson's poems paint an aesthetic earth with harmony and healing. The very first poem, "Solar Eclipse," with its dreamlike visuals, detail the 2017 solar eclipse. The surreal light radiates and expands across the land, and the experience unites every being. Dodson writes:

> In these moments, the whole land pauses,
>
> bonded by an offbeat happening that urges
>
> us to recognize there is something larger,
>
> something more majestic…
>
> (3.18-21)

In this pause, a brief respite allows us to contemplate not only the beauty of the moment, but also our connections with the woodlands and the splendor of a Divine Creator.

In her poem "The Morning as Bride," dawn's light is shifted slowly from moon to sun. The moon "is suspended/ like a glowing pearl" (2-3), waiting behind the veil of clouds like a bride who greets the groom. We are reminded to look for "what unexpected beauty the day may hold" (25).

Even the smallest creatures, those beings we often overlook, are beautiful and useful. Dodson's poem, "Mussel Power," reminds us that little-seen creatures perform "colossal" (2.19) workings every day of our lives. The speaker points out that mussels "spend their long lives/ buried partly in the riverbed sediment" (2.15-16), but they filter pollutants from "gallons of water" (2.19). These tiny creatures have purpose.

Dodson's poems draw the reader close enough to hear Earth's voice. The earth laughs; trees tell their stories; water and stone are messengers; and the river speaks.

For a person who was born here, or, for people who have fallen in love with this region, no matter where you are, Appalachia, in all her motherdom, will beckon you. The mountains follow you everywhere, imploring you to remember who you are and what made you. In Dodson's "Haunted by Hollers and Hills," the speaker remembers with fondness "where soup beans and cornbread/ sit welcomingly on an inherited stove" (3.11-12), and how "the tongues of ancestors speak" (3.13). One might *try* to move away, to change, to forget Appalachia, and forget our collective selves. Yet the speaker reveals that in homebased Appalachia, "*this* is the one true place where I can/ most commune with the green earth—" (4.21-22).

In *The Medicine Woods*, Dodson's love, devotion, and concern for Earth are evident. Her poetry allows us to *hear* the soil. In "Earth Laughter," she writes:

> There are healing echoes
> of laughter—
>> laughter—
> resounding joyfully in the soil.
> (1.1-4)

And she brings the woods home in a more personal, intimate way in "The Language of a River":

> My river has a tongue honeyed
> with the ancient argot of hill folk,
> the riparian idiom of my people... (11-13)

But this river, the Clinch River, the speaker says has "... no code-switching, its accent,/ as unfeigned as water star-grass (19-20).

The woods are also a place of healing, offering respite, retreat, and meditation. In "Feeling the Electric Earth," the speaker hunts for "sassafras and yellow root, forest medicine and mountain lore" (4-5). In these mountains, healing may come in the form of wildflowers, herbs, roots, bark, and just plain *being*. The woods offer a place to meditate and restore oneself. And the poet reminds us in "Mid-Morning Meditation" that we need not meditate closed indoors:

> This day there is no buckwheat cushion
> In a Zen-graced corner of a warm room.
> Today mindfulness walks in the woods.
> (2.6-8)

The woods—the very Earth—is the place to "find well-being" (4.26).

Forbears gaze at us from behind Dodson's words. The speaker in "Feeling the Electric Earth," mentions root hunting "in my ancestors' Tennessee woods" (1.3), and releasing a skink "the way I had seen my Mamaw do" (3.21). In the quiet hours, the faint, distant sounds of our ancestors remind us that they, too, had a share in the same air we breathe, the same water we drink, the same land we walk upon and live upon.

The Medicine Woods also takes on a more serious tone. The poems offer a grave warning about our earth and how we care for her—or how we do *not* care for her.

In "Ecology for Eli," about a Union soldier in the Civil War, Dodson reminds us that aggressions begin when we avoid dialogue and nonviolence. When humanity splits large enough for war, the earth splits large, too.

> Trees were massacred—about two million—
> armies axing them for firewood and bridges,
> destroying the habitats of birds and bats,
> the roots of life shattered, ravaged, stolen.
> The trees left standing often bore their own
> Battle scars, *perfectly riddled with bullets.*
> (3.22-27)

The poem "Mariposas," bemoans how much people (including the poem's own speaker) are oblivious to their impact on a region. The speaker also mourns humankind's devastation:

> As bulldozers annihilate the forests,
> and pesticides poison quaffing insects,
> perhaps these flitting souls with broken
> wings resurrect in broken places…
> (36-39)

In "The Ancestors," Dodson tells us that our own predecessors also give warning:

> ... the voices of our ancestors hasten us
>
> to preservation because the future
>
> will not exist in a vacuum but must be
>
> linked to a remembrance of the past.
>
> (1.5-8)

The book's last poem is titled "We." Dodson writes that we are "heedless of the impact of our choices" (5). Her poem reminds us that we are simply "travelers here" (23), that this place we inhabit is "borrowed from our children" (25). As such, we must collectively treat the planet better. If we don't, this region, this mountain "will diminish daily" (26) until nothing.

Her poems also connect with spirit. In "Transient Art in the Gloaming," the Great "Artist" (1) paints the earth with jewels. The Creator is found in even the smallest things, yet the earth needs succor. So, we must answer the call. And

> ... we must pray healing, dream healing, weave healing,
>
> Speak healing, paint healing, write healing,
>
> Bring healing back...

I highly recommend *The Medicine Woods*. Danita Dodson is a true, soulful poet of Appalachia, and a rare gem in today's poetry. Her poems take me back to my roots—figuratively and geographically. They are written with elegance and grace, and they glide along the mind like a summer breeze. That is not to say, however, that her poems are like cute, fluffy bunnies. No, her poems store tremendous word power. Through them, I hear the earth sing and laugh. Through them, I see wildlife and green life. I taste the creek's crisp, cool water and sassafras root and soup beans and cornbread. I *feel* tree barks and grasses and little creatures. Her poetry journeys to find the medicines of air, earth, water, and spirit. Danita Dodson wants to share these experiences with you, too. You may be transformed, or, perhaps experience a reawakening... if you consider our interconnections in *The Medicine Woods*.

21
Christine Noble Govan:
Mystery at Book's End

by Edward Francisco

G ROWING UP IN THE SHADOW of Lookout Mountain in Chattanooga, Tennessee, a city socially stratified according to altitude, I fell under the spell of native author Christine Noble Govan, whose specialty was children's mystery novels set in or near the city's scenic attractions. A prolific writer of more than fifty novels, Govan occupied two entire shelves at my elementary school library, showcasing such titles as *The Mystery of Moccasin Bend* (1957), *The Mystery at Plum Nelly* (1959), and *The Mystery at Rock City* (1960). The only drawback to having so many of her books in the library was that I could only check out one at a time. That fact forced me to devour them. I even convinced myself, for a time, that I alone was Christine Govan's target audience and that she wrote the mysteries exclusively for me. I was beginning to understand the impact a writer can have on a reader eager to suspend disbelief in service to a compelling story and a gifted storyteller.

It wasn't just the familiar place names, either. I happily identified and saw myself as a member of a coed club of young sleuths known as the Lookouts. Their specialty was solving crimes committed by adults. The kids were smart, savvy, and persistent. Their personalities were unique and engaging. Govan could never be accused of creating cardboard cut-out characters. They were, by turns, bored, irascible, curious, and excited. They never expected adults to entertain them and would have found the idea anathema. More than anything, I wanted to be part of their gang. I refused to believe they were fictional characters.

In 1964, I encountered my literary idol face to face for the first time. The occasion was the annual Plum Nelly Clothesline Art Show which first occurred in 1947. To this day, Plum Nelly sells the wares of local, regional, and occasional worldwide artists during a single October weekend. Plum Nelly got its name when its founder, Fannie Mennen, hosted the event on her property at Lookout Mountain. In Southern parlance, Mennen's brother-in-law declared, "Your place is plum out of Tennessee and nelly [nearly] out of Georgia." The name stuck.

My eleven-year-old self stood in line with other kids for Mrs. Govan to sign our books. I'd bought mine—*The Mystery at Rock City*—from the Scholastic Book Services available for order at school. Christine Govan was warm and gracious to the children filing by. Her smile never flagged and shone as bright as the sun on that crisp October Saturday. I submitted my book shyly and she responded generously by thanking me for being one of her young readers. Her filigreed signature was the art of a bygone era.

The next time I encountered Mrs. Govan was as a junior in college. In the intervening years, I'd acquired some information about my literary heroine. I discovered that, although born in New York in 1898, she lived most of her life in Chattanooga. Her father, Stephen E. Noble, died when Christine was four years old, prompting the family to move to Sewanee, Tennessee, because her maternal great-uncle Charles Todd Quintard lived there. After several years, the family moved back to Chattanooga where Govan (née Noble) completed high school.

Afterwards, the future author enrolled as a scholarship student at the University of Chattanooga but left because her family needed her financial support. Certified to teach first grade, Christine Govan taught briefly at a rural one-room school. In June 1918 she married Gilbert E. Govan, a bookstore owner, originally from Atlanta. They had three children: Emmy, Mary, and James. Despite her domestic responsibilities, Govan's approach to her work was deliberate and calculated. She vowed to publish two books each year.

One particularly interesting factoid about Govan's life was her decision to become an early member of the NAACP and to support the Civil Rights Movement in the largely Jim Crow South. Her best-selling trilogy

Those Plummer Children focused on interracial friendships. Editions were published in England, Denmark, Germany, Japan, and Sweden.

I met Mrs. Govan for a second time when I was twenty. She was seventy-five. A mutual acquaintance introduced her and my father. When my dad said what a fan of her work I was, and that I was majoring in English in college, and that I aspired to be a writer, Govan extended an invitation for me to visit her on the mountain. My father arranged a meeting during Christmas break.

I was filled with dread that escalated into full-blown terror. What twenty-year-old aspiring to be a writer doesn't harbor a suspicion that he or she is a fraud? Mrs. Govan would see through my façade. It's one thing, I told myself, to want to be a writer; it's another thing to write and see one's work published between covers. Despite being three-quarters of a century old, Christine Noble Govan was hard at work writing novels. She'd just published *Danger Downriver* (1973) at the time I visited her.

She entertained me with all the graciousness and hospitality I should have expected. My jitters melted in a matter of minutes. She asked me about my favorite authors. I confided that a course in Shakespeare had ruined me for vocations in medicine or law. I wanted to write and to teach the works of other writers—like Shakespeare. I'd done most of the talking, but at this point she offered the only piece of writer advice I was to receive: "Always measure yourself by the best, and you'll never be disappointed." When I groused that words sometimes failed me or that I lacked inspiration for stories, she spoke up gently: "Can you recall a day of childhood in stark clarity?" I nodded that I could. "Then you'll never lack for material."

For the better part of an hour, I bent Mrs. Govan's ear. Years later, when reflecting on the kindness she afforded me that day, I recalled a maxim attributed to St. Francis of Assisi: "The first duty of loving is listening." Christine Noble Govan loved her literary landscape, loved the characters who inhabited it, and loved the real-life boys and girls transformed by the exploits of the Lookouts. If she were here for another hour, I'd thank her that some small measure of the grit, boldness, and generosity of spirit demonstrated by her child sleuths had rubbed off on me. If there's a better way to sing an author's praises, I don't know it.

MOUNTAIN REGION

22

Freak Show: Confessions of a Modern Southerner

by Edward Francisco

I T STALKS LIKE A SHADOW and hugs like a straitjacket. I wear it like an off-the-rack, ill-fitting coat. At times, it tightens round my throat like a scarf threatening to strangle me. It's closer than my own skin. It itches in spots beyond my reach to scratch. I didn't ask for it but received it anyway—like a deformed child one has little heart to defend against taunts and slights and ridicule. Only I'm the child misfit, and there's no other way to be me except accepting that I am, in a word, irredeemably, irreducibly, irreversibly—Southern. Nor can I reconcile the existential duality that being southern imparts: defending the indefensible, loving the unlovable, hiding what won't stay hidden. Never permitted the luxury of abstractions, like the doubting apostle Thomas, a Southerner will demand to see the nail prints. Too often, ours has been the stuttering cadence of a repeating decimal not subject to change.

Typically, a body adapts to changes imposed on it. Ours refuses. It behaves aberrantly, stubbornly, perversely, even criminally, at times. We're a seasonal side show. If... I were God (Everybody else is pretending to be Him or Her. Why can't I?), I'd erect a razor-wire fence around the eleven Confederate states and turn us into a theme park. Tourists could drive by and wave. Signs would warn not to get too close as we have a tendency to bite the hand that feeds us. We could put on a spectacle for them. After all, we've had 400 years of practice. A Montana "Patriot" waving a Confederate flag? If there's one thing I can't stand, it's a Johnny-come-lately, amateur-ass racist. Step aside, boys. You're out of your league. Watch how pros do it!

Ours is a complex and messy history inviting of despair: Quentin Compson's violent denial in *Absalom, Absalom!*, his self-told, self-repeated lie about the South, "I don't hate it!" before plunging into a New England river frigid in the extreme. Inhospitable extremes of hot and cold best define the Southern temperament—never tepid, never lukewarm, never in moderation.

No less than Mississippi native and Nobel Laureate, William Faulkner, intuited that the heat and humidity spawned a Petri dish of… acid bitterness, violent relationships, ignoble histories, and gloomy memories. In fact, visitors to the South in the nineteenth century frequently alleged heat to be a causative agent for the South's corrosive and peculiar character. How else to explain it? A Vermont tourist, a journalist from Montpelier, was shocked that Southern girls seemed to "blossom" earlier, achieving puberty sooner than lasses from other parts of the country. Explanation: a veritable greenhouse effect stoking hormones.

Obviously, early physical development translated into promiscuity to outsiders sniffing self-righteously at the lax morals of Southerners. A more useful explanation might be that the sticky, broiling heat encouraged Southerners to shed clothes whenever possible. I have a theory that skinny dipping originated in the rural South and required only one rule for participation: What happened underwater stayed underwater. Brilliant and boisterous man of letters, Robert Penn Warren, put a finer edge on it when he said sexual intercourse is a "chief form of amusement in the south" because "it's inexpensive and easy to procure." Let me just say it. We Southerners are sexy as hell. Others know, too. According to a recent national survey, the Southern accent was rated sexiest in America.

What to make of our impulsive, hot-headed, lust-in-the-dust collective spirit? Why, own it, of course. Let's face it. We're a convocation of the guilty. Our sins are writ large, a fact of which we are reminded constantly. We can make no excuses. However, if cultural psychosis is the hand we've been dealt, then maybe we should exploit that hand in ways that benefit us all. Our best writers have always known who we are and have often written about us with a devastating sense of humor, refusing to pull punches when we behaved foolishly, knowing when more was at stake than our egos. A week or so ago, I came across a thesis, chuckling at the title, "Freedom at the Freak Show: Carnivalesque Imagery in the Fiction of Flannery O'Connor, Eudora Welty, and Katherne Anne Porter," writers steeped in our mad, crafty, wild, and absurd legends perpetuated by what one author calls "agile Southern furies." Surely our craziness has much to teach the rest of the country.

Don't assume you're immune to our disease if you only just moved here and are a transplant, either. Once here, you're infected. You'll know by the elongation of vowels and softening of consonants in your speech. Your genes will mutate under our influence. Your children will sound like us.

Don't despair, though. Our best people have risen above the din and confusion of petty hatreds to do some remarkable things. For every Bull Connor, we've witnessed the rise of a Martin Luther King. For every race-baiting journalist, we've encountered the outspoken courage of a Hodding Carter. For every segregationist preacher, we found a Reverend Ralph Abernathy and Will D. Campbell praying in our midst. For every gun-toting thug in the coal fields of Harlan, Kentucky, we beheld a stalwart Florence Reece standing her ground and singing "Which Side Are You On?"

Our checkered history offers us ample evidence of being authentic, if nothing else. It also encourages us to be humble on occasion, humility being a gift whereby we learn to tolerate, even embrace, foibles common to us all. There's a saying in the South: "He may be a son of a bitch, but he's our son of a bitch." If we like you, we'll be loyal to a fault.

My meditation wouldn't be complete without sharing the concluding stanzas of Robert Penn Warren's poem, "Founding Fathers, Early-Nineteenth-Century Style, Southeast U.S.A." In this era of fierce generational strife, Warren reminds us of our essential connectedness to those who came before and those to follow and the common denominator uniting us all:

… and they died, and are dead, and now their voices
Come thin, like the last cricket in frost-dark, in grass lost,
With nothing to tell us for our complexity of choices,
But beg us only one word to justify their own old life-cost.

So let us bend ear to them in this hour of lateness,
And what they are trying to say, try to understand,
And try to forgive them their defects, even their greatness,
For we are their children in the light humanness, and under the
                                        shadow of God's closing hand.

23

War in Coal Creek

by Delonda Shown Anderson

A CITY IN EAST TENNESSEE RESTS quite unobtrusive and timeless against a misty mountain backdrop. Historic architecture lines the old main street that once felt the drumbeat of a booming industry. Rocky Top was once Lake City, but the area was originally named Coal Creek. Pioneers first settled the area in the mid-1800s and found the banks by the cool, crisp creek amenable. Every region has that chronicle of events that inevitably defines a place. So it was with Coal Creek, Tennessee. At the turn of the twentieth century, the small, vital city was beset by war and disasters unspeakable and horrific. For Coal Creek, tragedy exposed a buoying people with an inner strength and tremendous fortitude. I'd like to take you on a journey to explore this unique place. And our first stop is the Coal Creek War.

By the 1850s, the major industry in Tennessee was coal, thanks in large part to short-line railroads, and Coal Creek had the most coveted coal of all. It has always been a cheap resource with a big profit. In fact, it was so cheap that anybody who had an iota of wealth took a gamble. And Appalachia was rife with coal—fifty million acres. So, in October 1867, Coal Creek exported their first railcar of the fossil fuel. After this, coal camps—company owned communities for miners and their families—sprang up across the Appalachian Mountains.

Though coal barons experienced prosperity, the region otherwise suffered. The South and Appalachia were bankrupt after the Civil War, and it just so happened that the prison system was in dire need of reform. Prison upkeep was too expensive, and the facilities were overcrowded and dilapidated. To amend the prison dilemma, the Tennessee State

Legislature passed a convict-leasing law in 1866. Prisoners were rounded up and "leased" to the coal mines as free labor. They were housed on or near the premises in stockades and kept under guard.

Needless to say, the convict-lease system didn't set too well with the working miners. As time went on, the miners' wages and workdays were slashed. Yet, between 1870 and 1890, the convict-lease system stuffed Tennessee's pockets with close to $770,000 (between sixteen and twenty million dollars today). The miners understood what was happening. Companies paid little to nothing for convict workers and received greater profits.

A coal miner wasn't paid by the hour, by the day, or even by the job. A miner was paid by the weight of coal he extracted—specifically, by the ton. Every day a mineworker loaded the coal he dug into an empty rail car. He put a "small brass tag with his number stamped on it," which assigned the load to his name. A weighman worked "at the tipple where the coal was weighed" and allocated the weight to each miner's account. The coal miner was then paid with a currency called 'scrip,' which could only be used at company stores in or around the coal camps. If a miner refused to do business with a company store and went elsewhere, he could lose his job.

Weigh tag (center) from Coal Creek, Tennessee, and scrip from Block Mining (L) and Westbourne Coal Camp (R).

By 1891, the convict-lease system had caused twenty-five years of job and wage uncertainty, and a score of unresolved grievances left the miners with few options. One of the grievances involved the weighman for the Tennessee Coal Mining Company in Briceville. The miners were suspicious of the weights and numbers so, in accordance with Tennessee law, they requested a "checkweighman," a person appointed to investigate the workers' claims and check the company weighmaster's numbers. The coal company agreed. The miners hired their own checkweighman. And the company *disagreed*. As a further affront, the coal companies tried to force the miners to sign contracts that were set in stone, but the terms just about eliminated all their rights. A signed document meant a miner had no right to a checkweighman, no right to accept a salary of cash over scrip, and no right to refuse to work. But perhaps what angered miners most was the statement that gave employers unconditional authority and took away the miners' right to unionize. They refused to sign and, one by one, walked out.

The Tennessee Coal Mining Company responded by evicting the miners and their families, and by closing the Briceville Mine in April 1891, locking out the miners. The company mockingly reopened the mine on July 4—Independence Day—with convict-lease labor. Forty convicts were brought to Coal Creek and ordered to demolish the now evicted miners' homes and build a stockade to house more prisoners.

On July 14, the anniversary of Bastille Day, the miners met to discuss bolder actions. After midnight on July 15, three hundred miners successfully besieged the Briceville stockade, collected the convicts and their guards, and put them on a train to Knoxville. They sent word to Governor John Buchanan asking for his help. The governor traveled to Briceville, "accompanied by a battalion of state militia" to hear the miners' grievances. Unsurprisingly, he offered no assistance. The following day, he returned to Nashville but left the militia in Coal Creek. Status quo continued.

On July 20, around two thousand armed miners stealthily advanced to the Tennessee Coal Mine stockade. Hidden from sight, they sent three men to inform Colonel Sevier, commander of the militia, of their demand for the convicts' removal. When the colonel tried to capture one of the three men, that man gave a signal, and "at once the two thousand miners sprang to their feet and marched in awesome demonstration to the stockade." The colonel was outnumbered and surrendered. The miners marched the convicts, guards, and militia to Coal Creek station and put them on a train to Knoxville. After this, they went to another mine in Briceville and repeated the same actions.

Governor Buchanan traveled back to Knoxville and met with a newly formed mining committee. The miners would temporarily comply with the convict-lease system if they were pardoned for their nonviolent uprisings; and if the governor called a special session of the Tennessee General Assembly urging the overturn of the convict-lease law. Upon his return to Nashville, the governor called the special session in August 1891. The legislature denied the miners' request, and further, made it a criminal offense to interfere with convict labor. Anyone who did so faced up to five years in prison. The miners and Tennesseans as a whole were stunned.

On Halloween night, 1500 armed miners disguised themselves and marched with purpose to the Tennessee Coal Mining Company where they released 163 prisoners outright—free—into the hills. Then they set the stockade on fire and watched it burn to the ground. They repeated these actions at the Knoxville Iron Mine, releasing 120 convicts before setting fire to the guard house. They "battered down the stockade door with a sledgehammer" at the Cumberland Mine in Oliver Springs and freed two hundred convicts before burning it down. Community sentiment sided with the miners as Coal Creek's locals provided the convicts with food and clothes.

The coal and leasing companies hesitantly extended an olive branch. They halted their convict-lease participation, rehired the free miners, and restored their rights. The miners and the community were relieved. Peace at last.

In December 1891, however, Governor Buchanan, faced with public criticism, sent the convicts back to the mines with military reinforcements. The stockades were rebuilt stronger and larger, and prison workers came to Coal Creek once again. The miners resumed work, but, little by little, injustices grew within the coal walls. The prisoners were forced to work full time while the miners worked part time, a scant one to three times a week. Any miner who participated in the uprisings was "blacklisted" and fired. The best places in the mine to work were given to "scabs and blacklegs."

In August 1892, the situation erupted for a final time. The Tennessee Coal Iron and Railway Company cut a good portion of the miners' workload by half. Mineworkers all over the region were outraged. They trekked to the stockades, overpowered guards, looted, gathered convicts, put them on a train to Nashville, then torched the buildings. The situation volleyed back and forth. The governor returned convicts, rebuilt stockades, and sent more troops. The miners sent the convicts off, burned the stockades, and became bolder in spite of the troops. In the largest show of united force, three thousand miners throughout East Tennessee congregated at Coal Creek. They hijacked two trains, released more prisoners, and burned more stockades. The governor called for additional troops and requested volunteers all over the state. The miners dug in and prepared for all-out war. But "when the train loads of soldiers bearing field guns and Gatling guns arrived in Coal Creek they began to retreat."

Those who stayed fought doggedly. Troops arrested and detained miners to encourage total surrender. The fighting miners made attempts to free their fellow comrades. They seized General J. Keller Anderson after feigning surrender. The fighters' ringleader, Bud Lindsay, pointed a gun at the general's head and told *him* to surrender. Anderson "straightened himself up, threw out his arms in the face of Lindsay's pistol and told him to 'shoot and be damned.'" He was taken unharmed.

Coal Creek Miners

Coal Creek Miners Posing, 1893.

General Samuel Carnes was brought in to secure order and rescue Anderson. When Carnes arrested over three hundred Coal Creek citizens, a good portion of whom were likely the miners' families, the mineworkers surrendered, and the war ended. Five hundred miners were arrested and around twenty-seven were killed. At least seven were killed on the other side. Three hundred miners were indicted for "conspiracy, for carrying arms, or for murder, but only a handful" went to jail. The aforementioned Bud Lindsay's detention was harrowing. Since he was the ringleader who threatened General Anderson's life (several times), he was hanged by the neck three times and was cut down right at the point of death each time. Skirmishes emerged again in 1893 but were quickly quelled.

History may report that the Coal Creek miners' insurrection was unsuccessful. But a closer look suggests otherwise. In 1893, less than a year after the miners' war, the General Assembly called for the end of convict-leasing. In 1895, the leasing contracts were allowed to expire. The following year, a mere four years after the Coal Creek war, the Tennessee Legislature abolished the system for good and new prisons were built—Brushy Mountain (1896) and Tennessee State (1898). This journey to explore Coal Creek exposed a little Tennessee city that helped changed the nation and helped pave the way for future union organization.

24

Coal Creek: Fraterville

by Delonda Shown Anderson

A FTER THE COAL CREEK WAR, coalminers garnered a new respect, reclaimed their jobs, and formed unions. Coal companies gained a skilled workforce and restructured the industry better than it was before convict-leasing. Families were relatively happy, and normalcy and stability returned. Ten years after the Coal Creek War ended, however, an uneasiness settled on the periphery. The journey in Coal Creek continues at the Fraterville Mine. Consider the following scene:

She awakened on a beautiful May morning well before dawn, sat on the bedside, and glanced back at her husband who clung to a few more minutes of sleep. She washed, dressed, put her hair in a bun, and tied an overused apron around her waist. She approached the cookstove with confidence, opened the left hatch, filled it with wood, and lit it with a timber. When breakfast was ready, she set a modest table and covered it with biscuits, homemade blackberry jam, hand-churned butter, coffee, and buttermilk. Next, she woke the children and readied them for school. Her husband stirred in the bedroom—a swish of water from the basin, the rustle of his clothes, the tread of his boots. Coal dust puffed under the bedroom door. After years in the mines, the black dust rooted in and became part of them all. He walked through the kitchen and told her how good it was to wake up to such a fine smell in the morning. He took his seat at the head of the table, pulled on a pigtail or two, and giggles abounded. She packed his lunch pail and wrapped biscuits for the children. He patted his stomach and bragged about marrying a good woman. She chuckled, chastised him lovingly, and informed him only the Lord was *good*. His footsteps shuffled toward her, and she handed him his lunch. He put his hand on her shoulder and their eyes met. He kissed her forehead and gently pinched her chin. He turned to the children, ruffled the boys' hair, and told them all to do good in school. He looked back as the door closed behind him. She prayed with all her heart that God would keep her husband safe three miles down the dark place. Forty-five minutes later, at 7:30 a.m. on May 19, 1902, her face grew colorless as the earth trembled, and the dreaded bell clanged tragedy.

The name *Fraterville* means "village of Brothers." The Fraterville mine was owned by the Coal Creek Coal Company and was the oldest in Coal Creek, opening in 1870. Major E. C. Camp was president and general manager of the mine. A former Union Civil War officer, he was opposed to convict leasing and hired qualified miners, paying them in cash instead of scrip. Camp's son, George, learned the business first-hand, working as a coal miner before succeeding his father as supervisor. The Fraterville mine sat adjacent to the Knoxville Coal and Iron Company's abandoned mine and was considered one of the safest mines in Tennessee.

Fraterville Mine Accident, 1902.

When the explosion occurred, the whole camp felt the earth rumble. Witnesses saw smoke, flames, and wreckage shoot up in the air from the mine's opening. After the bell rang, all the camp inhabitants ran toward the mine. Two search and rescue teams were immediately formed. The first team met deadly gas at two thousand feet. Subsequent teams sifted through rubble, falling slate, mounds of blasted coal, and shattered pillars. The initial impact of the explosion killed almost every miner. One miner was found alive, but his arms were contorted, his eyes were missing, and his legs were broken. Another miner was blown from the mouth of the mine and survived for a short time. The consensus for the number of deceased stands at 184 men. Various nationalities of men, aged sixty to twelve, all died together. Some recovered bodies were without limbs or heads. Twenty-six men and boys actually survived the initial blast and barricaded themselves inside pockets and passageways, stuffing clothes or anything they could around air crevices to stop the deadly gas. But their efforts were in vain. Some of the men survived several hours, long enough to write farewell letters to their families or friends. The letters are heart-wrenching:

To My Wife:—We are shut up at the head of the entry with a little air; but the bad air is closing in on us fast. It is now twelve o'clock, Monday... Now, dear wife, put your trust in the Lord to help you raise my little children. Ellen, take care of my darling little Lillie. Ellen, little Elbert said that he trusts in the Lord... If we should never get out we are not hurt, only perished. There are but a few of us here... Elbert said for you to meet him in Heaven. Tell all the children to meet with us both there.

(J. L. Powell)

From Henry Beach:—Alice, do the best you can; I am going to rest... Elbert said the Lord had saved him... We are all praying for air to support us; but it is getting so bad without any air. Howard, Elbert said for you to wear his shoes and clothing. It is now two-thirty o'clock... Oh, how I wish to be with you. Goodbye all of you... Bury me and Elbert in the same grave... There are a few of us alive yet. Oh, God for one more breath...

Dear Wife and Children:—My time has come… It is now ten minutes to ten o'clock Monday morning, and we are almost smothered. May God bless you and the children, and may we all meet in Heaven… To My Boys:—Never work in coal mines… be good boys and stay with your mother and live for Jesus.

(Powell Harmon)

One miner's twelve-year-old son had begged him for years to work alongside him in the mines. The explosion happened on the boy's first day. Father and son were found wrapped in each other's arms. They were the last bodies recovered.

The "piteous wails" and primal, guttural howls from wives, mothers, grandparents, children, grandchildren, friends, and fellow miners haunted the land for days. The disaster left at least ninety-nine women widows and almost 270 children fatherless. Some women lost husbands and all their sons. When the casket train came to Fraterville, only three men remained at the camp.

Coffins arriving for victims of Fraterville mine accident, 1902.

Several possible causes were given but no definitive answer was ever reached. The mine was closed on Saturday, re-opening Monday, the day the miners came to work. It is possible that, since the ventilation was cut off over the weekend, a buildup of methane might have occurred and could have been ignited by the lamps on the miners' hats (which were, ironically, open-flame). With the eruption of gas, coal dust caught fire as it circulated and further added to the explosion. Another theory was that a young, fifteen-year-old miner tapped into the adjacent Knoxville Iron and Coal mine. This adjacent mine was shut off and the methane accumulation spilled into the Fraterville mine. Once the breach was discovered, the miners made efforts to seal off the gases, but the occurrence of the explosion suggests the attempts were unsuccessful.

The Center for Disease Control and Prevention published a report in 2008 entitled "Explosion Hazards from Methane in Emissions Related to Geologic Features in Coal Mines" which intimates the cause was gas released from a falling roof. The finding states the gas "was liberated from overhanging strata by the 'creep' that had began [sic] with an unusual violence shortly before the explosion." *Creep* is when pillars are forced into the soft soil by the weight of the gradually sinking ceiling.

Another possible reason was company negligence. State Commissioner of Labor, R.A. Shifleft stated he inspected the mine in 1901 and found "the ventilation was not up to requirements" but acknowledged the company did make changes by installing a sixteen-foot fan for aeriation. The company, it was also discovered, did not have the required air pipes opening every ninety feet. Indeed, the coroner's jury found the coal company and Inspector Shifleft negligent at the inquest. The charges were later dropped. On the stand, owner George Camp testified that the Fraterville mine had an exceptional safety record for the past thirty-three years. He produced documents stating the company made all safety modifications told to them by inspectors. One newspaper stated,

> George Camp, the young man who has grown up as a comrade
> to the dead men and became skilled in the mining business under
> the tutelage of the man now dead, wept bitterly on the stand.

Camp also defended Fraterville's ventilation furnace operator, Tip Hightower, who lost two sons in the blast, touting his trustworthiness and excellent work ethic.

Regardless of the cause, the fact remained that the worst mine disaster in Tennessee history had occurred, and the grief-stricken community was in serious need. The state legislature proposed relief funds for widows and orphans. Businesses and patrons throughout the region offered financial assistance. Coal Creek wrapped community arms around the hurting. The pain is still felt today, over one hundred twenty-three years later. Some of my own people were killed in the disaster:

Peter C. Childress (father, 48 y.)

William L. Childress (son, 18 y.; newly married 2 days before explosion)

James C. Childress (son, 15 y.)

John C. Childress (son, 12 y.)

Noah Daugherty (35 y.)

William (W. B.) Goodman (35 y.)

Many were buried in Miner's Circle at Leach Cemetery in Rocky Top. The plot was designated especially for the miners who died in Fraterville. When I stand among the graves arranged in a circle, a gentle breeze greets my face and I sense them there all together, united forever. Protective love engulfs me, and I thank them all.

25

Coal Creek: Cross Mountain

by Delonda Shown Anderson

C OAL CREEK'S HISTORY TRANSPORTS US to a cold December day in 1911 in Briceville, Tennessee, and we arrive at the Cross Mountain mine.

Coal camps in Appalachia were cheerful in December. Christmas garland most likely bedecked the walkways. Various tin toys, dolls, and trains adorned company store windows as Nativity plays and Christmas parties neared; and snowfall descended, soft and magical. Camp houses probably adorned their walls with children's artwork, Christmas cards, or holiday-themed newspaper. A family trudged the backwoods to find the perfect Christmas tree. Once it was cut down, dragged home, and set up, the tree was most certainly decorated with stringed popcorn and homemade ornaments. Children gazed at the empty space beneath and filled their imaginations with teddy bears, dolls, jigsaw puzzles, crayons, and tin cars. A coal miner had to work additional days to afford a merry Christmas.

On a frosty December 9, 1911, at around 6:30 in the morning, eighty-nine miners entered the Cross Mountain mine with Christmas hopes of their own. On that December day, less than an hour later, a violent explosion occurred in Cross Mountain, evoking memories of the Fraterville mine disaster in 1902. Only five men came out alive.

The Cross Mountain mine at Briceville, located nearly five miles from downtown Coal Creek, was owned and operated by the Knoxville Iron Company and had been operational for over twenty years. The mine was labeled a "Class B" drift mine that produced about five-hundred tons of coal each day and never "had a serious accident." The mine was quite large and far-reaching. The area where the men worked was five-hundred acres, two-hundred fifty of which was a functioning work area. The shaft went down two miles inside the mountain. The entryways were large—from 2,500 to 3,000 feet. Brattices, or, "partitions used in a mine passage to confine the air and force it into" the work area, were mostly "slate and waste material ten or twelve feet thick and packed tight." Near the entrance, a seven-foot electric fan sat one-hundred feet down in an airshaft and was used to force out bad air and bring in good air.

Boys working at Cross Mountain Mine, 1910.

The mine was supposed to be inspected every two months. Two new mine inspectors were hired in 1911: State Inspector George Sylvester on June 1 and Deputy Inspector Richards on July 14. The mine had not been evaluated all year before the two men were employed. After their hiring, the mine was inspected on August 3 and October 30 but no issues were found. J. F. Hatmaker performed another inspection six days prior to the explosion and had given the mine a favorable report.

The initial blast caused flames to shoot out from the mine openings up to three hours later. Panic and fear spread just as fast as the explosion itself. The number of workers on dayshift at Cross Mountain were some-where between 126 to 156 men. At least eighty-nine men descended two miles to their working area. Others escaped because they hadn't fully entered the mine before the explosion occurred. One man, Hugh LaRue, avoided the disaster because his wife begged and urged him to stay home. Mrs. LaRue told him about a dream she had where she

> saw scores of miners with their heads blown off being carried out of the mine entrance. That she and her little children stayed at the mine's mouth watching the unfortunate coal diggers being carried out.

Though a Knoxville Iron Company official "minimized the extent of the explosion... declared that they believed many if not all the men in the mine would be rescued alive," the community knew deep down the ominous occurrence meant certain death for all of the men in the darkness.

Family members hurried to the scene at the mine entrance. Wives and mothers moved "as close as the restraining ropes would permit around the entrance of the mine... they begged to be allowed to enter the shaft and search for their husbands and sons." Miners all around Coal Creek stopped working at once and rushed to the site. As a matter of fact, volunteers came from just about every mine in the region: Jellico, Oliver Springs, Middlesboro (KY), and southwest Virginia. Estimates reveal at least ten thousand people—miner and non-miner—came to help.

Search, rescue, and recovery teams were immediately organized by George P. Chandler, president of the Tennessee Coal Company. Rescue teams were divided into groups of fifty men. Every crew worked two-hour rotations inside the mine. The first rescue efforts were stalled due to debris. The teams had to excavate it by mule since the electric cars were destroyed. Flames and fire were another deterrent that had to be extinguished before continuing. It was imperative to "remove the debris and force fresh air into the inner most recesses of the mine," not only for the miners who could have survived but also for the rescuers who risked their lives. Poison gas (carbon monoxide) halted the rescue process, but some were undeterred, working without food, sleep, or pay, until "they were carried out overcome by the noxious gasses." A few of the rescuers even had to be resuscitated by using a "pulmotor" (essentially, an oxygen machine).

Better rescue equipment and methods were used at Cross Mountain, some for the first time. The United States Mine Bureau developed mine rescue crews who came to Briceville with twenty-five "oxygen helmets," the equivalent of today's gas mask. These rescuers were able to go farther distances into the mine for longer periods of time. Canary birds were first used to detect the presence of poisonous gas at Cross Mountain. Initially, miners thought this idea was ludicrous. However, after seeing the method's success, they soon realized the bird's usefulness. If the bird didn't live, the miners couldn't go inside without an oxygen helmet.

The author's great grandfather, Lawrence Monroe
Goodman (R) working at Block, ca. 1930s.

Eighty-two men died suddenly and violently from the explosion. Two other men who survived the blast succumbed to carbon monoxide. It was reported that rescuers heard "them knocking on the walls of the mine." The situation seemed hopeless for the rescuers and the community. Almost sixty hours after the incident, five miners were rescued *alive*: William Henderson, Milton Henderson (son), Arthur Scott, Theodore "Dore" Irish, and Irving Smith. William Henderson, who, incidentally, was found by rescuers sitting and casually smoking his pipe, said about the group's experience:

> With our coats we fought back the after-damp that came through the cracks in the brattice and then stuck our coats and other articles of wearing apparel in the hole of the brattice... We remained in this room quietly for several hours burning one light and taking turns eating. Late Saturday evening Arthur Scott and Dore Irish left the room and attempted to make their way back and reach the entrance of the mine through the overpass. That was the last we saw of them. The next morning, we made our way, the air having been purified by the fan into the entry... ran into gas and were forced to go back... where the air was pure. We remained there until discovered tonight.

All of Briceville was overjoyed. Women rushed to see if one of their husbands had been found, but "the wives of none of the rescued men were there, some of them being ill and hysterical. The scenes at the homes where the men arrived were affecting."

The sounds of grief renewed when the train from Knoxville came to Briceville carrying 175 coffins. Such a numerous volume had to be a jarring sight for the community. Bodies were so badly disintegrated, they couldn't be prepared for burial, so they were all buried in their work clothes, "consigned to their graves unrecognized and unidentified by their widows and mothers."

Inspector George Sylvester was chosen to investigate the cause of the explosion and presented his conclusions to Tennessee Governor Ben Hooper. Sylvester believed the blast was caused by "mainly, if not wholly, a dust explosion," ignited by "a small amount of gas present in the air." But he couldn't "decide with any degree of certainty the exact point from which the explosion started or its initial cause," but, based on the evidence he found, it spread "in the lower part of the mine from one entry to another..." Further, he proposed another possibility, admittedly without evidence, a hefty chunk of coal might have fallen in one of the rooms the previous night, circulating dust that could have caught fire by a miner's open flame lamp.

A new graveyard was created at Laurel Branch for the miners who lost their lives. Like Fraterville, the graves form a circle—the ancient symbol of eternity—around a monument that reaches toward heaven and honors eighty-four brave souls.

This stop at Cross Mountain has ended the Coal Creek journey. I hope I have successfully depicted this region as an Appalachian community who comes together, near or far, rich or poor, from various nationalities, to offer help or to stand on principle.

26
Freeing Free Hills

by Edward Francisco

I N THE YEAR 2000, MY sons Erik and Gabriel and I set out to create a video documentary of the people living in Free Hills, one of America's last remaining Black settlements established before the Civil War. Located in hardscrabble Clay County, Tennessee, near the community of Celina, the Free Hills have been home to freed slaves and their descendants for more than two centuries. Residents tell the story of Virginia Hill, daughter of a prosperous North Carolina planter, who inherited her father's slaves, freed them, and bought property where they could live in relative safety and seclusion. Early accounts establish that the first slaves relocated in the rural wilderness were Virginia Hill's biological children. If so, Hill may have been motivated to ensure her offspring's safety as best she could. Too, she undoubtedly grasped the consequences of sexual relations between elite white women and enslaved men in the antebellum South, as historian Catherine Clinton explains:

> White women whose affairs with slaves were made known faced varying degrees of public humiliation. When a planter's daughter or wife was discovered to be pregnant by a slave, great pains were taken to cover up the pregnancy. The resulting child might have been sold into slavery, but infanticide was not an uncommon means of avoiding scandal.

Virginia Hill's manumission of her slaves may have been inspired by the best of intentions, but life in Free Hills wasn't easy from the outset. Tucked away in the Upper Cumberland region on the Tennessee-Kentucky border, Free Hills does not afford easy access, nor is farming viable, owing to geography marked by steep slopes and large outcroppings of rock. Trapping and fishing sustained early settlers who swept dirt floors and rode donkeys to accommodate the harsh terrain.

Despite difficulties, the community persisted, buoyed by the Free Hill Church of Christ, the historic heart of the community for two centuries, and the Free Hill Rosenwald School, built in 1929 with the aid of the Julius Rosenwald Fund, a grant program directed by Booker T. Washington. For a time, it seemed that Free Hills thrived as it was home to approximately 400 people between 1920 and 1950. Free Hill's Hill Top Café was a popular gathering spot for the locals. Juke joints sprang up where people came to drink beer and play blues music—with names like Bud's Snack Bar, the Blind Pig, and the Tip-Toe Inn. However, the community's ascendancy was short-lived.

When my sons and I visited Free Hills on the cusp of a new millennium in 2000, signs of dissolution were very much in evidence. The population had shrunk to almost 200. Once vibrant businesses had closed. The one-two punch came when the local garment industry relocated to Mexico and a home health firm closed its doors, shuttered its windows, and moved just outside Nashville. Unemployment in Free Hills soared. As an elder of the community explained to me: "There's nothing for young people here. They'll likely leave and never come back. Who can blame them?"

For the young people who stayed, the prospects were grim. It was no coincidence that most of the people I interviewed were older. My son Erik, at that time a social worker advocating for the elderly poor, had arranged for me to record conversations with some of his clients. The young folks he'd approached all balked. The reason became increasingly clear when I quizzed their elders about the greatest threat to Free Hills. It wasn't the economy. It wasn't the occasional terrors inflicted by the Ku Klux Klan. "Drugs" was the unanimous reply from everyone I interviewed. All agreed that crack cocaine was the scourge driving Free Hills toward extinction. (I'd read earlier that the National Trust had placed the Rosenwald School of Clay County, Tennessee, on its list of Most Endangered Historic Places.)

As strangers, we had no way of knowing the severity of the problem. Yet, we were about to glimpse—literally—a transaction taking place under our noses. While we were interviewing his grandparents, the couple's teenaged grandson traded an envelope for a fistful of cash handed to him by a white teen. The living room window afforded my son Gabriel, our videographer, an opportunity to record the drug deal in real time.

While our visit to Free Hills was emotionally draining, we had the option of leaving. In fact, it was inconceivable that anyone would stay given a chance to leave. There was just too much of what author James Agee termed the "cruel radiance of what is" in the faces of the people we met. Grinding poverty, frustrated potential, and institutional racism had leeched the life blood of Free Hills residents. Was it any wonder the young people turned to drugs? Without legal opportunities to secure a livelihood, they opted for illegal means, in addition to anaesthetizing themselves from the shards of the fractured American dream.

From several hundred miles away, I tracked the status of Free Hills to the extent I could. In the early 2000s, I read that the Drug Enforcement Administration (DEA) had conducted a sting operation in the Celina-Free Hills area for possession of controlled substances. Around that time, someone directed me to a Detroit based rap group who referenced Celina in their lyrics as a key location on the I-75 "drug corridor."

In 2016, Joey Garrison, a reporter for the *Nashville Tennessean*, wrote an article about the state of Free Hills. He reported that only seventy or so residents still called the community home. One of the remaining few, sixty-two-year-old Ollie Page, described it this way: "It scares me that one day it's going to be a ghost town." Page could have been sounding the death knell for one of the country's last remaining Black settlements populated by freed slaves.

On the ride from Free Hills down to Celina, I mused aloud, wondering what Abraham Lincoln would have thought of a unique, once vital, African American community established two decades before the 16th president signed the Emancipation Proclamation.

Steering the car around serpentine curves, my son Erik spoke up:

"His grandparents are buried about a mile from here."

"Whose?" I asked.

"Lincoln's."

"Are you sure?"

I'd read Carl Sandburg's *Abraham Lincoln* and later, Gore Vidal's interpretive biography, but I didn't recall that Lincoln had family connections in Tennessee.

Erik eased onto the shoulder and made a U-turn, pointing the car in the opposite direction on state route 53. In a few minutes, we pulled off, parking and exiting the car just yards from a Tennessee Historical marker alleging that Lincoln's paternal grandfather, Hannaniah, and the president's grandmother were buried on private property near Tinsley Bottom in Clay County. Erik knew the land's owner who granted us permission to explore the cemetery overgrown and choked with weeds. We found Hannaniah's grave marker affixed by the Tennessee State Historical Commission (THC).

"I don't think it's accurate, Erik," I said.

I knew that Lincoln was wreathed in folklore, making people eager to place him in locations that he never visited or stick him on a limb in someone's family tree. I suspected that was the case here. The next day, I visited the Celina Public Library. After a couple of hours, I found what I was looking for: an article written by an historian in 1912 discounting the possibility that Lincoln's grandparents were buried in Clay County. The historian's genealogical research revealed that Hannaniah Lincoln was actually the president's second half cousin. Obviously, I wasn't the first person to discover the error. I wondered whether the Tennessee Historical Commission knew of the mistake. The presence of the marker suggested they didn't.

The next afternoon I picked up the phone. The woman at THC was pleasant at first before discovering the reason for my call.

"Do you know how much those markers cost?"

"No."

"A thousand dollars each!"

I suggested in the interests of accuracy that the Commission take down the maker, bite the bullet, and erect a new one. During the rest of our conversation, the woman urged me, for all intents and purposes, to mind my own business. The marker wasn't coming down.

It was my initial immersion into the post-truth world where notions of "truth," "fact," and "reality" are malleable and not subject to usual standards of proof and verification. In fact, such slippery notions are merely "constructs" waiting to be "deconstructed." Did it matter whether the inhabitants of Free Hills died off? If that happened, did they ever really exist? When truth proves inconvenient, why not substitute a more convenient "reality" conducive to amnesia and not fettered by facts?

That seems to be the impulse of Governor Bill Lee and Republicans in the Tennessee legislature who passed a bill in 2021 banning the teaching of critical race theory in public schools at a time when such initiative is needed most. Avowedly, the GOP-controlled General Assembly now prohibits educators from "teaching things that inherently divide people." The lawmakers' ahistorical approach to problems still plaguing the body politic is an attempt to absolve themselves and their ilk of sins associated with racism. Their ritual magic insists that history conform to fantasy. The prescription for weaponizing lies and annihilating truth requires a series of insidious steps: Obscure the lens of reality, deny plausibility, and insist that a significant minority of the population invalidate their own experience, becoming invisible, in effect.

The Free Hills, in contrast, offer a stark testimony to the truth of America's tensions, contradictions, and disappointments clouding the vision of the Founders, of whom Virginia Hill was surely one. As for poor, beleaguered Abe Lincoln, he made a statement at Gettysburg before which we should all tremble: "Now we are engaged in a great civil war, testing whether that nation, or any nation so conceived and so dedicated, can long endure." To Lincoln's disquieting statement, the fate of Free Hills may ultimately supply the answer.

27

"Unwomanly Actions" in Appalachia's Labor Movement

by Delonda Shown Anderson

APPALACHIAN WOMEN MAY BE THE most unacknowledged and undervalued segment of our region. But that fact wasn't always so, particularly in the matriarchal Cherokee tribe, where lineage was matrilineal, meaning the descent was determined through the female line, and where women were completely independent. They could divorce and hold ownership. They had substantial diplomatic and financial power. They were active in decisions about governance and held advisory roles. Women were "heads of Cherokee households, and they worked hard, as they farmed and preserved, maintained monies and traded successfully, prepped hides and crafted necessities. White settlers—particularly male white settlers—were dumbfounded by the amount of power and equality Cherokee women had. The white man's repeated brutality and cultural purge of the tribe ensured that Cherokee women were suppressed and oppressed.

When immigrants came to this mountain region from the respective motherlands of Germany, Ireland, Scotland, Wales, and the Netherlands, women were often no more than baby-poppin' workhorses. Why do I think so and why use such harsh language? Well, I heard oral histories that centered around my great and great-great grandmothers. I've seen the vintage images of their happy, stout selves weakening year after year, work upon work, birth after birth, until they are back-bent, hollow-eyed, and skeletal by age 45. But our grandmothers and mothers have stories that will never be heard. Their histories and hard work are accounts that have lingered like mists across the Blue Ridge Mountains—ethereal and intangible. Our own stories are barely heard today, and, when they *are* told, they're as slow dripping as molasses.

In my opinion, the most historically unrecognized fact about Appalachian women is their role as laborer. Their "woman's work" wasn't deemed "real work," though I dare anyone out there to light a fire before dawn in a wood stove and make breakfast for a family of about twelve (after you've awakened and dressed the children), with no time for your own self to eat, then scatter feed for the chickens and gather eggs, then feed and milk the cows or goats, then plant, hoe, and tend the acre garden at temperatures above 90 degrees with one baby strapped to your back and the rest hungrily working their little fingers by your side; then, continuing the workday, revisit the wood stove, where you realize the kindling and firewood's empty so you chop wood and fire up the cook stove on such a hot day; boil water for clothes washing, then scrub them on a washing board; catch, kill, pluck, and singe a chicken (if you're lucky), make dinner for twelve from scratch because there is no other way; finally sit down long enough to hear the blessing and eat a few bites; boil water on the same stove for dish washing and bathing, wash dishes, bathe the children, and (if energy permits) bathe yourself; sew a quilt or churn butter or preserve food or mend clothes or make clothes; at night, read a verse from the Bible (if you're one of the few lucky women who could read) and say a prayer; then do your "wifely duties" and hope to God another mouth to feed won't come. But you know it will. And that's just *some* of the day. I dare anybody to say all that ain't work!

Women changed from the late 1800s onward. Appalachian women began to work outside the home and became a new workforce, and that's where I'll focus deeper. Jacquelyne Dowd Hall discusses Appalachian women and their role in textile's early labor movement in her article, "Disorderly Women: Gender and Labor Militancy in the Appalachian South." The article uses female narratives to chronicle women's overall contributions to the textile and mill workforce. The piece also breaks down the rayon industry in post-World War I and reveals the often-over-looked women strikers in that industry. Hall describes their fortitude and dauntless courage as they stand up for rights against an ever-growing corporate and state-wide Behemoth.

According to Hall, the reasons various textile companies selected Appalachia is due to the region's isolation and the pool of what the industry considered "uneducated" workers. Hall concentrates specifically on the rayon industry's Bemberg and Glanzstoff plants in Elizabethton, Carter County, Tennessee, where 30 percent of Bemberg's jobs and 44 percent of Glanzstoff's jobs were held by women, generally single, aged twenty-one and under. Through the women's personal accounts, Hall paints a picture of their hope and excitement at working in the mills. They regarded it as a means to escape from the drudgery of farm work, domestic work, and poverty. Once there, however, reality came fast and hard. The women worked long days and were exposed to the "caustic chemicals" used to produce rayon. The "petty regulations" smothered them, and they were even denied bathroom breaks. The women worked in this environment day after day with low wages and no raises. Yet men received higher wages *and* raises. This fair wage issue threw a lit match into a powder barrel.

On March 12, 1929, the teenage female Glanzstoff workforce banded together and walked out, convincing their counterparts to join them a day later. This small movement snowballed into a workers' rights avalanche. The Bemberg plant joined them four days later. The striking women gained support from unions, while town officials and plant managers secured Governor Henry Horton's assistance. Troops and armed guards were sent to intimidate and even wound protesters and picketers. A few Elizabethton businessmen kidnapped union officials, drove them across the state line, and told them not to return. The officials returned and the striking workers were livid at the businessmen's actions. One side's escalation stood against another side's intensification. In the end, the women had to concede, and, since the already weakened union had no power against such mounting pressure, the strike failed. Women were arrested. Workers were blacklisted and locked out. Some managed to ease back into their former jobs as domestic servants. Others found a way back into the mill when their married name gave them a new identity. Still others continued the fight for female workers' justice, the effects of which can still be seen today.

Hall further explains the textile industry's working conditions that contributed to female activism in the 1920s. Women were under such close observation that any trip away from their workstations was scrupulously supervised at all times—something their male coworkers did not experience. Women's appearances were heavily scrutinized, too. They couldn't wear makeup or jewelry, and they were required to wear uniforms purchased with their own money. They were even forced to "rent houses at high rates" from the local real estate developer. The article "Cotton Mill People: Work, Community, and Protest in the Textile South, 1880-1940," by Jacquelyne Dowd Hall, Robert Korstad, and James LeLoudis, describes the treatment of textile workers.

According to the article, cotton production surged in the mills before World War I, and the work was a monotonous ten-to-twelve-hour day where workers "walked, stretched, leaned, and pulled at their machines." Cotton fibers filtered through the air, stuck to every exposed area, and entered the lungs. The machinery was deafening, and the badly ventilated rooms generated a sweltering, smothering heat. One could easily see where the term *sweatshop* originated. Some mill supervisors were too severe with women and children, verbally intimidating them, and, at times, shaking the children. After World War I, the demand for cotton declined, so the textile industry as a whole looked for ways to cut costs. Supervisors pressured workers harder to make sure they didn't "waste time" by talking, drinking water, or using bathroom facilities. Supervisors constantly monitored with stopwatches, clocking precisely how much time a worker could complete every single task. This strategy caused such a fast-paced system that many workers couldn't keep pace. Business owners purchased faster machinery that did more work and cut out most laborers. To further agitate the situation, owners hired "college-trained supervisors" who had no knowledge of what work was like on the floor of the mill. Tensions escalated, and, as stated before, the situation led young women to strike in Elizabethton, Tennessee.

The tactics striking women used to make their voices heard were new occurrences in the mountains, and it got pretty violent, let me tell you. Once those teenage girls from the Glanzstoff plant decided they wouldn't put up with low wages and bad working conditions, the strike quickly escalated. After things settled down, the Bemberg plant fired two union members, sparking *another* strike in April 1929. The strikers countered the owners' tactics by joining forces with the United Textile Workers. Women not only initiated the strike, they also led the way, shouting and singing, marching, and protesting. They blocked roads with their bodies and refused to leave, even as threats heightened. Hundreds of strikers were arrested, "two houses were dynamited," barns were set ablaze, and "a water main leading into Elizabethton was dynamited." To help those who no longer had an income, women workers organized community resources and pooled together what they had. Eventually, mediators prevailed and reached a fragile agreement where "plants would reinstate former employees, would not discriminate against union members," and would hear grievances.

Hall also conveys the female worker's take on Appalachia's view of women in general. Bessie Eden, for example, says of Appalachian farm life: "The girls were supposed to do housework and work in the fields. They were supposed to be slaves." To be sure, the striking young women saw their mothers as strong, but they didn't want the hard, seclusive life they lived. Yet, though women successfully obtained the vote, they had little hope of advancement in any facet of life. Labor was (and arguably still is) no different. Women couldn't be supervisors in the textile industry. Women also earned significantly less than men, often due to jobs they were offered as opposed to jobs offered men. In other words, women couldn't do "men's work."

Appalachian women had an effective activist role in the textile labor movement. Hall provides a beautiful narrative of the women strikers. However, she doesn't mention a defining moment regarding women and textile labor near the era: the 1911 Triangle Shirtwaist Company fire in New York City. The fire allegedly started in a rag bin near the combustible chemicals the company used in manufacturing. The foreman tried to extinguish it, but the water hose was rotten and the valve was rusted shut. The fire spread. There was no sprinkler system. The seamstresses worked so close, they were just about "cheek to jowl," working by gaslight amidst narrow aisles and all the "clippings of flammable fabric" on the floor. The stairs were about thirty-three inches wide, dark, and unsafe. Of the four elevators, only one with a 12-person capacity worked, but it broke down. There were two stairwell exits. One was kept locked to prevent stealing. The other door opened inward. The outside fire escape was already in ruins. The horrific event occurred within the top three floors of the building (8th through 10th floors) but the firetruck ladder could only reach the sixth floor. Over six hundred people worked there, the bulk of whom were women. On that fateful March day, at around 4:40 p.m., the workers were preparing for the end of the workday at five o'clock. Most of the workers were immigrants who spoke little to no English. One hundred forty-six people died—123 women and 23 men. Some succumbed to burns or smoke inhalation; others jumped down the elevator shaft; still others jumped from the building onto the pavement below.

Although it wasn't located in Appalachia, the horrific event had to have some impact on female textile workers in the region. Hall also doesn't provide much detail on sexual harassment in the workplace, which was considered normal, routine behavior. Still, the article does an excellent job illuminating working women's extreme courage in throwing caution to the wind and bucking the system, despite the powerful storm around them.

28
Flooding of Hallowed Ground:
TVA and Appalachian People in the 1930s
by Delonda Shown Anderson

President Franklin D. Roosevelt
signing the TVA Act into existence, 1933.

IN 1935, EAST TENNESSEE MOUNTAIN man William Henry Hawkins grabbed his shotgun and marched with purpose out of his humble, box-frame home, where he lived with his wife and young daughter. He then drove to Norris Dam as a one-man show of force to stop the Tennessee Valley Authority (TVA) from taking his land. The situation quickly de-escalated without incident. A few nights later,

Hawkins peered out of his window and saw TVA removal workers walking around on his property, an act he regarded as an attack. It was out and out war. Hawkins encircled his home with brush and lit it on fire as a wall of defense against the removal men. The flames spread fiercely out of control and the fire burned down his house. Everyone inside escaped alive and unharmed. Hawkins eventually relented and agreed to move, so relocation arrangements were made near Jacksboro, Tennessee. Yet, a few days after the move Hawkins was pronounced insane, and, with his brother's signature, was committed to East Tennessee Hospital for the Insane. Hawkins' insanity diagnosis was not uncommon for many landowners during relocation. People were either driven insane from what they deemed government overreach and thievery or were declared so by family members—oftentimes for more nefarious reasons, like money-grabbing (i.e., taking advantage of government offers). Hawkins is listed in the 1940 census as living with his wife and daughter in Jacksboro, Tennessee. So, it seems he was released from the facility fairly soon.

President Roosevelt's Tennessee Valley Authority Act of 1933 was a grand scale government plan designed to provide much needed flood control to the Tennessee Valley area. The Tennessee River Valley includes states Tennessee, Virginia, North Carolina, Georgia, Alabama, Mississippi, and Kentucky. The region flooded unpredictably and caused a greater blow to people and their homes, land, and businesses amidst the Great Depression. The Act also provided a solution for Wilson Dam and nitrate-producing facilities in Muscle Shoals, Alabama. During World War I, the federal government bought the plants as part of the National Defense Act of 1916 to manufacture materials required for badly needed explosives. Once the war ended, the plants closed and remained dormant as congress debated over a decade about what to do with it all. President Roosevelt, along with congressmen like Senator George Norris, dealt with these problems by forming a federal system of dams that would solve navigation issues along the Tennessee River. The TVA's design would open clear waterways, transport fertilizer in cooperation with Alabama's Muscle Shoals dam, and improve farming and land management. The act also sought to produce wide scale electricity and power distribution, attract industry and manufacturing, bring jobs to the region, and increase tourist attractions in state parks and wildlife reserves.

With such possibilities, it would seem that citizens in the Tennessee River Valley shared mutual excitement for the opportunities generated by the TVA. Some people did take advantage of these new prospects while others, like Hawkins, defiantly rejected the measure. To accomplish such a prodigious feat, the TVA had authorization, via eminent domain, to flood tens of thousands of acres of land, and displace over 3,000 families from the Tennessee Reservoir area. By 1946, the TVA went on to purchase "over 1,129,000 acres" and "had removed 13,449 families from sixteen reservoir areas." The total number of "*persons*" removed is unknown. Some families rejected removal because they did not want to give up land that had been in families since the early to late 1700s. Therefore, actions taken by people like Hawkins were not uncommon. Those who resisted seemed willing to do just about anything to protect and keep their land from condemnation and flooding. In order to better understand why the people of the Tennessee Reservoir area had, and still have, grievance with the TVA, we must turn the focus to the makeup of the people living there, their history of government suspicion, and how the TVA treated them during and since the relocation.

Floodwaters rushed across William Henry Hawkins's property on March 4, 1936. Hawkins knew once the waters escaped from Norris Dam, he would never see his homeland again. Good things seem to always come with sacrifice, and the TVA did offer good things. Yet, those who made the hard decisions to allow their land to succumb to the floods have never truly received any acknowledgment for their sac-rifices. Instead, they seem almost like an echo, like a haunting, forgotten people whose legacy became merely pictures or interviews about the land they loved so much.

The first settlers of Appalachia came mostly from Scotland, Ireland, England, Germany, and Africa. European immigrants settled the area beginning in the mid-1600s, while Africans were forced to the area via the abhorrent slave trade. They all came with their own experiences of poverty, political violence, land ownership denial, religious persecution, and/or bondage. Settlers longed for a chance to farm and live off the land. As independent pioneers and formerly indentured servants, they took the opportunity to develop their ideal way of agrarian life in the backwoods of Appalachia. After Reconstruction, freed slaves also developed an agrarian lifestyle. Scotch-Irish and German settlers established homes on fertile lands along the deep gap valleys, or hollows, within the mountains.

How did they come to own this land? After the American Revolution, and with a newly formed country's reedy and tenuous economy, heroic veterans were offered large expanses of Appalachian land as compensation. Ridges and valleys allowed settlers a large degree of autonomy, as familial clans developed but had little interaction with others outside kinship groups, except when instances of social gatherings or turmoil or unrest occurred. These farming people depended primarily on the land and its resources to support their self-sufficiency. Despite obstacles from government and industry, descendants managed overall to maintain the agrarian lifestyle. Indeed, "By the 1930s, the region had become the home of the rugged Appalachian farmer of pioneer stock who produced little beyond the immediate needs of the family."

Appalachians have a historically bad relationship with government. Contentious sentiment goes all the way back to the settlers' countries of origin, with England's subjugation and land grabs, Germany's harshly enacted serfdom and persecution, and Africa's enslavement and exploitation. Mountain people's experiences with industry were also antagonistic. For one reason, businesses often decimated the region's land, crippling their agrarian lifestyle. The Appalachian timber boom, for example, annihilated large swaths of trees, the dearth of which caused intense erosion and worsened already problematic flooding. For another reason, industry often used dishonest, underhanded tactics against mountain people. For example: At the end of the 19th century, "outside speculators, land developers, and industrialists" found various ways to cheat Appalachians out of their land. Those business entities created "broad form deeds" that seemingly guaranteed landowners the title to all the acreage above the surface, while buyers supposedly held *only* mineral rights (i.e., the sole right to dig for, profit from, and own coal, copper, etc.). In reality, minerals were *connected* to the land. That aforementioned coal baron would likely have razed the land down to the bald, naked earth. Then, he would have torn through and drilled down, deep into the dark earth. So, the actual landowners effectively gave up land rights without realizing it. Mountain people lost "millions of acres of land" due to these tactics. And, if anybody knows mountain folks, they don't let things slide. They told tales of these experiences to subsequent generations through oral history. Up to the 1930s, Appalachians had been involved in their own fights with the U.S. government, from the Whisky Rebellion in 1791, to the coal wars and moonshine wars of the 1920s. Appalachian people viewed the TVA with greater suspicion because it was a government institution ran by a private corporation, a combination which, given the long, combative history, they vehemently opposed.

Mountain people had (and still have) deep connections with their ancestors through the land passed down to them. This connection and their agrarian, self-sufficient life meant their roots and livelihoods were fixed in that valley. Their strong relationship with the earth gave them a profound sense of place. When they gave up their land, they gave up everything they had ever known. All the landmarks that define community were gone. The TVA extracted millions of acres of trees and scorched the land to prepare for the reservoir flooding. This process left a shocking illustration for the loss of *place*, as the land sat otherworldly, bare, and smoldering. No more Sunday hymns echoed through the holler churches. Children's laughter no longer resounded there, and no ABCs or mathematical recitations would be heard there again. The loss of post offices disrupted connections with friends and family. Popular merchants and stores closed their doors to familiar customers. The clink of iron forges was silenced, and the flames of their furnaces were drowned beneath the water. Houses and mills were either torn down with hopes to relocate or left to inundation.

Appalachia's natural environment was turned upside down as the land flooded. The loss of wild game, gardens, medicinal herbs, and water sources, left the displaced person feeling the absence of sustenance. Fishing holes that provided catfish, bass, or crappie, were gone forever. Salt caves, mined for seasoning, meat preservation, and medicine, were no more.

Arguably, the most strongly felt loss was the forfeiture of connection with their ancestors and history. Appalachians along the reservoir area would never again walk the footpaths or live in the homes of their great-great grandparents, as they were accustomed. Even the deceased's resting places were dug up and relocated.

Relocation workers hired by the Tennessee Valley Authority saw Appalachian lives as more impoverished than agrarian. Some workers wondered how, given their perceived notions of poverty, these people could be content where they were. No doubt, poverty existed, and still does, in the Appalachian Mountains. The TVA thought they offered residents along the Tennessee Reservoir the chance of a lifetime. Many residents considered the whole process federal government interference. In most instances, they were paid for their properties, though it's doubtful the amount was sufficient. Prosperous families had an option to move into wealthier towns or cities, while poorer families had few options. If they declined to move, condemnation proceedings began. Many people were relocated *twice*. Imagine how that would feel. The most egregious relocations were those of African American farmers, who went from *owning* a home to "renting a company-owned house." They were offered no information on where to go, and were further suppressed being placed in unfamiliar, segregated areas during the Jim Crow era.

The entire ordeal left a bitter taste in the mouths of displaced persons, and they passed that sour cud onto their children. Descendants never forgot the government's use of eminent domain against their families. Subsequent years saw the abuse of these beautiful mountains through strip mining of cheap coal for TVA. Polluted waters and air remain visible testaments to government and industry disregard. And let's not forget December 2008, when over 5 million cubic yards of toxic coal ash sludge lumbered like a blob across the Emory River in Kingston, Tennessee. The sludge was tested and the following toxins were found: arsenic, copper, barium, cadmium, chromium, lead, mercury, nickel, and thallium. The spill buried wildlife, dozens of deer, and "ejected fish from the Emory River onto the river bank as far as 40 feet from the shore." Multitudes of river life were killed. Humans *may* have fared better. No one died during the spill. However, cleanup crews have developed life-threatening illnesses like tumors and lung cancer. They *still*, after seventeen years, need to be compensated for the sicknesses they suffered from in that job.

Monument at Norris Dam acknowledging Nebraskan Senator George W. Norris.

Grudges against government and industrial entities flow deep in Appalachian veins, a feeling intensified through a blatant unrecognition of Appalachian sacrifices. Today, a plaque exists at Norris Dam celebrating George William Norris "in recognition of his public service." But… no plaques of appreciation exist to thank the families and individuals who gave up their much-loved hallowed ground for the country's benefit. The only recognition Appalachians have is amongst themselves—through oral history told to succeeding generations. As mountain farmer William Wirt from Epperson, Tennessee, puts it:

> One day we were the happiest people on earth. But like the Indian we are slowly but surely being driven from the homes that we have learned to love, and down to the man we are not a friend of the Government for the simple reason that every move they have made has increased our poverty.

> We were told that if we kept the fire out of the forest that we would have plenty of range for our cattle, but we found that after a few years that there is no range left. We were also told that we would have plenty and increasing flow of water in our mountain streams furnishing an abundance of fish for sport and food. But I've found that our streams are drying up and the fish in the

ponds that are left are dying, and at times you can smell them as you pass along the highway...

Now what are we going to do, move on and try to fit in where we do not belong or undertake to face the situation and gradually starve to death? In the little mountain churches where we once sat and listened to the preaching of the gospel with nothing to disturb us, we now hear the roar of machinery on the Sabbath day. After all I have come to believe that the real old mountaineer is a thing of the past and what will finally take our place, God only knows.

29

Redneck Hillbilly

by Delonda Shown Anderson

W HEN MY BROTHER AND I were little, we raced to sit in front of the TV to watch cartoons on our three channels. (Five, depending on how you literally rotated the outdoor antenna, by hand.) Whoever sat down first could watch whatever cartoons he or she wanted. This "plan" was doomed, however, when it became the inception of an all-out brawl, with vicious scratches, hair pulling, and snot-slobbered rage. So, our mother gave us a choice: We could either take turns on Saturdays—one being his Saturday, the next mine—or we'd watch no cartoons at all. *Ever.* Needless to say, we chose the former. We both looked forward to *Looney Tunes*. I was thinking the other day about a particular *Looney Tunes* cartoon called "Hillbilly Hare." I'm sure you know which one I'm writing about—the one where Bugs Bunny outsmarts hillbillies Curt and Punkin Head Martin at every turn. Though I found it funny, I felt an unease, even then, and a sense of condescension. Now that I'm an adult and have the luxury of looking back, I wonder: From where did the term "hillbilly" originate? And, for that matter, from where did the term "redneck" come? How were these labels used? And why are they still used today?

Let us try to find the answers using a variety of sources, starting with the label "redneck." In the southeastern United States (including Appalachia), "redneck" is a term proudly used to characterize a certain way of life—one that bucks authority but is skewed toward authoritarian tendencies; one filled with huntin', fishin', and muddin' with an extra dose of carefree living; one that loathes government overreach but might benefit from government programs; one that prides itself in ancestor reverence but either forgets or doesn't know history as a whole. As a person born, bred, and fed in these mountains, I came to understand the term a little differently. In Bethany Bultram's book, *Redneck Heaven: Portrait of a Vanishing Culture*, the word "redneck" first occurred in the U.S. in the 1830s and referred disparagingly to Presbyterian religious protesters. Patrick Huber and Kathleen Drowne, in their article "Redneck: A New Discovery," found that the term was used in 1893 to "describe rural white laborers of the American South." The pair also say "redneck" first entered political dialogue in the 1890s when Mississippi "Democrats used it to denigrate farmers within their party who supported populist reforms." Farmers worked the fields all day long, and the sun blistered a red ring upon their necks.

I was taught the word came from coal miners who tied red bandannas around their necks to signify solidarity against hired gun thugs, horrible labor conditions, and corrupt practices. Patrick Huber, in a later 2006 article, "Red Necks and Red Bandanas: Appalachian Coal Miners and the Coloring of Union Identity, 1912-1936," discusses this in detail. Huber writes that wearing the red bandanna around the neck was a simple way for miners all across the region to identify a fellow union member—not only for unity, but also for protection. During the Red Neck War of 1921, aka The Battle of Blair Mountain, between 15,000 to 20,000 West Virginia miners of all ethnicities took up arms against a few thousand deputies and state militia, along with the infamous Baldwin-Felts Detective Agency. The miners wore the signature red bandannas and fought against strong arm tactics (brutality, forced evictions, and downright murder) and for the right to unionize. In his book, *The Battle of Blair Mountain: The Story of America's Largest Labor Uprising*, Robert Shogan says the red bandanna "became the hallmark of the insurgent army, leading both friends and foes to refer to them as 'rednecks.'" Interestingly, Huber indicates that those who fought against the miners wore white bandannas. During gun battles, the color significance was important. By noting these mining examples, one might deduce that "redneck" is rooted in protest.

We've seen the same red bandanna in our modern times. *The Guardian* published an article in 2018, "We are Proud to be 'Rednecks.' It's Time to Reclaim that Term," by Stephen Smith, Wilma Lee Steele, and Tina Russell. The article first explains the 20th century history of the miners using the symbolic red bandanna and deems them as West Virginian "revolutionaries." The writers lament today's corporate colonialism and corrupt politicians. Further, they say that poverty, "divorce, drug abuse, debt, incarceration and suicides" all swim together in a simmering pot that doles out the perfect misery soup. "The more we suffer," they say, "the richer some folks get." The article then discusses the modern "redneck" reference. In August 2018, West Virginia's teachers, school workers, janitors, and bus drivers in every district went on strike. "Thousands… stormed the capitol—many wearing their red bandannas." Smith, Steele, and Russell end by saying, "So call us rednecks. We wear that red bandanna with pride." The website Redneck Revolt: Putting the Red Back in Redneck presents another modern interpretation of the label. They profess to be "a national network" with "a pride in our class as well as a pride in resistance to bosses, politicians, and all those that protect domination and tyranny." Further, they claim to be "pro-worker" and "anti-racist." They, in my opinion, come closest to the ideal of the miner rednecks in the 1920s.

Let us move to the term "hillbilly" to find its origins and usage. The term suggests more of a connection to the land, to the majestic mountains, and the hills and valleys. If you're born or transplanted in these mountains, that land connection is palpable. I would imagine, even if you're a visitor, the aura is unmistakable. That's not to say the term "hillbilly" is better or worse than "redneck." Hillbillies declare their love for the land while, at the same time, abusing her resources. Hillbillies might feel disdain about stereotypical portrayals of them or their commodification, but they love watching *The Beverly Hillbillies* or buying a corn cob back scratcher—or, worse, a corn cob, shall we say, for lavatory use.

Merriam-Webster Dictionary defines "hillbilly" as "a person from a backwoods area." The Oxford English Dictionary goes a step further by saying a hillbilly lives in a "mountainous area, esp. of the south-eastern U.S." In his review of Anthony Harkin's book, *Hillbilly: A Cultural History of an American Icon*, James N. Gregory says the term first caught on in 1900 as an amusing depiction of the Appalachian and Ozark peoples. He goes on to say it had a snowball effect and transformed into the same backward character we have seen portrayed all our lives.

Moreover, Richard Drake, in his book *A History of Appalachia*, lends a bit more detail to the incident, saying a reporter used the word "hillbilly" in the New York Journal to describe "'free and untrammeled white' citizens living 'in the hills' with 'no means to speak of,' who 'dresses as he can,' drinks whiskey and 'fires off his revolver as fancy takes him.'"

Yet, the term "hillbilly" was around even before 1900. According to our familiar Patrick Huber and Kathleen Drowne in another article entitled, "Hill Billy: The Earliest Known African American Usages," railroads increased upper-middle class travel to the region, so, mountain folk became the fascinating new creature to ogle under a giant bell jar. It was only a matter of time before some remark was made about "hill people." The pair found the earliest use in an 1893 *Dallas Morning News* article called "History of Whitecapism." The article brought Mississippi's white terrorism against African American communities to the forefront, and described the instigators as "Cane Hill billies":

> The negroes… work for less money and serve their employers more faithfully and obediently than the 'Cane Hill billies' as District Attorney Hudson denominates them. The whitecaps have found another reason for their hatred. These negroes stand well with the good white people… Thus they have placed themselves in more harmonious communication with the better element of the whites than the 'Cane Hill Billies.'

Huber and Drowne also reference articles from the Indianapolis African American newspaper *The Freeman* to bolster this use of "hillbilly." The articles reveal the shameful treatment African American soldiers received at the time of the Spanish-American War. Reporter J. A. Jones writes in an 1898 article, "Southern Sentimentalism," that "A gang of 'hill billies' down in Texas, refused to receive their pay from a Negro paymaster." Huber and Drowne claim this use of the term indicates that the African American South had already known about this label for a while before Jones's article was published, as the term's characterization seemed to carry "distinct connotations of white racism and bigotry."

Another "hillbilly" reference predating 1900 comes from an agrarian newspaper, the *Cleveland Ohio Farmer*. The term appears in an October 1899 letter, "We Hill Billies." The unnamed scribe reveals his fellow "farmers living on these river hills are dubbed 'Hill Billies' by the villagers along the river. We don't like it 'a little bit.'" Such an open aversion implies the derogatory and/or racist undertone just might have been correct.

The hillbilly character has been used for decades as a means to promote or entertain. In the 1920s, for example, "hillbilly music" and "hillbilly records" were highly successful, according to Jeff Biggers in *The United States of Appalachia: How Southern Mountaineers Brought Independence, Culture, and Enlightenment to America.* As is the case with the entertainment business, a tasteful thing often sours. Musicians were purposely dressed down "with outdated work clothes and oversized hats, and promulgated the harebrained stereotypes of hillbillies."

The hillbilly image has also been used to sell a variety of products, from moonshine to country sausage. The word has been taken and manipulated, even by persons who proclaim to be our own yet write faux elegies. (Just to pinpoint the betrayal—it's the *elegy* part.) Today's "hillbilly" embraces the term as something different from the country bumpkin, the quasi-racist, or the ignorant. For mountain people, "hillbilly" is a badge of pride that takes us all the way back to pioneers and Revolutionary War veterans who settled the hills. Each time a hillbilly trudges uphill, strides on a walkway, fishes in a lake, or traverses a creek, he or she adds to the footprints of thousands—Native American and settler. In my own family, my mother proudly declared she was a hillbilly. And she saw it the same way: a pride within and among the hills.

Now we've come to the end of our investigation. The terms "redneck" or "hillbilly" certainly have plenty of history. Not only that, but modern Appalachia has pretty much subsumed them into the culture. I also think a greater acceptance of Appalachian lifestyle exists now as opposed to past decades. People are interested in things that Appalachians, regardless of sides or identities, have been doing all along: gardening, sustainable living, herbal medicines, upcycling, etc. People seek to learn from Appalachians face-to-face or by reading books like the Foxfire Series. Perhaps this type of exposure has created a better understanding. The internet and social media have revealed more of Appalachia's beauty and uniqueness, more so than the ugly and stereotypical. Television also plays some part. Old shows like *The Waltons* or *The Andy Griffith Show*, though admittedly romanticized, are still considered treasures in TV world. Similarly, movies like *Where the Lilies Bloom* (1974), *Matewan* (1987), *The Education of Little Tree* (1997), or *Songcatcher* (2000); and documentaries such as *Mountain Talk* (2004), *The Appalachians* (2005), *Hillbilly* (2019), and even the intrusive *American Hollow* (1999), offer unique glimpses of Appalachia, from redneck to hillbilly to everyone in between and outside. As to the offensive images, stereotypes, labeling or emotional manipulation—those people who are determined to humiliate and make their little jabs, or control and cut deep, will always exist. And a label is very hard to escape. Perhaps for this reason, mountain people have turned a derogatory term upside down and made it their own.

30
What We Don't Do Anymore

By Delonda Shown Anderson

PEOPLE ARE OFTEN HORRIFIED WHEN I explain how much a scene in the movie *Deliverance*, based on the James Dickey novel, reminds me of my family and fills me with such fond memories. No, not *that* scene, though I can't blame anyone when the mind instantly leaps to that part. This scene occurs much later, after the pig squealin' and the killin' and the rapids crushin' and the cliffs and whatnot. The remaining characters gather at a large dining room table, surrounded by a slew of mountain people, and the juxtaposition of experienced horror versus the goodness in front of him brings Ned Beatty's character, Bobby, to tears. In the book, Dickey writes that the house was "booming and knocking with people and light." Further, Dickey records the following foods atop the "long, swayback pine table": "fried chicken… potato salad and heavy, course biscuits and gravy and butter and collards and lima beans and big hominy and turnip greens and cherry pie." So it was with my extended family—plenty of people, warmth at the table, and our bellies full of good food.

Every so often when I was a child, my family and I traversed outside the deep holler to the homes of my grandparents or great-grandparents or great aunts and uncles, and, let me tell you, it was a large family affair. I remember those gatherings vividly, and they weren't just at holidays or reunions. My brother and I were usually in a sort of stunned, silent awe watching our cousins run wild and rambunctious throughout a house or hearing them hootin' and hollerin' outside. And our eyes sparkled like rock candy in the sunlight once we saw the long dining room table over-flowing with food.

When we went to my great aunt Gladys's house, she inevitably pulled me aside, bent down to my little ear, and whispered,

"You see them pickles? They're bread'n butter pickles. I knowed you liked 'em and I took a jar out just for you. You go own'n have some, now. But don't tell nobody."

And that was *before* supper. I felt so special each time I went there and that jar of pickles was sitting smack dab in the middle of the table *just for me*. I was a tiny spectator in the large world of an enveloping mountain family. Times like these enabled my mind to capture and tuck away snapshot images of my great-grandfather Goodman's smile, my great-grandmother Goins's face, my Mamaw Shown's busyness, my aunts and uncles parading or even arguing. All these visuals are encased within a buzz of hummed words I can't recall, but the hum lingers. And anytime I want, I can pull up a memory from those gatherings and my ancestors are *still* here with me. Even when my sons were younger, we had our own family gatherings at my parents' house in the holler, full to the brim with the same foods, the same special feeling, and the same rambunctious nature inside the children.

Ah, but time fades, people change, and loved ones leave. After my father passed away, it seemed like those get-togethers left with him. My mother could no longer care for the large, four-bedroom house in the holler that she and my father built with their own hands (and that's not hyperbole); so she was forced to sell it, along with the dining room table where we all sat just about every weekend for dinner or supper.

Not too long ago, the COVID-19 pandemic was all around us in every pocket of our nation and in every "corner" of the world, and the isolation made one remember those old days when families gathered together eating and singing and playing and talking.

Recently, I considered how we as a nation don't do that anymore. We don't eat together anymore as a large family unit outside our immediate family (and sometimes not even with them). Even before the pandemic, we were all so busy zipping here, running there, fast and chaotic at all times, scarfing down whatever greasy burger slid down our gullet in the car on our way from point A to point B, and burning our candles until the ends were gone. Does anyone really remember why the candles were burning in the first place? Those times are lost opportunities to be present, to be in the moment, to be still.

But true dining instances are so impactful. They enable families to know one another, to be close to each other, *even* if "Old Uncle Cletus" (or the like) is drunker than a skunk and spouting off nonsense. Every member adds value and color to our families. Plus, things have a way of balancing out. If you have an Old Uncle Cletus in the family, you have a Great Aunt Gladys.

Passing food from one kin to the next is such an intimate gesture that enables us a tangible experience with an imprint of our bloodline. And think of the love that went into these homecooked meals from harvest to preparation to serving, consuming, washing, and cleaning. At the dinner table, topics along the lines of fishing, deer hunting, childrearing, jokes, or swimming holes may occur. Oral histories are told and, if we're fortunate, our old, wise kin build upon those histories. Folklore and storytelling abound. Arguments sometimes breach the conversation, and, should a person storm out, that's just another opportunity for reflection, understanding, or, in some cases, avoidance. Togetherness adds to the story of our history.

And, too, "family" doesn't have to be blood kin. One can look to that old saying about family: There's the family you're born into and the family you choose. Sometimes, a family is comprised of both blood relatives and soul relatives.

I write all this not because I'm criticizing or harping. I write this because I'm guilty, too. Yet certain times allow me to be more contemplative, to acknowledge regrets and missed opportunities. One day, I hope that somewhere along the line maybe, just maybe, I can be a little child's Great Aunt Gladys, too.

So, thank you, James Dickey, for *Deliverance*. I'm sure such an author never imagined the impact just a few lines, or a simple scene, could have on a person. And, ironically, it's not even *that* scene.

MOUNTAIN CULTURE

31

Sin Eater

Short Story by Edward Francisco

I'VE GOBBLED ENOUGH SIN TO last a lifetime, though my craft doesn't attract followers the way it once did. Customs die hard in the coves and hollers of these mountains, but the old ways eventually fade when them that practice the rituals start dying off, one by one, taking the knowledge with them. It's honest work, and I come by it honest. My daddy was a sin eater, his daddy before him. It's in our blood. I didn't figger I had a choice to opt out of being what I am.

It's lonely work. Folks tries to avoid us. It's like we're lepers. That is, until they need us. By that time, some one or other of their kin is dead. That's when they seek us out—them that ain't skeered or don't mind that other folks sees us as given to unholy practices or even witchcraft.

Used to be, there was an old preacher hereabouts that warned against me from the pulpit even as I was minding my own business, rarely stepping foot outside this old cabin at the way end of the holler where I've spent my whole life. I left only when called. Then one day, the preacher died, and I got a knock on the door. His wife's oldest boy, probably one of the very scoundrels that tipped my outhouse over on Halloween, stood there, hands thrust in his trouser pockets.

"Whadya want?" I asked, glad for a chance to see the rascal face to face in the light of day.

"Mama needs you," he said. "Daddy's dead."

I stared at him a long minute, guessing him to be in his late teens, a tall, lanky boy sporting a cowlick over his forehead.

"I thought yore daddy was a preacher," I said finally.

"He was," said the boy. "But Mama needs you."

The boy had no way of knowing that a sin eater won't ever refuse to eat a dead soul's sins. We take an oath to do what needs doing. Still, I wanted the boy to sweat some before I agreed to go with him. I wanted him to look me in the eye so I could see how much of his daddy's seed was in him.

"You going to be a preacher too?" I asked.

His weight shifted from foot to foot.

"No," he said. "No."

"Good. Let's go then."

"Don't you need a coat?" It had started snowing.

"No," I said, not bothering to tell him that a man in the habit of swallowing hellfire don't get cold. I'm naturally furry anyway.

We set out. The boy must have thought me odd the way he kept snatching sideways glances at me. Maybe it was because I ain't had a shave or haircut in years. Why should I? Company don't never call, unless, like the boy, they're fetching me to take on some sinner's sins. Otherwise, folks shy away because of the way I look or what I do. I can't say which. To tell the truth, I ain't seen myself in years so I don't know what I look like. I don't own a mirror. Most folks don't know it, but a mirror can swallow a person whole. A mirror is the devil's plaything. I ain't the devil, but I like to pride myself on knowing how he thinks. It's the only way to survive in this world.

On we trudged up the dirt road leading to the boy's cabin. The boy was quiet, a fact that made me almost like him. I don't like wasting words on fools. I didn't know if the boy was a fool, but his daddy was, so there was a good likelihood that some of his daddy's foolishness had rubbed off on him. Still, I had to talk to the boy. There were things I needed to know.

"When did your daddy pass?" I asked. The cabin was in view. The snow fell straight down from the sky without a wind.

"Yestiddy evenin', about six," the boy said.

"Almost a whole day ago," I said.

"Why?" the boy asked. "Does it matter?"

The Bible says to answer a fool according to his folly.

"If it didn't matter," I said, "I wouldn't have asked."

It wasn't my place to school the boy on points of the craft. I was surprised that he'd sought me out in the first place.

"Why did you come get me?" I asked.

"It was Mama's notion," he said.

"Yore daddy was a preacher," I said.

"What does that have to do with anything?"

He sprang back as if stung by a serpent like the ones kept in a box down at his daddy's church. I didn't ask if his daddy had died from a snakebite. I didn't care. The boy acted like he did because he knew there was bad blood between his daddy and me going back years.

"Are we going to stand here shivering," I asked, "or are we going in?"

The boy lurched ahead. I fell into step behind him. The snow was powder under our feet. The boy mounted the steps of the cabin and rapped on the door to let his mama know we was there. Stepping inside, I saw the old lady sitting in a rocker, rocking furrows in the floor. She made no effort to rise.

"I've fetched him," the boy announced in a tone as if to say he'd paid a debt and was wiping his hands clean of the matter.

"I seen you have," said the old woman.

I looked around and saw the dead preacher laid out on a wood slab girded by saw horses. Somebody had throwed a quilt over him and duct taped his eyes shut. The smell of death wasn't on him yet. The cold in the room had slowed the decay. The boy took his coat off and hung it on a peg over the mantle. He stood before the fireplace warming his hands.

"How'd he pass?" I asked the old woman.

"Poison."

"Snake venom?"

"Poison."

I walked over and gave the man's corpse a close look.

"The boy said it happened yestiddy evenin'," I said.

"Thereabout," the old woman said.

"Why did you seek me out? I figger I'm the last person he'd want doing soul work over what's left of him."

"He's dead. He ain't got a say," said the old woman. She hadn't stopped rocking.

"He was a preacher," I said. "Don't you want a preacher to say some words over him?"

"He may have been a preacher," she said, stabbing a finger at his corpse, "but he did a lot of unpreacherly things in his time."

"Just so's you know," I said, "I had a calling same as him."

The old woman's eyes never veered from the dead man.

"I don't believe none of that," she said. "I don't know as I ever did."

"That's my way of saying it's my line of work," I said.

"You'll get your money," she said.

"I'll need a loaf of bread and a bowl of beer."

"It'll have to be *shine*," said the boy. "We ain't got no beer."

I nodded. Truth told, I like the taste of *shine*. If it's a good batch, it goes down smooth and cleans the palate.

The old woman snapped her fingers, and the boy slouched off into the kitchen to retrieve my needs. He came back shortly. I took the bread and *shine* from his outstretched hands. The old woman kept rocking.

I placed the loaf of bread on the preacher's chest as was my custom and set the glass of *shine* on the wood slab. The old woman and boy watched on. I lifted the loaf of bread over my head, lowered it, and bit into the crust before setting the loaf back on the preacher's chest. I swallowed the *shine* and set it back down, too. The words I spoke was ones heard from the dawn of time.

"I give easement and rest now to thee. Come not down the lands or in our meadows. And for thy peace I pawn my soul. Amen."

I turned to face the boy and the old woman.

"You ought to bury him now," I said.

"Did it take?" the old woman asked. "I don't want him taking another step on this earth."

"He's gone on," I said.

The boy disappeared into the kitchen.

"He'll start to smell now," I said. "You should bury him."

"You know now, don't you?" she said.

"The bread—it ain't tainted, is it?" I asked.

"I wouldn't do that," said the old woman.

"You did it to him," I said, pointing at the preacher.

"He had it coming," she said. "You ain't done nothing."

"Everybody's got sins nobody knows about," I said.

"He had it coming," said the old woman.

"Well," I said.

"Your fee?" she asked.

"I won't be needing it."

She nodded.

"You need to bury him though."

"I may be needing you again," she said.

I nodded. With no words left to say, I braced against the cold, turned my back on the tiny light of the cabin, and stepped into the darkness for the slow walk home.

32

J. D. Vance's *Hillbilly Elegy,* A Book Review

By Edward Francisco

"Shut up, you fucker... You smart-ass. If I wasn't crippled, I'd get up right now and smack your head and ass together."–J. D. Vance, *Hillbilly Elegy*

M Y SUSPICION IS THAT J.D. Vance tries to shock his readers by pretending he's unfazed by his family's white trash doings. For Vance, it's all *de riguer*—Mamaw's obscenities, Mom's whoring and alcohol fueled violence, Papaw's churlishness and unexplained disappearances. The message of Hillbilly Elegy? Vance loved them anyway—rogues, scoundrels, sociopaths—one and all. Not only that, but the author is able to penetrate the surface of appearances, discovering the inherent good in his people: "She [Mom] was definitely the smartest person I knew" and "He [Papaw] taught me that lack of knowledge and lack of intelligence were not the same." What to make of these contradictions that don't seem the least disturbing to Vance? Then there are cracks in his narrative where pieces of the story appear to fit.

For example, the locations where the narrator claims to have spent his childhood shift underfoot without warning. It is understandable that his family moved from Kentucky to Ohio in an effort to escape grinding poverty. It's also credible that Vance's mother and third husband, Bob, squandered a hundred thousand dollars a year of combined income. Never having had money, they didn't know what to do when their fortunes reversed. However, Vance seems to exaggerate his hardscrabble circumstances and the violence to which he was exposed as a result of his hillbilly origins. At one point in the book, he admits that, although his mom and Bob had blowups over money, "Bob never was physically abusive." Nor was young Vance's experience unique or even much a departure from the norm in his Middletown, Ohio, community:

> Mom and Bob weren't that abnormal. It would be tough to chronicle all the outbursts and screaming matches I witnessed that had nothing to do with my family. My neighbor friend and I would play in his backyard until we heard screaming from his parents, and then we'd run into the alley and hide. Papaw's neighbors would yell so loudly that we could hear it from inside his house, and it was so common that he'd always say, "Goddammit, there they go again." I once saw a young couple's argument at the local Chinese buffet escalate into a symphony of curse words and insults. Mamaw and I used to open the windows on one side of her house so we could hear the substance of the explosive fights between her neighbor Pattie and Pattie's boyfriend. Seeing people insult, scream, and sometimes physically fight was just a part of our life. After a while, you didn't even notice it.

The author would have us believe that these behaviors are residual effects of hillbillies transporting their legacy of "irritability, aggression, and anger" to a new locale only to face social circumstances they were ill-equipped to handle. A simpler explanation may be that violence attends poverty not unique to hillbillies. Otherwise, how did Vance manage to escape, and from what exactly is he escaping? There's certainly none of the physical or psychic scarring of Dorothy Allison who shows the lingering manifestations of trauma:

> "Let me tell you about what I have never been allowed to be. Beautiful and female. Sexed and sexual. I was born trash in a land where people all believe themselves natural aristocrats. Ask any white Southerner. They'll take you back two generations, say, "Yeah we had a plantation." The hell we did.

"I have no memories that can be bent so easily. I know where I come from, and it is not that part of the world. My family has a history of death and murder, grief and denial, rage and ugliness—the women of my family most of all.

"The women of my family were measured, manlike, sexless, bearers of babies, burdens, and contempt. My family? The women of my family? We are the ones in all those photos taken at mining disasters, floods, fires. We are the ones in the backgrounds with our mouths open, in print dresses or drawstring pants and collarless smocks, ugly and old and exhausted. Solid, stolid, wide-hipped baby machines. We were all wide-hipped and predestined. Wide-faced meant stupid. Wide hands marked workhorses with dull hair and tired eyes, thumbing through magazines full of women so different from us they could have been another species."

Vance never wants his readers to forget that, despite being "disadvantaged," he attended Ohio State University and Yale Law School. In fact, his purported reason for writing *Hillbilly Elegy* was to answer two questions disturbing him since his first days as a student in law school: "Why has no one else from my high school made it to the Ivy League? Why are people like me so poorly represented in America's elite institutions?" Unfortunately, Vance fails to answer either question. But he does give us clues to his thinking.

Ever popular among self-styled conservatives, like Vance, is the notion of "grit"—the resilience enabling an individual to achieve extraordinary feats through perseverance and passion. An enthusiast writing about grit, Angela Duckworth, argues that "grit can be learned, regardless of IQ or circumstances." Vance falls right in line with Duckworth's thinking. He admits to finding plenty of support from his "intellectual fellow travelers in the Republican party" who support Vance's political domestic agenda:

We can easily create a welfare state that accepts the fact of a permanent American underclass, one where family dysfunction, childhood trauma, cultural segregation, and hopelessness coexist with some basic measure of subsistence. Or we can do something considerably more difficult: reject the notion of a permanent American underclass.

Whether he intends to or not, the writer is situated in cultural privilege enough to insist on having it both ways: being a part *of* the tribe while being apart *from* the tribe and conveniently choosing when to be which. Vance tells us that he "never felt like a foreigner in Middletown." Yet, he's comfortable chumming with Charles Murray, co-author of *The Bell Curve*, the controversial 1994 book arguing that a cognitive elite drives society, while ethnic-racial groups with lower IQs drain resources, contributing to stagnation. Like Vance, Murray recommended the elimination of welfare policies that encourage poor women to have babies:

> The technically precise description of America's fertility policy is that it subsidizes births among poor women, who are also disproportionately at the low end of the intelligence distribution. We urge generally that these policies, represented by the extensive network of cash and services for low-income women who have babies, be ended. The government should stop subsidizing births to anyone rich or poor. The other generic recommendation, as close to harmless as any government program we can imagine, is to make it easy for women to make good on their prior decision not to get pregnant by making available birth control mechanisms that are increasingly flexible, foolproof, inexpensive, and safe.

When all is said, I can only respond with a fair amount of cynicism, suspecting that J.D. Vance's encomium to his upbringing is a ruse, of sorts—window dressing for a more sinister purpose. Though I never knew her, except in Vance's own words, I can almost hear his mamaw's stern warning echoing in my ears:

"J.D., a hillbilly with a little education is a dangerous thing."

33

Vera and Bill Cleavers'
Where the Lilies Bloom,
A Book Review

by Delonda Shown Anderson

T WO KINDS OF HOLLOWS EXIST in the mountains. The first kind is the nice, pleasant, winding road that leads to a lake or park out in the boonies. The second kind is an offshoot from that nice road and it snakes down into a deep, dark holler. I grew up in the second kind, a holler within a hollow, if you will.

Our house sat on the side of a hill, surrounded by trees galore. You name it, pretty much anything outside bamboo or palm surrounded us. The earth was rich and dark, and smelled like sweetness, rain, and mild patchouli. We traipsed through the woods, crossed streams and creeks, and stopped at an amazing little waterfall. We had seasonal foods and access to some medicines via wildcrafting, but if I listed everything, I could likely fill the whole article.

To be sure, life wasn't easy. We had our share of hardships, stirred in a batter of trauma, misery, and grief, sprinkled with anger and oppression. Suffice it to say, we knew poverty—dull, abject, and age-old. When something broke, we either fixed it or gave it new purpose. Food had to stretch, clothes had to endure, and shoes had to last.

Yet, none of us were dumb or filthy, as we are often portrayed. Before the internet was a thing, my mother made sure our family had *two* sets of encyclopedias, and we were grateful to have them. The holler even had its own book-sharing system. Whenever our family read and finished books, we traded them with another family, and vice versa. But one book in particular spoke to me like no other at that time. I couldn't relate, necessarily, to the plot (well, perhaps an element here or there), but I did find commonality with the lifestyle. To this day, it conjures up all those old mountain scenes, smells, and feelings.

Where the Lilies Bloom is a young adult novel co-authored by Vera and Bill Cleaver, published in 1969 by Harper Teen. The book was a finalist in the National Book Awards for Children's books in 1970. The story centers around the Luthers, an Appalachian sharecropper family consisting of a widower father, Roy Luther, and his four children: Devola, Mary Call, Romey, and Ima Dean. The land they work is owned by a man named Kiser Pease, who is quite smitten with the oldest daughter, Devola, but Roy Luther vehemently objects.

Roy Luther is sick and knows he'll die soon. Since Devola is "cloudy headed," he gives fourteen-year-old Mary Call several big responsibilities: take care of his burial, be proud of who she is, keep the family together, and don't let Devola marry Kiser Pease. Mary Call becomes the new head of the family, and the story develops around her and the Luther children and how they survive and stay together without their father.

Mary Call narrates the story and reveals so many Appalachian customs and ways through her viewpoint. Folk medicine and wildcrafting are a huge part of the story as the children journey in the mountains, collecting herbs and roots, then drying and selling them to the local grocer.

Living in certain parts of Appalachia means living fairly isolated. *Lilies* addresses the toll this takes on a person. Defeatism and despair are often countered by hope and optimism. At the children's worst point in the story, Romey says, "The Lord has forgotten us. This land is forgotten. *We're* forgotten. We're forgotten people." Mary Call has her own thoughts:

I looked at my brother and I thought, It's the truth… I thought about a man's hold on life, how painful its struggle… And something within me stirred and my spirits lifted…

This land isn't forgotten and neither are we. It just seems like we are out here in all this snow and cold and quiet.

... I thought about spring, how it would come again. How the mountains would turn fresh-green again and wave upon wave of returning warblers would come flashing across them wildly singing. The bluets and the trillium and lilies—all of the spring lovelies would bloom again. Spring would come—it always did.

Appalachian poverty is often propagated within a family. This entrenched impoverishment is addressed near the beginning of the book when Mary Call says of her father:

He's let things beat him, Roy Luther has. The land, Kiser Pease, the poverty. Now he's old and sick and ready to die and when he does, this is what we'll inherit—his defeat and all that goes with it."

Yet, poverty is countered by a profound mountain connection and clever resourcefulness. When the Luthers need some type of income, they find their mother's wildcrafting book. Mary Call is inspired:

And with excitement in me beating hard I carried the book to the cold kitchen and built a fire in the wood stove and sat beside it until the night was gone and read about ginseng and mayapple and goldenseal and all the rest of the medicine plants that grow wild in the green forests of Appalachia—plants which drug companies the world over gladly pay for.

The story also presents realistic experiences within mountain families and doesn't sugarcoat. Families are united but they sometimes argue and say hurtful things to one another. Stressors are a huge factor. In the book, Mary Call becomes exasperated with her siblings. When wildcrafting one day, she's frustrated by their lack of effort and lashes out at Devola and Ima Dean who leave. She and Romey are left to finish. Mary Call tells Romey, "I've got the worry of all of you on me," then she and Romey have a heated argument:

Romey shuffled his feet and released a sigh. "Well, I'm sorry you've got the worry of me on your mind. I didn't ask to be born. I wish I hadn't've been."

"Yeah? Well, maybe you'll fall off the mountain today and kill yourself and be out of your misery. Get the dishpan."

Romey thrust his jaw out. "Get it yourself. I'm not your slave. You're the hatefulest person alive, Mary Call. If Roy Luther was alive you wouldn't treat us like you do."

"Just get the dishpan, Romey, and shut your trap. I haven't got any time to stand around here this morning and listen to you whine. We've got work to do."

The Luther children endure a series of harsh trials, seemingly one after another, but they do so all together. They find that human will and determination are powerful characteristics. Flaws and weaknesses are part of a humanness that can't be denied. The mountains provide solace and Earth's regeneration provides healing in all aspects of their lives.

Aside from the run-on sentences and comma splices, I guess the only thing I didn't like about the book (though I'm not bothered by it anymore) is the fact that Vera and Bill Cleaver weren't Appalachian. I didn't discover this fact until my mid-20s. I was genuinely shocked that writers who weren't *from* Appalachia could write something so connected *with* Appalachia. I'd say any person from these mountains, young or old, who reads the book would agree the story seems to be told by a native of the region. But that they did so makes them good writers worth reading.

Vera Fern Allen Cleaver was from South Dakota and William Joseph Cleaver was from Oklahoma. I found them to be pretty amazing writers, really. Both served in the Air Force. Neither graduated from college, yet they coauthored over a dozen young adult novels with "a particular interest in mountain children," and they published hundreds of short stories.

In 1974, United Artists made *Where the Lilies Bloom* into a movie, filmed in Watauga County, North Carolina, directed by William A. Graham, and starring Julie Gholson as Mary Call; Jan Smithers as Devola; Matthew Burril as Romey; Helen Harmon as Ima Dean; Rance Howard as Roy Luther; and Harry Dean Stanton as Kiser Pease, among others. The soundtrack was performed by The Earl Scruggs Revue. You may recognize Rance Howard as Ron and Clint Howard's father. Jan Smithers went on to play Bailey Quarters on *WKRP in Cincinnati* and other television appearances. Harry Dean Stanton has a considerable filmography, a good portion of which are TV westerns. The other three child actors made no more films.

The movie mostly "goes by the book," deviating here and there without notice, really. I don't know much about film's technical aspects in general, but I do know what's well done. The movie doesn't disappoint. Several wide shots offer panoramic views of the gorgeous North Carolina mountains. The setting provides an authentic visual and feel. The actors were spot on—with their performances, characteristics, and dialect. Stark differences are presented between the wealthier Kiser Peace and the struggling Luther family.

I can't find a thing I didn't like in the movie, really. I highly recommend *Where the Lilies Bloom*—both the book and the movie. Out of a possible ten stars, I give them both an eleven.

34
You Cain't Whup a Bear

by Edward Francisco

IT STARTED AS A LARK. Six of us guys sat watching TV one evening in our college dormitory lobby. Someone absently picked up a copy of the local newspaper lying on the sofa.

"Hey, here's something we can do," Joe M. Announced. (Names are abbreviated to protect the chronically stupid.)

"Doesn't anyone want to know what it is?" Joe continued.

"What is it then?" someone asked, irritated that Joe was talking during an episode of *Soul Train*, a music-dance television program that aired from 1971 to 2006, featuring performances by R&B, soul, and pop artists.

"It says we can win $300 just by wrestling a bear."

In our time with him, Joe had earned a reputation as a shameless schemer, an incorrigible huckster, and an inveterate liar. A native of Memphis, Joe claimed he'd attended high school with Cybill Shepherd when she dated Elvis. He swore he'd been invited to a party Elvis once threw for her. Each guest was given a pink Honda Cub 50 and urged to ride wildly about the grounds of Graceland. Elvis led the caravan.

Joe went on to explain that the bear grappling event was to occur at intermission during a pro wrestling tournament at the local National Guard Armory.

A big, beefy, slow-talking Texan named Ray halted Joe's prattle.

"Look, ain't nobody can whup a bear. Thems is wild animals. I'm the biggest person in this room, but I got more sense than to try to tackle a bear."

Ever since October, Ray was expecting a call from the Draft Board. One fateful autumn evening we'd all gathered around the selfsame TV we were watching now. The occasion was the annual draft lottery, during which every nineteen-year-old able-bodied male in the country would discover whether he could continue his education or be plucked out of college and issued a one-way ticket for an all-expenses paid vacation to Saigon. The war in Vietnam was raging, and a good portion of the American public was starting to see the absurdity of our involvement there. The absurdity trickled down to the selection process itself.

Imagine our collective shock when a shapely young woman wearing a bikini was designated to draw slips of paper from two barrels, one containing the names of the months, the other revealing numbers from one to 365. The order in which she drew people's birthdays was the order in which young men would or wouldn't be drafted. On separate sheets of paper, we wrote our dorm mates' birthdays. The first date drawn from the barrels was March 4. "Ray's birthday." For a moment he sat motionless as a stone. I broke the spell of silence.

"Ray, you okay, man?" I asked.

Ray stared straight ahead.

"I'm fine," he said, then paused. "But I'm going to kill that whore in the bikini."

The recollection of that evening led me to conclude that wrestling a bear wasn't nearly as dangerous as being ambushed in the shadows by the Viet Cong.

Meanwhile, Joe was working hard to diminish the dangers of tussling with a four-hundred-pound black bear.

"He'll be on a leash. He's got a handler. It only costs thirty dollars to enter. It's not like it's a grizzly."

"I'll donate to the cause if you'll wrestle the bear, Joe," quipped Ricky, my college roommate of two years.

"Not me!" Joe protested. "I'm pudgy. See."

He pinched a roll of fat hanging over his belt.

"If not you, then who?" Ray sneered.

"Francisco," Joe declared confidently. "He knows Karate."

"Kung-fu," I corrected.

"All the better!" Joe seconded.

I could detect a shift in the lobby's magnetic field. Those assembled were musing at the prospect that I might prove victorious in my epic battle with the furred colossus, given my superior martial skills. I felt my manhood increasingly on the line. Summoning every molecule of bravado, I heard myself accept the challenge, outlining three conditions.

"First, I get $100 of the $300 prize money. Ya'll can split the rest. Second, you buy me a steak dinner two hours before the match. Third, you supply me with a quart of Jack Daniels to sip on the way to the venue."

The event was on! Word traveled throughout the dorm that in forty-eight hours I'd be pitting my fighting prowess against a North American black bear with nightly experience in the ring. For two days I tried psyching myself. Attempting to allay my panic, I strode to the library one night and sat for two hours studying the habits and anatomy of black bears. Then it hit me. The newspaper pictures of wrestling bears always showed them rearing on back legs to gain a height advantage. For some reason, human opponents faced the bear straight on, mano-a-mano, trying to grapple with an animal enormously strong and deceptively fast. I reasoned that a bear's paw strike wasn't as fast as Sugar Ray Leonard's jab, but it didn't have to be. There was more than 400 pounds of impact behind the swat. Often as not, the bear slapped most of its opponents silly. When the would-be warriors folded onto the canvas, the bear's torso came down like an avalanche. The unfortunate human victim, if quick enough, rolled under the ropes, out of the ring, and onto a cold and unwelcoming floor. Most pictures showed the handler rewarding the bear with a Coca-Cola.

At once, I saw what the puny pugilists had gotten wrong. It was a matter of physics. I abandoned their failed strategies, adopting logic as the golden arrow in my quiver of bear-baiting ploys.

After a hearty meal at the steakhouse on the eve of the competition, we piled into someone's car where I sat in the back seat. The front seat passenger passed me the requested bottle of Jack Daniels. I broke the seal and swigged, all pretenses of sipping gone. At first, the whisky cleared my head.

"I've got this!" I announced triumphantly.

My bravery escalated by the minute. Unfortunately, alcohol and testosterone impair the judgment and retard the memory. I barely recalled the pro wrestling card I'd watched before the intermission when the bear was led into the ring. I sprang out of my seat, barely cognizant of slaps on the back and urgings to join the line of human centurions awaiting their turn with the bear. I tried to focus. In my alcohol induced fog, I recited my painstakingly developed game plan. I just had to remind myself to follow it. Of the two fighters in line before me, both succumbed to the bear's prowess—one fighter thrown from the ring, one pinned to the canvas. It was my turn. I slid under the ropes, stepping onto the ring's surface. People I didn't know cheered me on. The bear's handler had the behemoth tethered to a chair. To my relief, the bear was muzzled.

I sized up my opponent, telescopically pinpointing my targets of attack. I'd earlier surmised that bears have knees, giving the creatures a center of gravity located between the bear's hind paw and below the knee joints. If possible, I had to attack the beast at the knee. A side or crescent kick wouldn't be effective.

Instead, I'd need to body roll a step or two toward the bear's paws but under his knees. Then I'd scissor one of the bear's legs and roll in the opposite direction. The bear couldn't help but topple. It was an immutable law of physics. I congratulated myself for my superior cognitive ability.

What I didn't count on—the discovery of every Darwin award winner who prefaces a suicidal feat with "Watch this!"—was that the bear would be startled by *me*. In retrospect, it made sense. If I slipped beneath the beast's line of vision, that alone would activate his startle reflex. That knowledge came too little too late. I rolled. The bear stutter-stepped backward a pace, making his legs inaccessible to me but making my chest accessible to him. His front paws began the slow-motion descent downward before landing squarely on my pecs. The air squeezed out of me in a rush. The bear's handler, a toothless old man trickling snuff from his mouth, was laughing it up, deliriously enjoying my misery. With my last gasp of air, I squeaked out: "Get him off!" The old man waited a few seconds before tugging the bear's chain and pulling him off me. I saw stars, then heard the distant underwater voices of my buddies shouting for me to get out of the ring. As if by instinct, I rolled under the ropes, dropping with a thud onto the floor. My dorm pals hoisted me to my feet. I don't recall saying it, but they say I said in a tone of battle-tested authority.

"Boys, you can't whup a bear."

I enjoyed a brief period of notoriety for simply getting into the squared circle with what scientists call Ursus americanus. For some time, people asked what it was like to wrestle a bear. I'd warn against comparing a bear with a large human. "It was more like wrestling a Volkswagen Beetle. You couldn't hold onto it, but you didn't dare let it go."

Years later, I related my erstwhile exploit to my friend David Brown. David was drawing a deck of Hillbilly Tarot cards at the time. Deriving inspiration from my experience, David featured me on a card—wearing a coonskin cap and taming a bear.

Hillbilly Tarot created by Dr. David Brown.

I appreciated David's effort to reproduce my epic struggle with the beast. However, I was no bear whisperer and certainly no Saint Francis. I came clean, telling David then what I'm saying to you in my best hillbilly twang just for the occasion: "If it's one thang I know fer shore, it's that you cain't whup a bear." Trust me, friends, I can bear witness to it.

35

Goat Man

by Edward Francisco

WE SOUTHERNERS CHERISH OUR "CHARACTERS"—EC-CENTRICS and outliers who intensify the spiciness of life. Take William Faulkner. To his neighbors in Oxford, Mississippi, Faulkner was "Count No 'Count," a little bitty fellow who put on airs while sport-ing a limp and a cane and donning a cape for his morning walks around the town square. Not until the author won the Nobel Prize in 1949 did public sentiment toward Faulkner begin to thaw. Nowadays almost ev-eryone in Oxford claims at least a peripheral biological tie to America's greatest literary Titan—even down to the young Vietnamese clerk at the Jitney Jungle who once gave me directions to "Uncle Bill's" Rowan Oak Estate.

Or how about the zany performances of the Southern Belles, and good ol' girls in the hit TV series *Designing Women*, its creator, Linda Bloodworth Thomason. One scene showing our affection for odd sorts involves Julia Sugarbaker, played by Dixie Carter, explaining to a visitor why we accommodate family members who appear at times to be a "bit off":

JULIA: "I'm saying this is the South, and we're proud of our crazy people. We don't hide them up in the attic. We bring 'em right down to the living room and show 'em off. See, Phyllis, no one in the South ever asks if you have crazy people in your family. They just ask what side they're on.

PHYLLIS: "Oh? And which side are yours on, Mrs. Sugarbaker?

JULIA: "Both."

Of course, we don't have to restrict ourselves to literature, TV, and film to unearth an honest, true-to-life "character." Those readers of a certain age may recall hearing about or seeing an itinerant wanderer who from 1930 to 1987 was a fixture on the Southern landscape while riding in a ramshackle wagon drawn by a team of goats. He was dubbed by all who saw him as the "Goat Man," or variously, "Billy Goat Man."

Born Charles "Ches" McCartney at the turn of the century in Iowa, McCartney ran away from his family's farm home at age fourteen. Soon afterwards, he found himself in New York where he met and married a Spanish knife thrower ten years his senior. McCartney became part of the act, serving as his wife's near-miss target. With the advent of the Great Depression, the duo gave up carnival life and unsuccessfully attempted to make a living as farmers. Fed up with poverty, his wife walked out on him one day before dawn. He married at least two other times, reputedly selling one wife to an interested farmer for $1000.

Having been fond of goats since his days of working on the farm, Ches McCartney hatched the idea of using a goat cart to travel the country as an itinerant preacher. He claimed to have covered 100,000 miles and visited all states but Hawaii, explaining that his goats couldn't swim that far, and even if they could, "they'd just end up eating the grass skirts off the hula dancers."

Wherever McCartney and his goats made an appearance in one of innumerable locales throughout the Southland, crowds flocked to see him. Of course, some smelled him before catching sight of the eccentric wanderer. The goat odor was so stifling as to announce his presence before he arrived. Between marriages, he claimed not to bathe, explaining how he and his goats didn't mind one another's ripeness. At dusk McCartney's habit was to park his wagon and goats on the side of the road, build a bonfire, and chat with locals. He always left them with a message: "Prepare to meet thy God."

Whether his intent or not, the Goat Man invoked a carnival atmosphere wherever he traveled. In his book *America's Goat Man*, Darryl Patton describes McCartney's vehicle of choice:

> McCartney's iron-wheeled wagon was large, rickety, and garishly decorated with a clutter of objects he found and collected along the road. It contained a bed, a potbellied stove, lanterns, and lots

of trash, and was pulled by a team of around nine goats, with a few trailing behind to occasionally push and serve as brakes on downhill stretches of road. His traveling goat herd sometimes numbered up to thirty.

We could expect that someone so obviously Gothic would attract a writer like Cormac McCarthy. In his 1979 novel *Suttree*, set in and around Knoxville, Tennessee, McCarthy's protagonist Sut converses with the Goat Man on the outskirts of Dixie Lee Junction:

Sut: What you wants with these goats anyway?

Goat Man: Little or nothin. Good fresh milk. God's best cheese.

Sut: You have any other animals? Dogs or anything?

Goat Man: No. Just goats. I think a fellar gets started with goats he just more or less sticks to goats.

My own experience with the Goat Man occurred when I was five. My parents and I were traveling home from a visit with my grandparents in north Hamilton County, near Sale Creek, Tennessee. The road we were on, Highway 27, was a two-lane ribbon with shoulders wide enough for cars to pull off safely. A line of vehicles was forming. One or the other of my parents exclaimed, "It's the Goat Man!" Daddy eased our Buick off the road's edge and onto the grass.

There in the field, the Goat Man tended his signature campfire surrounded by his goats. We exited the car, joining other curious onlookers. Children ran wildly about. Approaching, I caught sight of him. Sporting long hair and a grizzled beard and wearing threadbare, scruffy clothing, he might have been an ogre in a scary dream. But there he sat in the flesh, hawking postcards featuring a picture of himself and his goats. One card cost two cents.

"Would you like a postcard?" Daddy asked.

Of course! Who wouldn't? Daddy dropped two wheat ear pennies in my awaiting palm.

"Go ahead. Give them to him," Daddy urged.

I moved gingerly. The closer to the Goat Man I got, the mor pungent was his odor. He held out a rusty hand with a postcard. I breathed again when the transaction was completed.

"When you get home, you'll need to take a bath and wash the goat off," my mother said once we were back in the car.

The next morning, I took my card to kindergarten with me. Children crowded around to see my picture of the Goat Man and his goats. When the teacher asked me to put it up, I placed it in the cubby labeled with my name. Thinking it secure, I went about the hard work of playing. When parents started picking up kids, I scurried to my cubby only to discover my postcard gone. Some nimble-fingered kindergartner had stolen it.

Ches McCartney continued his rickety ramblings throughout the South for years afterwards, eventually living out his last days in a nursing home in Macon, Georgia. He died in 1998. Found in his possessions were copies of the Bible and *Robinson Crusoe*. At the time of his passing, he was believed to be in his late nineties. However, true to the spirit of his legend, he had claimed to be 106.

36

Look at Her

Short Story by Delonda Shown Anderson

H E LEFT WORK EARLY AND didn't expect her to be home. But the hazy air from a fresh shower greeted him as soon as he opened the door. A pungent linen soap pierced his nostrils. He saw her straightaway at the small kitchen table in her pink bunny bathrobe, her hair wrapped in a towel. Her legs were crossed, one of which swung back and forth as she daintily chewed a salad. She was hunched over, focused intently on her phone. He quietly put down his briefcase.

Look at her, he said to himself. A sourness pierced his jaw and traveled like a current through his body. Not that she was unattractive. He raised an eyebrow. On the contrary, she was stunning and built like a brick shithouse, as the saying goes. Not that she wasn't submissive. Also, on the contrary. She was that and more. She was every good woman for every bad man.

He met her three years ago at the ice cream shop where she worked. They married soon after. She was seventeen. He was thirty-two. She was thin, average height, with long, red tresses. And, oh, her eyes. They were light hazel—the misleading kind that seemed vacant but thoroughly searched through a man. More than just about anything, she won him with those eyes. That and her vigor. Every night, twice or thrice or more. *But*, he thought, *everything gets old*. He rubbed his bearded chin. *Never thought I'd say that bout sex*. But it was true. Everything he adored, the vitality, the fieriness, the syrupy sweetness, now made his stomach churn. The pressures of husbandhood strangled him, even in his sleep, and he had little room for a way out. He cocked his head and sized her up a minute. Her brain was still high school. Of course, he'd married her young and never gave her a chance to be anything else. But, like every woman, she was smart about spending money. And divorce wasn't an option. She'd use her wiles to win over an attorney and take him for everything. Everything.

Look at her, he thought. Her eyes fixated on her phone as her thumb pressed and swiped. *She doesn't even know I'm home... so focused on that damn phone. What's she looking at?* He moved stealthily and looked over her shoulder. She smelled cool and clean. He gazed down at the phone screen. *Ahh.* He rolled his eyes. *Recipes.* The perfect, dutiful wife making sure "her man" has dinner. He had a deucedly mischievous thought to scare the life out of her. So, he leaned down, put his lips to her ear, and, in his deepest voice, asked,

"So, what's for dinner?"

She screamed, dropped her phone, banged her knee under the table, and knocked her salad on the floor. He squatted down and grinned, amused at her reaction. She held her knee and flashed her eyes at him. His smile dimmed like a bright day's dusk. He saw a flicker of something in those hazels, something besides that candied expression. Something more *real*. Then she reverted to the same sweet little thing. He stood up.

"Charles!" she yelled. She released her knee and limped toward him.

Here comes the baby talk, he thought. A bit of food came up in his throat and he swallowed it back down.

"Oh, Charlesy-Warlsey," she said, slathering him with facial kisses.

He jerked away from her.

"Julie, stop."

Her bottom lip stuck out like a toddler's.

"You're a grown woman," he said, loosening his tie. "Act like it."

"Oh, okay," she said. "I'll do better."

Julie cleaned up the salad pieces and looked at each morsel with subtle disappointment. *She'd just prepared it*, he thought, *likely took only a few bites*. A piece of wilted lettuce stuck to her pinky and she devoured it. Suddenly, an image popped in his head of her being sickly and emaciated. His eyes widened. He stepped back and propped himself against a wall. *I could just starve her*, he thought, smirking. He contemplated it for a minute, indulged himself with the thought of shutting her up in a room and feeding her smaller and smaller portions until, eventually, she received no food at all. His own stomach floated with a delightful wickedness. When his eyes returned to the present, she was standing in front of him, smiling. He jerked back a little, then sighed. *Not possible*, he thought. He could already hear her cheerfully singing his praises, a la baby talk, behind the locked door, thanking him for any morsel he gave her.

"Don't worry about the salad, Sweetie," she said, stretching up on her tiptoes and kissing his forehead. "You look so sorry about it."

She dumped the fixings in the compost jar, then washed her hands. As she dried them, she dropped the dishtowel then surreptitiously bent down, exposing her young, sugary backside. She turned, sly and shameless, and smiled at him. He pretended not to notice. Her cheeks flushed as she stiffly tugged the robe down. He turned toward the stairs, then looked back. Her head hung low and her body shook through hurtful tears. He liked that. Or maybe she was... laughing? *No*, he decided. *She's clearly upset.*

He made his way to the bedroom and shut the door behind him. He changed into sweats and a t-shirt, then turned to the bathroom sink and splashed water on his face, dowsing away every smothery kiss and every sweetness. He stared at himself in the mirror. *Not a bad looking man, really*, he thought. He pulled back his brown bangs, jutted his chin, and studied both sides of his face. Little wrinkles here and there and a few blemishes. He never had blemishes before. *Marriage*, he reasoned. *Stressful as hell.* He flexed his bicep and smiled. Women at the office found him attractive, though. He ran a hand across his face and looked deep into his reflection. His smile faded. *Yes, it's true*, he thought. *Everything gets old.* Why should he waste another day being miserable?

After some time, he descended the stairs. She was on the phone, dressed in a pair of blue jean cut-offs, a pink tank top, and crisp, white tennis shoes. Her hair was pulled up high in a ponytail. Finished with her conversation, she placed the phone in her bag and retrieved a compact mirror. She puckered her lustrous pink lips, then, clearly satisfied, clacked it closed. She caught him glimpsing at her and smiled. He grabbed his laptop from his briefcase and made himself comfortable on the plush sofa. He had work to do.

"Charlesy," she said, skipping toward the couch.

She came from behind and wrapped her arms around his neck. He stiffened.

"I didn't know you'd be home early today. I already made lunch plans with Monica, then to the grocery store. But..." she said, running her fingers through his hair and placing those pretty pink lips by his ear, "if you want me to stay home, I will. You know, you do things to me, Charlesy."

He spotted her reflection through the window. Her body undulated in the most grotesque way. *Go with Monica*, he thought. *Leave.* His wife spent a lot of time with her "BF," and he could never express how grateful he was to the girl. He pulled away from Julie and opened the laptop. She swiftly rose.

"Can I bring you anything while I'm out?" Julie asked.

Yeah, a gun, he though. He sat there, solid and rigid, and flirted with the idea—how he'd shoot her, where he'd shoot her. Would he cut up her perky limbs? Or bury her in the backyard? *Too messy*, he thought. *Too complicated.*

"No, thank you," he replied. "Have a good time."

"Okay. See you in a few hours..."

"Mmm hmm."

She squealed and made a cheerleader move before she went out the door. He hurried to the window and watched her leave. God, he thought, even her driving's perky. He returned to the couch and his laptop. He had work to do. His fingers rested atop a-s-d-f and j-k-l-;. But he stared at the screen, numb and tired. He couldn't remember the last time he was genuinely happy. As a matter of fact, most of his emotions left him a long time ago... right after he married Julie. She was draining the life out of him. The less he shone; the more she sparkled. He chuckled. Yes, even her driving was perky. *Her driving.* He sat up straight. *I could cut the brake line*, he thought. His lips slithered into a devilish grin. He played the scenario over and over in his head like a bad action movie. She'd drive her perky self around the curves, rush her perky self through the guard rails, and plunge her perky self down a cliff. He imagined her screaming shrieks losing volume as she rushed to her fiery death.

The next thing he knew, he woke from a deep nap, his laptop closed on the coffee table in front of him. He sat there and listened to the paper bags rustling in the kitchen. *She's home*, he thought. *A respite no more.* Her phone rang to a K-Pop snippet. He looked askance at her wiggling to the tune. She swished past the doorway to check on him. He feigned sleep and listened to the one-sided conversation.

"Yeah, that was fun," Julie said softly. "We should do that more often. Oh, he's asleep right now. I'll hafta be quiet."

She put groceries away as she spoke.

"What?"

The kitchen chair moved across the floor and he heard her plop down onto it.

"Tomorrow's perfect! Oh, God, finally. Thank you, Monica. What do you mean 'will he come?' I think he will when he finds out it's the opera."

The opera, he wondered. *The opera?* He quietly grabbed his laptop and searched. *By God*, he thought, it's *The Phantom of the Opera*. His favorite. He grinned from ear to ear. Suddenly, his eyes widened and his breath left him for a second. *There*, he thought. He saw the opportunity. She'd look beautiful in her finest dress. He'd wear a three-piece suit, buy her flowers—her last flowers. *The whole day, I'll be a gentleman. She deserves at least that much.* He'd be overly attentive, extend his arm for her, and they'd walk forward to the opera house, stopping at the crowded intersection of 4th and Maynard—the busiest, most dangerous four-way intersection in the city, maybe even the state. He couldn't count on two hands how many pedestrians had died on that four-way in just six months. *Beautiful*, he thought. He'd lead her farther to the edge of the sidewalk, wait until the traffic light turned, and, while cars zoomed past, and as the crowd was caught up in their own separate universes, he'd put his hand flat on her back, kick her heel, and just push. He closed his laptop and toyed with a mournful, teary-eyed script. *She lost her footing, detective. There was nothing I could do. How am I gonna live without her?* He'd be absolved and free.

"Over," he said aloud.

"What's over?" she asked.

His shoulders jolted and he gasped. He cleared his throat.

"Oh, nothing. Just work. How was shopping?" he asked.

"Great," she said.

"That's good."

She sat beside him on the sofa.

"I have a surprise for you, Charlesy."

"Oh, yeah? What's that?"

He stretched and yawned and put his arm around her waist. To his surprise, she stiffened. But she quickly melted and nuzzled into him. *Tonight*, he thought, *her last night on this Earth, I'll give her my everything.*

"Monica bought us tickets to the opera tomorrow night. Some phantom thing or other. I know you love the opera. How 'bout we go?"

"Well," he said, rubbing her arm, "I think that sounds just perfect. Just perfect."

He kissed her, and she hungrily moved into him.

"No," he said, sliding away.

He stood and scooped her up in his arms. He held her there and looked into those pretty hazel eyes, then continued,

"Not tonight. Tonight, we're gonna do things *my* way."

"Oh, Charlesy…"

Her sultry lips burrowed into his neck. He carried her into the bedroom and shut the door.

The next morning, they had breakfast together, and, truth be told, he enjoyed being with her. He almost—almost—had second thoughts, until he mentioned they should go play tennis together. She danced and performed a few high-kicks at the thought of it.

"I'll wear my best skort and top!" she exclaimed.

"Great," he said dully.

That evening, he took her to the upscale *Bonté Française*. She looked absolutely gorgeous in an emerald-green dress. Her red hair was curled just right in spirals down her back, and her black heels and matching bag were lovely. He was glad he'd chosen this night. *She'll die young and beautiful*, he told himself. The *maître d'* came to the table and told him he had a phone call at the front.

"I don't know why they didn't just call my cell," he said, perturbed. "How'd anyone know I was here?"

The head waiter shrugged and smiled, then led him to the phone. When he returned, Julie was closing her purse. A glass of wine sat in front of him.

"I ordered you a glass," she said. "You love it so much. I hope you don't mind."

He gave a slight shrug, kissed her, and said,

"Thank you, Beautiful."

"Who was on the phone?" she asked.

"Don't know. The phone was dead."

Dead. He looked at his watch. It's getting close to that time.

"Honey, we'd better be—"

"I'm going to the ladies' room," she said. "Be right back, Charlesy. Then we'll be off to the opera-wopera. I'm so excited!"

Yes, he thought. *So am I.*

He hurriedly drank the wine, gestured for the check, and paid the bill. She returned, looking vibrant and eager, her eyes bright as stars. He extended his arm. She smiled, put her arm in his, and off they went.

As they walked, his stomach grew queasy. He guessed it was nerves. *Won't affect my plans at all*, he told himself. *If anything, it'll help during the police interview. I'll be sick with grief.* They walked casually toward the sidewalk. Finally, they reached the intersection. The pedestrian light flashed yellow on the countdown. He released his arm, moved close to her, and crept nearer to the edge. People, as he predicted, were practically shoulder-to-shoulder, back-to-back. He had forever before the light changed. *Enough time*, he thought. *Enough time.* Someone was a little too close behind him, but that didn't matter. His head swam with dizziness, but he steadied himself. *What's wrong with me?* He hurriedly put his hand on Julie's back and moved his foot near her heel. *Now*, he thought.

Suddenly, someone behind him pushed hard. He tried to draw back, but the force was too great as he stood on the edge. The traffic never stopped and he felt the piercing blow of metal across his shins, his thighs, his back, his chest. The pedestrian light turned green and people scurried away from him. Others circled around him. The pain was unbearable at first. Blood pooled around him, warm and comforting.

His eyes looked wild in a frantic search for Julie. He saw her standing among the circle. *Look at her*, he thought. *So beautiful.* Someone held her hand. He followed the connection. *Monica?* Both women wore a wry, sinister grin. Julie put her head on the woman's shoulder. *Monica shoved me*, he thought. And, for the first time in years, he really laughed, even though it was excruciating. At the irony of it all; at the *Phantom*; at the night sky full of stars; at the sirens drawing near. He laughed until the darkness came.

37

The Strange Case of David Lang

Short Story by Edward Francisco

I WAS NAMED FOR MY GREAT-GRANDFATHER, David Lang. David has long been a source of speculation and fascination owing to his disappearance near Gallatin, Tennessee, on September 23, 1880. He supposedly vanished into thin air while walking through a field near his home. Nor was his disappearance without witnesses. It was twilight. The afternoon sun had dropped behind the hills. Yet, even in the grainy light, David's wife and children, sitting on the porch, saw him disappear.

As a boy I was teased beyond thought at the story of my great-grandfather. Imagine my delight when his saga appeared in 1959 in a book titled *Stranger than Science* by Frank Edwards. Edwards' account squares with the stories I've heard at numerous family reunions:

> David Lang had not taken more than half a dozen steps when he disappeared in full view of all those present. Mrs. Lang screamed. The children, too startled to realize what had happened, stood mutely. Instinctively, they all ran toward the spot where Lang had last been seen a few seconds before. Judge Peck and his companion, the Judge's brother-in-law, scrambled out of their buggy and raced across the field. The five of them arrived on the spot of Lang's disappearance almost simultaneously. There was not a tree, not a bush, not a hole to mar the surface. And not a single clue to indicate what had happened to David Lang.

Before my grandmother, David's daughter, died in 1965 at the age of eighty-seven, she told me as I sat in wide-eyed wonder what happened afterwards.

"Six months or so later, my brother and I were playing near the spot. I don't know why. We were just drawn to it. It was, after all, the last place we'd seen him alive—assuming that he was, in fact, dead."

That last bit always intrigued me. Did my grandmother harbor a suspicion that her father's disappearance had been the result of some inexplicable supernatural phenomenon? As a boy, I'd also begun to investigate paranormal subjects. I had a special interest in UFO sightings, radioactive mutations, and time travel. By some odd confluence of circumstances, had my great-grandfather been plucked out of this dimension and placed into another one? Was he a quantum being? My grandmother would bring me out of my reverie by returning to the spot of her father's disappearance.

"As I said, my brother and I were drawn to play there. About six months later, we were searching for four-leaf clovers on Daddy's grave—that's how we'd come to think of it. All of a sudden, we heard our father's voice—both my brother and I heard it. It seemed to be coming from the base of a large rock. He was calling to us. We tried to answer but with no success. An hour later the voice faded. We never heard it again. Years later we hired an excavation crew to dig on the site. It didn't take long before they struck a solid floor of granite. No sinkholes were found, no wells, no Indian burial mounds—just rock."

My grandmother's stories lured me to the place of David Lang's disappearance. I half-heartedly hoped that he would call out to me from under the big rock. Maybe I was under my grandmother's suggestive spell, but I sometimes thought I detected the echo of a voice I'd never heard. Breezes in the trees can play tricks on the ears.

My grandmother's death only intensified my interest in unusual happenings. I devoured as much information as possible on such diverse subjects as UFOs and alien abductions, séances and Ouija, the Illuminati and secret societies throughout the ages. I collected coins in order to detect Masonic symbols in U.S. currency. I spent hours contemplating the possibility of time travel. To that end, I wore out three copies of H. G. Wells's *Time Machine*. I also encrypted codes and memorized the Cherokee alphabet, developed by a club-footed chieftain named Sequoyah, whose English surname, enigmatically, was Guess.

High school found me abandoning these interests in favor of other pursuits. Girls, cars, and sports comprised the reigning trinity of my teenage years. Girls, in particular, were just as mysterious as Stonehenge or Area 51. In short, space aliens had nothing on a species of nymphs whose innocence inspired in me the rankest sort of lust. No wonder Odysseus had ordered his crew to tie him to the mast of his ship so he couldn't jump into the sea in pursuit of sirens.

Senior year offered time to re-evaluate my priorities. I decided to enroll at Vanderbilt University to pursue a double major in English literature and particle physics. I wasn't unaware that these subjects were at far ends of the academic spectrum. What I hoped, I now think, was that I'd find a theory unifying all fields of knowledge. What can I say? I was young. Shouldn't youth be a time of enthusiastic speculation?

I didn't give up on girls—certainly not. Nashville offered plenty of opportunities for romantic couples desiring to couple. Music bars like the Mercy, eateries like Holland House, and art crawls through the galleries on Fifth Avenue and the arcade, were part of an elaborate courtship ritual leading back to dorms where inebriated couples needed no justification for enjoying some midnight delight.

That was mostly on weekends. Vanderbilt is often termed a "Southern Ivy." Its professors and courses proved rigorous during my days there. Classes, labs, and study sessions often meant sleep deprivation. There never seemed to be enough of me to go around. A date on a weeknight could ruin a GPA. At times I envied my great-grandfather's seeming ability to be in two places at once.

Then one day two seemingly random events occurred but with such synchronicity as to erase any doubt they were somehow connected in ways unfathomable to me. The first took place in my eight a.m. American lit class. I'd been unable to read the assignment the night before because I'd been writing a physics lab report, already two days overdue. My English professor, a man in his fifties with a shock of white hair and a goatee, and wearing a sport coat embodying Vanderbilt's ideal of the shabby, genteel college don, told us to open the book to page 243. There on the printed page was Ambrose Bierce's story "The Difficulty of Crossing a Field." As was his habit, the professor provided a summary of the piece, knowing that half the class was barely awake at eight, the other half hungry for having skipped breakfast.

"In this story," the professor said, "a man is seen crossing a field, then disappears from existence."

But wait! That's what had happened to my great-grandfather. I strained to hear what else the professor was saying.

"Such a story could be thought of as a foreboding prophecy of Bierce's own unexplained disappearance."

Bierce disappeared? I cursed under my breath for not having read the story and the accompanying biographical notes before class. The professor went on to say that Bierce's disappearance was one of the great mysteries in American literary history.

Between classes, I rushed to the library, looking up Bierce and his work, awestruck that the author had written about a disappearance like one experienced by my great-grandfather. I got chill bumps as I read the inspiration for Bierce's story: a sensational narrative evincing historical accuracy based on testimony by witnesses. In this account, said to have occurred on a morning in July 1854, Bierce reported the fate of a planter named Williamson, who lived six miles from Selma, Alabama, who vanished before the eyes of his wife and child, and a neighbor and his son.

I could hardly tear myself away, but I'd spent all night working on the physics report and needed to attend class in order to turn it in. As it was, I was late on entering. I took a seat in the back. The young man next to me reeked of marijuana. In 1973 pot was pervasive on campus. When people weren't toking, they were popping amphetamines like candy. Some nights it was the only way to prop up when studying. The professor was in mid-lecture—something about a thought experiment by an Austrian physicist named Schrodinger. The professor read a passage from our text summarizing the experiment:

A cat is placed in a steel box along with a Geiger counter, a vial of poison, a hammer, and a radioactive substance. When the radioactive substance decays, the Geiger detects it and triggers the hammer to release the poison, subsequently killing the cat. The radioactive decay is a random process so that there is no way to predict when it will occur. Physicists say that the atom exists in a state known as superposition—decayed and not decayed simultaneously. Until the box is opened, an observer can't know whether the cat is dead or alive.

A person didn't have to be a theoretical physicist to understand the implications of Schrodinger's theory. In a quantum dimension, a thing could be in two places at once, could, in fact, be both alive and dead. Just because I was dead in this dimension didn't mean I was dead in another. Envisioning time as a continuum meant that I was already dead at some point in the future. In that nanosecond in class, I had the undeniable sensation that a spark had crossed a commissure in my brain, resulting in an instantaneous linking of disparate entities: my great-grandfather's bizarre disappearance, Ambrose Bierce's prophetic vanishing act, and the paradoxical time-bending properties of quantum physics.

My epiphenomenal moment didn't last long. People diagnosed with temporal lobe epilepsy sometimes describe experiencing an aura. There's even a menu of diagnostic auras. If I had an aura that day, it dissolved quickly. Still, I was determined to discover what role I played in the cosmic theater of space-time.

However, every new discovery meets resistance almost at once. It's as if with every intoxicating insight, a corresponding impulse arises to slam shut the windows of perception. The demon of doubt rears its head.

My own misgivings emerged with a reporter's attempts to prove that my great-grandfather's disappearance was a hoax—a species of folklore perpetrated after the publication of Bierce's story inspired by a mid-century planter's disappearance into the vortex of time. I was furious! Why was one story easier to believe than another? The reporter even conjectured that David Lang never existed. If so, then what did that say for me?

Still, I found mention of another reporter's account, including an interview with David Lang's daughter, Sara Lang, my grandmother! The reporter noted that Sara was reluctant to grant the interview but granted it to substantiate her family's earlier claims about her father. She had verified the events of that day, acknowledging how eerily strange it was to be the daughter of the ghostly David Lang. She'd said little else, a fact consistent with my grandmother's shy character and her almost obsessive desire to shun publicity beyond the scope of her family. Remember. My grandmother died in 1965, years before the Internet with its ubiquitous splash of images and lurid appeals of self-promotion. Hers was a mindset that doesn't exist anymore. She was born and lived in a southern version of the Victorian era. She was a genteel lady and, as she was fond of saying, a lady's name should appear in the newspaper twice only: once, when she was born, and once, when she died.

"These stories—do what you will with them," she'd said to me.

I promised to revisit them in the future. That point would not materialize for years. After Vanderbilt, I pursued graduate degrees in English literature at Harvard, then at Christ's College, Oxford. On completing the D. Phil. at Oxford, I returned to the happy coincidence of an available professorship at Vanderbilt. I aced the interview, was hired for the position, and settled into a comfortable life as a gentleman scholar. I taught and conducted research. Two years later, I married my graduate teaching assistant. We had two children in fast succession—a boy and a girl, named David and Sara. Oddly, my wife chose both names. Our children are grown now. David teaches art at Vandy. Sara is an osteopath in Memphis. She's expecting in November—a boy, according to the ultrasound. As for my wife and me, it's as if we've hurtled through our children's lives in a time machine. Imagine the bewildering effect of prolonged cosmic jetlag. That's how it's been for us these past few years.

Up until a few months ago, the only touchstone with any reality I'd known could be found only in dreams. In one of the dreams, I was a boy, walking hand in hand with my grandmother across the expanse of a field. She stopped and pointed to the spot where her father had disappeared. He seemed to vanish with the haze. I don't know how to explain it except to say that my quantum state of dreaming seemed more real than the hours and days ticking off the clock with its assumptions of real time. Was I coming unhinged—besieged by regressive psychosis? I felt shaky and diaphanous. My doctor prescribed Beta blockers to stop my hands from trembling. The only time I seemed to relax was when attending the extraordinary lecture series hosted by Vanderbilt's physics department in the Central Library. Lectures were open to the public, but I always received curious stares from the scientists who sensed that I was a creature not of their world. After all, mathematics, not words, comprised their code of communication. Sitting in the auditorium, I sometimes wondered if I'd taken a wrong turn, pursuing literature instead of physics. I suddenly felt as if I were living in two dimensions—torn between opposite modes of apprehending human existence.

However I might wish to pursue another life, I'd been hired to teach literature, and that's what I'd done for almost thirty years. I consoled myself by thinking that if I hadn't gone into literature, I might never have read Bierce's "The Difficulty of Crossing a Field," a story that haunted and intrigued me and that, in proprietary fashion, I'd come to claim as my own. For years I scoured the story for a key to the mystery of my origins and to the cosmic landscape swallowing up my great-grandfather before his family's eyes. I sometimes intuited that through the medium of the story Bierce was speaking directly to me across a continuum of space and time.

So great was my obsession with Bierce that I offered a graduate seminar on his work two years ago in the fall. One brilliant October morning, I drove to campus, pulling into my reserved parking spot. On exiting the car, I dropped a Cross pen that I assumed rolled under the vehicle. When I bent to look, there was no pen in sight. I got back in the car, pulling into the parking space in front of me. Exiting the car once more, I scanned the lot. Still no pen. A young woman, an assistant professor in the history department, pulled in the spot beside me.

"Lose something?" she asked, striding over to help look.

She joined in the search. "Looks as if it's vanished," she said finally.

"Has anything like this ever happened to you?" I asked.

"Once," she said, "a few years ago. My daughter was a baby. She threw her pacifier out the car window. My husband and I looked and looked for it but never found it. I suspect that there are cracks in the space-time continuum and that things disappear all the time."

Had she said that? Did she mean it?

"Even people?" I ventured

"Maybe. It would have to be an awfully big crack, I would think."

A week later, Nashville hosted its annual Southern Festival of Books on the capitol mall. Publishers, authors, and editors occupy booths, selling books to the throng of conference goers and tourists converging for the event. A fixture at the conference is an author who bills himself as an investigative mythologist, whose ranging interests include aliens, alchemical symbolism, and esoteric geometry. He theorizes that, like

Rome, Nashville's seven hills comprise "light centers" like those found on the site of Stonehenge or the Mayan ruins. I've visited those ancient artifacts and can attest to a confluence of strange, almost psychedelic, sensations associated with those places. Nashville, according to the author, emits the same patterns of energy.

"If you could unfold the universe," the author told me in our last discussion, "the cosmic-axis would be on the spot where you're standing."

Although regarded by many of the locals as a star-gazing fanatic, he is the only person I know who'd ever investigated my great-grandfather's disappearance. He also knew more about Nashville's history than anyone I know.

"I'm curious," I asked before leaving his booth. "Was Ambrose Bierce ever here?" Bierce, the cosmic trickster, seemed to make the rounds. It was safe to assume he'd been here too.

"December 1864. Battle of Nashville. Union side."

In subsequent weeks, I visited Peach Orchard Hill, site of a two-day clash that broke the resistant back of the Confederate army in Tennessee. Bierce had been a cartographer during the war. Had he mapped this battlefield? Was I walking in his footsteps?

A month later, I picked up a copy of Nashville's weekly entertainment magazine, *Metro Pulse*. Between classes, I browsed its contents when something caught my eye, then struck me with the force of a hammer. It was a full-page splash ad for the 2013 season for the Nashville Opera. Among the chamber listings: *The Difficulty of Crossing a Field*. Imagine my shock when learning the name of the composer: David Lang! In what quadrant of the universe had I been not to have heard of this David Lang? He'd won a Pulitzer Prize in music and written an award-winning opera based on a story by Bierce, a writer, who by all rights, belonged to me. I stood in direct line of succession to the original David Lang. How many David Langs were there? My temples throbbed. I logged on to my computer to ask my question. In the snap of a genie's fingers, it found the answer: 1,216 people in the U.S. were named David Lang. Did we all exist at once, or did some of us disappear only to spring up in another dimension with only hazy recollections of our former state—what Wordsworth called "intimations of immortality"?

To make things worse, David Lang's online bio contained the following paragraph:

In 1999, Lang and playwright Mac Wellman based their opera The Difficulty of Crossing a Field on a short story by Ambrose Bierce, about an Alabama planter named Williamson who purportedly vanished while walking across a field in 1854. Bierce's story recurs in urban-legend form, in which, coincidentally, the vanished man is often given the name David Lang.

Not only had the composer David Lang co-opted my great-grandfather and his disappearance, but he'd also conflated my real ancestor with the character in Bierce's story. Undoubtedly, David Lang the musician was attracted to the story because his name was the same as my great-grandfather's. That was no coincidence, a synchronicity, perhaps, but no coincidence. Siting at my desk, I envisioned the gifted composer as a time-traveling thief, wiggling in and out of dimensions, stealing identities in the name of David Lang, then arranging them like notes on a score to be played like a celestial ensemble at the end of time. I felt diaphanous again—like a ghost walking over my own grave.

Of course, there was another, more disturbing possibility. My ancestor had disappeared, stuck between the walls of time. A diaphragm between this world and that had reverberated with sounds of his voice which his children heard six months after he'd vanished. What if my great-grandfather had felt his way along the warp and woof of time's curtain until finding a portal, enabling him to re-enter this temporal world on a finite continuum designated on the calendar as January 8, 1957—musician David Lang's date of birth? What if the composer was my great-grandfather? Or, a more disturbing prospect—and one just as likely: What if my great-grandfather was me?

I attended the opera, staged exactly a century after Bierce's disappearance, long a subject of speculation and controversy. Consult a literature anthology, and you'll find that the year of Bierce's death—1913—is almost always followed by a question mark. No one really knows what happened to him, just as no one knows what happened to the planter in Alabama in 1854 or to David Lang in 1888.

Legend has it that Bierce went down to Mexico and joined up with Pancho Villa and his forces during the Mexican revolution. Someone reported that he was later executed by a firing squad. The problem is that these rumors don't square with the fact, attested to by friends, that Bierce found Villa reprehensible and would likely never have joined his ranks. Then where did Bierce go? Did he engineer his own disappearance, or did the cosmos engineer it for him? How many people on the surface of the planet disappeared each day? And what of other famous disappearances in history—Amelia Earhart, entire ships in the Bermuda Triangle, and the lost colony at Roanoke?

These were my thoughts as I sat watching David Lang's alluring and eerie opera based on what Bierce billed as fiction. Lately I'd noticed a phenomenon while teaching I'd never experienced before. I'd chalked it up to a widespread attention deficit disorder inspired by the memetic bombardment of e-mail, texts, and twitters. The phenomenon manifested itself in the following way: I'd offer some information or instruction, and, after a discernable lapse, someone would ask me to repeat what I'd said, with my words, to my thinking, still hanging in the ether. It was on the order of saying, "We'll have a quiz on Thursdays," only to have someone ask, a bit later, "Will we have a quiz on Thursday?" This echoing pattern began to occur so frequently that I started checking my watch, seeing how long it would take for someone to ask me what I'd just said. On average, the lag time was two minutes. Odd that. I could only wonder: Were they two minutes behind the cosmic clock, or was I two minutes ahead? Did thoughts travel at different speeds? I couldn't help thinking of the words of Alice's mad rabbit: "I'm late! I'm late! For a very important date!"

On my way home from the opera, I recalled something from an astronomy class I'd taken at Vanderbilt thirty-five years earlier. It was that it takes light 4.37 years to reach the earth from Alpha Centauri, the star closest to our solar system. That meant that if Alpha Centauri exploded, it would take 4.37 years for observers on earth to notice its absence. By analogy, would it take my students two minutes before noticing that I'd had a heart attack and died? In that period of time, would I be both alive and dead, theoretically speaking?

I went home, finding my wife asleep. Not wanting to disturb her, I sank onto the sofa in the sunroom, glass of Chardonnay in hand. The more I sipped, drowsier I got. I was beginning to feel like the speaker in Poe's poem: "Once upon a midnight dreary, while I pondered weak and weary…" I decided to stretch out, too tired to make my way to bed. My eyes folded on the next lines of the poem. I never knew if I finished reciting them: "While I nodded, nearly napping, suddenly, there came a tapping, as of someone gently rapping, rapping at my chamber door."

There he stood, a misty figure in a Victorian gentleman's broad coat. It was not the image I expected, making it plain to him.

"But you were a farmer," I said.

"A gentleman farmer," he said in a soft drawl. "They left out that part of the story."

"Are you the southern planter or my great-grandfather?

"Does it matter?"

"I suppose not."

I could have been staring at my own face in a mirror—or mirrors. The effect was like one I'd experienced as a boy getting a haircut in the barber shop. The barber had mounted a mirror on the wall directly in front of his chair and a mirror on the wall behind it. Sitting in the chair, I could see an infinite succession of ever shrinking images of myself, exact replicas disappearing in a continuum. David Lang and I were seeing our past and future simultaneously.

"Are you and I the same person?" I asked, taking a sharp breath.

"Not exactly," he drawled, "though we obviously share the same DNA. Our psychic fingerprints are different, however."

I nodded.

"Did you ever wonder," he asked, "why you're interested in the things you're interested in, why you pursued the career you did, why you married the woman in the next room?"

He clearly intended the questions as rhetorical.

"Everything," he said, "everything in your life has led you to this point in time." He paused, letting it sink in, before resuming. "Your childhood fascination with the disappearing David Lang, your curiosity about physics, and your odd penchant for always being a bit out of synch with time—are all manifestations of the David Lang that you've been in the past or will be in the future."

"How many of us are there?"

"Oh, my," he said. "Try to imagine an infinite number of David Langs living in an infinite number of dimensions running parallel to one another like cosmic strings."

"But you and I are both in this dimension, at this point in time."

"Do you recall from your physics classes years ago at Vanderbilt a concept known as superposition?"

"Yes. It occurs when two or more waves in the same place are super-imposed on one another, meaning that they're all added together."

"Right!" He clapped his hands approvingly, sensing that I under-stood. "The principle of superposition tells us that waves cannot affect one another: one wave cannot alter the direction, frequency, wavelength, or amplitude of another wave."

"Then how do you explain the presence of more than one David Lang in a single dimension?" I was thinking of the composer Lang, almost sure that he was a time traveler, too. My next thought was what if we met, would we superimpose upon each other, becoming one person?

"It will aid us conceptually," he said, "to consider the ancient symbol for infinity: the shape of a sideways figure eight, or a snake eating its own tail. The figure folds upon itself at only one point."

"The point of superposition," I said.

"A point of timeless infinity. Another way of putting it is that we David Langs always arrive on time when it comes to disappearing."

"You've discovered the blueprint of the universe. Why not go public with it?"

"Do you recall the Inquisition? Throughout history, David Langs have popped into this world, intent on sharing esoteric knowledge, only to find extraordinary resistance. We've been drawn, quartered, hanged, drowned, and burned at the stake. The Illuminati? It's why they went underground cloaking themselves in a tapestry of symbols decipherable only to a few. While we're on the subject, I wouldn't tell anybody about this dream if I were you. Your wife already suspects that you're mentally ill given your habit of trying to decipher codes in the diagonals of cross-word puzzles."

"Where will you go?" I asked.

"Go? Everywhere. Nowhere. Do you recall the origin of the word *utopia*?"

"It's a Greek pun meaning no place and every place at once."

"Utopia—that's where I'll be," he said, with the conviction of a man who, like me, would experience no difficulty crossing a field.

38

What Was on Her Mind

Short Story by Delonda Shown Anderson

D ETECTIVE GOWAN STOOD ACROSS FROM me and fiddled with some recorder. He perked up when another detective entered the room.

"Name's Bob," said the other detective. "Detective Bob Kroy." He slid a paper in front of me.

"Sign this before you make your statement. Says you're tellin' the truth—to the best of your knowledge, of course."

He offered me a pen, and I caught a glimpse of his fingernails and torn cuticles. My eyes scanned the ball-point and made their way toward his wrinkled shirt and skewed tie. I smiled, wry and distant, and took the pen in that exaggerated elegant way that powerful men seem to love. "Bob" was a nail biter and that, in addition to the rest of his appearance, was pretty much all I needed to know about him.

Detective Gowan, on the other hand, was as dapper as the devil. Least ways, how *I* viewed the Fallen One. His hair was all nice, suit pressed, nails manicured. He had a baby-faced shave and intense blue eyes—the kind that told me somewhere back a long time ago, one of his ancestors was Melungeon. He spoke like he was *from* here, but not. Like he'd tried for years to squelch our way of talk.

After Gowan checked the recorder, the machine tutted a few clicks, then it was "on." Gowan indicated the time, the date, my name, and the reason for the recording. He sat down, looked at me intently, and asked,

"Now. Anything she complain of?"

I just looked right back at him, kind of stunned by the suddenness. He continued,

"Anything she say about him?"

I remained silent.

"Looking back, do you recall anything unusual? Bruising? Cuts?" he asked, leaning forward, pen in hand, and, since the recorder kept rolling, I figured he was noting my reactions.

I raised an eyebrow, then smiled.

"She rubbed her back some," I said. "I just thought she's tired, you know. From workin' s'damn much."

Gowan flipped through several pages in his notepad with a furrowed brow.

"Says here Posey McLeeny never worked," he said.

"I mean—well, no. She didn't work a nine-to-five. You'd just hafta live her life to know what I mean," I said.

His eyes searched my face and he studied me like I was one of those optical illusion paintings, trying to find the lie hidden in plain sight.

"Mmm hmm," he said. "Tell me about the last day you saw her. Friday, you said?"

"Yessir, it was Friday," I said, and began to unravel everything Posey told me.

I had no idea how Posey came up with such talk. I never knew what was on her mind. She was the brainy type. You know, the kind of person who's so smart she's scary. I'm sure she had a right high IQ. One day she'd discuss some famous artist like Mary Cassett or some photographer like Eddie Adams. Another day, she talked me through slaughtering a hog—dragging it to the scalding water, scraping off the hair, disemboweling it from groin to gullet, and various other preparations before freezing the butchered meat. Time after that, she schooled me about writers like John Fox, Jr. and Rebecca Harding Davis, or Walker Percy and Flannery O'Connor. Et cetera. And, on occasion, she chatted about the Lord and the beatitudes and forgiveness.

I immensely enjoyed her company, and she was always happy to have visitors, so, when *my* Earl agreed to help *her* Earl fix his truck, I asked if I could ride along and *my* Earl allowed it. That day was sweltering, as I recall, about ninety-seven degrees, and the heat was stagnant with no breeze whatsoever. My Earl's truck had no AC so all that hot, Southern air propelled through the windows. Sweat beads trickled down my back and gummed my t-shirt as my nostrils were plagued by a mixed aroma of acrid pencil lead, chemical exhaust, and musty locker-room. But I never said nary a word. I wouldn't have dared. As Earl journeyed deeper in the holler, toward all the dark, magical places, the trees' shade eased the air. The McLeeny house rested atop a hill in the distance like a brazen pimple. My stomach butterflied with anticipation about what topic Posey had on her mind this time.

When we reached their house, her Earl stood near his old rattletrap smoking a cigarette and Posey walked the rows in their garden with a bushel basket. When she saw us, she eased the basket down, took a towel from across her shoulder, and rubbed her face and hands. She walked toward me and hugged me timidly. My smile quickly turned. Her face was quite blanched and her eyes darted across the ground, like she tried to find some kind of answer there. To what, I wasn't sure, but I'd had that look myself sometimes and I figured it was what it was. My Earl and her Earl stepped toward the vehicle while we women moved to the kitchen. I sat at the table and she put on coffee.

One thing about Posey—she was *obsessed* with a clean house. At least to me, she was. As I sat there, my eyes tried their damnedest to find a sliver of grease, a dust bunny, a mark on the wall, anything out of place. Never with Posey. Even the floor looked like you could lick the corners and come up empty.

She was a natural beauty, too, with long, brown hair; and she never wore makeup that I ever saw. She had a wicked sense of humor and she was filled with life and spirit. Her face brightened when she entertained visitors. But… that day, she seemed somewhat deflated and she moved slower than usual. Less perk, you know? Her gait was a little off and she wiped the kitchen table with more measured motions.

"Somethin' wrong?" I asked her.

She turned away gingerly and scrubbed the spotless counter-top. Her breath was tight and shallow and she shivered like a jackhammer. I started to rise until she stopped, turned to face me, and asked,

"You ever thought about dyin'? I mean, really? I mean about *how* you're gonna die?"

She went back to scrubbing. I was flummoxed. I never knew what was on her mind.

"I have every intention of puttin' that off, even though Preacher Beaufort said we started dyin' the day we's born," I answered.

"Oh," she said flatly and started toward the coffee pot. "Coffee's done."

She poured us both a cup, then sat hunched with her heels on the chair's stretcher, hugging her cup between her hands.

"I don't mind dyin'," she continued. Her eyes were dull and absent. "Hit's just how bad it must hurt, you know? Every time I git a papercut, I thank, 'Damn, it must hurt to git stabbed.'"

Posey turned to face me. She took a sip of coffee and cast her eyes at me over the brim.

"Burnin's gotta be just horrifying. Or maybe the smoke gets to you first. Either way, I don't thank I'd like that," she said.

She turned and looked out the kitchen window. Her green eyes seemed far away, like her soul separated from the world for a time. Then again, I never knew what was on her mind. She gasped and winced simultaneously, reached for a towel, and wiped a little track of spider web waving from the sill. It was a familiar frantic motion. She sat back down slow and easy. Usually, she was happy, jumping here for this, going there for that, making these, fixing those. At least *I* thought she was happy. Both our cups were empty. She placed her palms on the table and strained to lift herself up.

"You're tired, Posey," I told her. "Why don't choo let me get the coffee?"

She ignored me and tottered toward the coffee pot, then refilled our cups. She sat back down, reached in a basket under the table, drew up some yarn in her lap, and knitted.

"And I cain't stand bein' choked, so I wouldn't wanna die from hanging or strangling. And poison'd make your guts bleed out, so—:

She stopped, looked harshly at her knitting, and undid a row.

"No, I remember when I's first in high school," she continued, as the knitting needles clicked, "and I had a teacher who talked about Woolf. Went on and on about that woman's writin'. Then one day, Woolf walked right into the water and never come back. I'd like to read something she wrote one day. Maybe that'n where she talks about having her own room, her own space," she said, then paused in her knitting and glanced nervously at the front and back doors.

She knitted feverishly then. At least, *I* saw it that way.

"I ain't read her stuff neither. I imagine she wuddn't too smart, seeing as how she just walked in that water," I said, chuckling nervously.

"I guess she just got plumb tired, you know?" she said, ignoring me. "Takin' it ain't easy. 'Specially when you're walking all over life's eggshells. And they ain't nowhere to hide. Nowhere a'tall. You ever thought about that? Somehow, I reckon Woolf knew thangs wuddn't right."

She stopped knitting and looked again out the window, past the trees, toward Ford's Lake.

"But that water… imagine what a salvation that'd be," she said. "So serene. And forgivin'."

She put her head down and stared a long time at the floor. I just sat there with her, and I reckon that was support enough. Besides, it did no good to guess what was on her mind.

Both Earls' footsteps clunked on the porch. Posey jolted up and winced. Her hand reached behind her back toward her kidneys. That's what I saw, at any rate. Her face turned as pasty as biscuit dough and a cold sweat rose from her pores. I reached for her and started once again to rise. But the screen door creaked open, then her Earl and my Earl laughed and talked and came in like cold wind. Her Earl bounced toward her, smug, with his hands in his pockets.

"Well, Pose, we got that ole jalopy runnin'," he said to her.

He put his arm around her neck and pulled her close. She pushed her hand against his chest and her upper lip curled.

"My ole lady here," he said, as he pulled her head to his mouth and kissed her crown, "knew just the right man to call. That man ri-chonder."

He pointed at my Earl, then winked at me, and said,

"Gotchee a good man right there. Ain't tat right, Pose?" he asked her. "Ain't Earl Sharpe a good man? If innybody knows a good man, hit's my wife. Ain't 'at right?"

"Oh, would yunz quit? Just hush. All I did was jiggle a wire or two," my Earl said, who strolled toward the kitchen table, stood behind my chair, and squeezed my shoulder.

"And I shore do presheate it," Posey's Earl said. "I really do. I cain't pay ye money, but I'll cutchee some wood 'fore winter. Will 'at do?"

"Naw," said my Earl, "I won't take one iota. You'n Posey are like my own kin. Yunz are family, pyoor and simple."

"Well, I shore do thank ye. *Family*," said Posey's Earl, squeezing her head in an old-fashioned noogie. He winked at my Earl as he continued, "Joo hear that Pose? We're like *family*."

She scrambled from his grip and hurriedly sat down at the kitchen table across from me. Her eyes were as wild as a trapped rabbit's. She looked down and scowled. I was curious so I looked down. Both Earls' shoes were a gaum of mud, dirt, and grass. She eyed her Earl fiercely, but that didn't last too long because he eyed her back in kind, and she bowed her head.

"Can I gitchunz somethin? Coffee?" her Earl asked.

"No, no thank you, Earl," I said. "Posey's been right hospitable, as always. Thank you for the cumpnee."

I nodded at her and our eyes met. Hers *said* something, but I had no idea what. My Earl squeezed my shoulder hard and said,

"We need to get on outta here. Me and her's got a date with a bushel of beans."

We all said our goodbyes and they walked us as far as the front porch. As I waved from the truck, I caught sight of her Earl's fingers pressing hard on Posey's arm, the kind of grip that'd leave finger marks or bruises. She stood stoic, almost rigid and at attention. At least that's how I saw it. But that's the last time I saw her. Then *you* called and asked me to come here and give a statement.

"Did you ever think she planned to do it, *this* way?" Gowan asked and calmly slid a picture of Posey's dead Earl on the table.

If this picture was supposed to shock me, it didn't work. I could've cared less.

"He was found by his fishing buddy," Gowan divulged.

"Well," I said coolly, "she never said anything about it. I never knew *what* was on her mind."

I glanced away from the picture and, instead, gazed at the detective with my brown, doe eyes. He cleared his throat, then shuffled the knot of his tie.

"Did you ever know of her to own or operate a boat?" he asked, opening a fresh document box.

"A boat?" I asked and snickered. Detective Gowan dropped a manilla file on the table and sifted through papers.

"Yes, a boat. Old Walt Shoopman owns a bait shop near Ford's Lake and he," said the detective, skimming a piece of paper, "told me he saw a woman at Copperhead Boat Dock. Apparently, this woman had a hard time getting a boat started sometime after the murder. Said she finally got it started and zigzagged across Ford's Lake."

Out of nowhere, he slammed the palm of his hand on the table. I have to admit, I flinched a little. I'd heard such noise before, though, and it was nothing to me.

"Now!" he exclaimed. He put his elbows on the table and clasped his hands together. He seemed pleased with my reaction. "Just answer the question, ma'am. Did you ever know of her to own or operate a boat?"

"No, never. Never a boat, never a car, never a bike, never a wagon, never a nothin'," I said. "She wutten never allowed to have such."

Gowan sat back, then, squinted his eyes, and sized me up. I sat back and smiled.

"I see you don't care much for this Earl," he said, tapping the picture with his finger. "Everything I read on your face tells me you thought this man," he said, still tapping, "was a son of a bitch. Well, Mrs. Sharpe, I don't believe much in vigilante justice. He might've been a son of a bitch, but that didn't give anybody rights to blow his face off with a shotgun while he was in bed."

"You asst the question, detective. I give you the answer," I stated, unfazed. "I meant simply; she never drove *anything*."

"Were you aware of her plans?" he asked.

"No," I said.

"You two were awful close. What's that old cliché? 'Thick as thieves'?" he asked rhetorically.

"I wouldn't say we's close, really," I said, nonchalantly. "Mountain women ain't afforded such luxury of goin' out'n all. Only times I saw her, I's with my husband."

Gowan's eyes blazed.

"Accessory to murder, Mrs. Sharpe. I might divulge that the house was clean. We never found the weapon. No shells, no ammo. Dusted for prints and found none. Clean, Mrs. Sharp. Except for a toothless hacksaw in the yard, and this here," he said, tapping the picture of Dead Earl. "Ain't no way in the world one woman can make a crime scene so clean."

I'd had enough at this point and had little else to say. I looked at him and stretched out my wrists in front of me.

"Arrest me if ye want, detective. I been here six hours and gave you my statement. You cain't make French fries without potatoes and I cain't say I did what I *didn't*. I never knew nothin' about what she planned. I never knew what was on her mind."

He sat back in his chair and took a good, long, hard look at me. He shook his head, reached inside his shirt pocket, and gave me his card. He told me I was free to leave the station, but not the county, until the investigation was over. He watched me as I walked out the door—a little too attentive for my liking.

My Earl waited in the parking lot and he was standing by his old truck when I came out. His eyes wore an odd expression of disbelief and his lips flattened with determination. He held out his hand and, surprised at the chivalric gesture, I reached for it. As soon as I did, he snapped his fingers and opened his palm. I reached in my purse, pulled out Gowan's card, and gave it to him. I rolled my eyes as I hoisted myself up on the passenger side, then turned to face the open side window as he drove us home. We passed by Ford's Lake, and my mind formed a mental map of all the places the water connected. It rested at the center of five counties. Posey's words came to my mind about dying and water and *what a salvation that'd be*. I'd pondered about it so much my head pounded, and I thought my brain might ooze out my ears. The heat was intolerable sickening. At least something of a breeze came through the window. I closed my eyes as we traveled the long, long miles beside the lake until a thought hit me. I jerked back from the window. I turned my head and glanced at Earl, then at the water, then back at Earl and back at the water. *No weapons. No fingerprints. No shells or ammo. Clean. Except for a toothless hacksaw.* I knew then. Right then and there. I finally knew exactly what was on Posey's mind. And I smiled. I closed my eyes again and imagined that shotgun sawed in pieces and thrown at the bottom of that lake. I imagined she made it to one of those counties, and that I might pass her on a street sometime and think I know her but can't quite place her. She'd change everything, of course—a different hair color, some pretty makeup, rich dresses and jewels. I snuggled into the thought.

My Earl softly placed his hand on my leg and my body tensed. He turned his head and gave me the kindest look. He always looked at me that way before it came. He steadily vice-gripped his fingers across my thigh. I prided myself that I didn't even wince. It was a message. *Keep your mouth shut and be the demure little woman I want.* Or else. Our eyes locked for a dozen seconds or so. His pupils dilated and his grip hardened further, enough to snap the bone. I gritted my teeth but never betrayed how bad it hurt. He swerved to miss an oncoming truck, let go of me, and cackled. I didn't care. Things like that didn't bother me anymore. Not anymore, I thought. Not anymore. I twisted again toward the window and let my thoughts meander across the lake. Posey, I thought. Posey. A pocketful of posies. Ashes, ashes. I turned in my seat and faced Earl. I gently held his rough hand and smiled. His eyes were etched with confusion as he searched my own. I gazed back toward that water, that salvation. I smiled at his profile. He never knew what was on my mind.

39

Danny Laemon

Short Story by Edward Francisco

H E HAD IDIOT WRITTEN ALL over his face. He smelled bad too, like he'd been swimming with crawdads in a sewer. Mama made me promise not to make fun of his poorly brushed teeth or the way he came to school sprouting hair in all directions. But Mama never had to sit by him on a bus either. She never had to learn how an idiot can make a fool out of you.

Maybe it was the excitement of the field trip or the way the bus jolted as we boys split the air with a chorus of our favorite anthem, "Thunder Road." Maybe Danny thought the revenuers in the song were actually after him. Whatever the reason, he couldn't hold it a second longer.

At first, the warmth was pleasing, the way sleep feels just before someone rouses you up for school, or when a window fan blows over your face and you can barely keep your eyes open. Only when you realize that whatever it is that's causing you to be warm is also wet, do you begin to get suspicious.

We'd almost reached the part in the song where the bootlegger was "roarin' out of Harlan" and "revvin' up his mill" when I discovered I was sitting in a puddle for which existed only one possible explanation.

Arching half out of the seat, I saw my hand rise and slap Danny in one fluid motion. His face registered the shock instantly, surprising me. He was slower gargling up the single syllable that would call attention to us.

"Hey!"

In the time it took for him to say it, I was able to unleash a flurry of blows atop his head. I could swear the spots I was pounding were hollow. He lifted his arms in defense, eyes blinking, lips bubbling with saliva that quickly gathered in little reservoirs at the corners of his mouth. From the back of the bus came the inevitable monkey chant.

"Fight! Fight! Fight!"

Danny tried to cover up, but I would locate an opening and deliver a strategic thump, my teeth clinched in the fury that attends justifiable homicide. I would have killed him, too, if Old Miss Sweet's rusty hand hadn't clamped to my ear, giving it a vicious tug.

"So you want to fight?" she challenged. "I'll give you a fight."

She was clutching Danny's hair like a clump of crabgrass. Finally, she succeeded in separating us.

"My stars and garters! I can't believe you've done this. And to think we have guests on the bus."

She was referring to the parent chaperones, a hapless group of mothers who attended every field trip and knew only one recipe for brownies.

"You don't understand," I sputtered. "He wet on me."

I'd be careful not to say *pee*. Saying *pee* could get you in serious trouble. It was one of the ironies of fourth grade that you could get in more trouble for saying *pee* than for actually peeing on somebody. I never quite figured that one out. I think it had something to do with the girls. Presumably they stopped knowing what *pee* meant and even stopped peeing by fourth grade. By junior high school, they even stopped sweating. They perspired briskly.

Old Miss Sweet's face softened, the prune lines around her mouth relaxing in an expression of mute hesitation. Her eyes were almost sympathetic. It was clear she didn't know what to say. Forty-three years of teaching ten-year-olds came to her rescue. Faced with the prospect of admitting the truth, Old Miss Sweet opted for the sweetly idiotic.

"That's no excuse for starting a fight," she gently scolded.

I couldn't have been more shocked than if she'd said Superman was a communist or Japan made fine and durable goods.

"Just let Danny Laemon pee on you and see how you like it!" I blurted.

Now I'd done it. I said *pee*. I really had. And there'd be hell to pay. I was fairly certain I wouldn't visit the playground for the rest of the year. That's what had happened to Ronnie Thatcher. We'd been asked to recite a poem and Ronnie had recited his, but not before explaining how it could be sung to the tune of "My Bonny Lies Over the Ocean." Ronnie's version went like this:

> My brother lies over the ocean.
>
> My sister lies over the sea.
>
> My father lies over my mother.
>
> And that's how they created me.

Miss Sweet had said "My stars and garters!" that time too. Then she'd sent Ronnie to the office with a recommendation for him to be paddled, kept after school, and a note sent home to his grandmother who was his legal guardian. Now, I anticipated all that would happen to me. I could see from the blood in Old Miss Sweet's eyes there was no other possibility. Fortunately, one of the mothers came to my aid.

"Here," she offered. "This towel should help."

Where she came up with a towel, I couldn't say. It was just mother magic, I suppose. Miss Sweet was obliged to thank her and stop thinking about how I'd wanted Danny to pee on Miss Sweet too.

"Maybe the boys can just sit on the towel," the mother suggested.

I had no intention of sitting by Danny ever again. I hadn't wanted to sit by him in the first place. Who did? I'd earlier plopped down farther in the back with some friends of mine, including Terry Crutcher. Terry was the coolest boy in the fourth grade, and we called him T. C. for Top Cat. It was Terry who'd introduced us to cigarettes, and we were looking forward to reaching the top of Lookout Mountain where a famous battle had taken place and where we would engage in some diversionary tactics of our own, escaping mothers and teachers while enjoying some smokes in the high dense weeds on the crest of the mountain. Later, under cover of camouflage, we'd even pee into the Tennessee River hundreds of feet below.

But Terry and my friends were splitting their sides now with laughter. A quick hot glance showed their smug little hands clapping, their faces crumbling at my discomfort. Only inches away, Danny Laemon was rocking back and forth in the seat, his plastic grin intact and victorious. My eyes narrowed in slits of the most intense hatred I'd ever felt for anybody.

Miss Sweet ordered us into the aisle. Already the seat of my pants had soaked up a considerable portion of the flow. Twisting my head over my shoulder, I stared at my backside. I might as well have sat in a puddle. Just behind me a little red-haired girl with a constellation of freckles turned to her seat mate and said, "Ooh! He's got Danny Laemon's pee all over him."

So much for fourth grade girls being unfamiliar with the concept. Besides, as I pointed out, it wasn't my fault I had to sit by Danny Laemon. At the last minute, Old Miss Sweet had invoked seating by alphabetical order. Because my last name started with *L* too—the only thing Danny and I shared—I'd been forced to change seats. Now look what had happened.

As Old Miss Sweet and the helpful mother discreetly dried off the seat, I cut my eyes over at Danny whose tongue had slipped through his half-parted lips and was licking the tip of his nose. I mouthed a threat to him. "I'll kill you," I said, without saying it. It didn't matter that my mother had told me to observe the golden rule when it came to Danny. In five minutes' time, I'd suffered indignities my mother wouldn't be forced to endure in a lifetime. The towel disappeared into one of the ubiquitous bags mothers carried on such occasions.

"Now sit down and no more fighting," ordered Miss Sweet.

I couldn't believe my ears.

"No way!" I protested. "I'm not sitting by that—retard."

My classmates jeered and tittered in approval.

"That's enough!" roared Old Miss Sweet. "What would your mother say?"

I didn't care. I honestly didn't. In fact, I would derive delicious pleasure in showing my mother my soaked backside and especially in explaining how the golden rule didn't apply to idiots like Danny Laemon. That's because, unlike the rest of us, they didn't understand rules at all.

"I don't care," I said. "I'm not sitting by him. I'll sit in the floor first. I wanted to sit by my friends anyway."

Miss Sweet had her back to the mothers, strategically poised so only I could hear what she was saying.

"You ought to be ashamed," she whispered, rebuking me in tones I expected to hear only in Sunday school.

"Well, I'm not," I answered defiantly. "I'm not one bit. I didn't want to sit by him a little while ago, and I don't want to sit by him now."

Old Miss Sweet's face settled into an ageless expression, one I had difficulty reading. Maybe she was reflecting on the futility of all her efforts to civilize generations of small savages. That was a problem teaching for years in the same community. You got to see the fruits of your labors firsthand. Even my mother had been taught by Old Miss Sweet, though Miss Sweet was forever assuring me my mother had been a good girl, earning nothing but A's, even in conduct. It was a legacy I could have lived without.

Miss Sweet wagged her head in disgust, turning in the aisle to face a portrait of surreal children's faces, all twisted with pleasure at the opposition I was showing to Miss Sweet's unreasonable adherence to the golden rule. No wonder she and my mother had gotten along so well.

"All right, then," announced Miss Sweet. "Since Travis Love"— she'd said both my names—a sure sign of trouble—"doesn't want to sit in his assigned seat, I'm going to ask for a volunteer. Who is willing to sit by Travis even though his trousers are soaked?"

It was a brilliant flanking maneuver. The results were predictable. Little girls pinched their noses while the boys hooted in mock aversion, one or two pretending to escape through the windows.

"Let me repeat myself," said Miss Sweet. "Is there anyone who'll volunteer to share a seat with Travis Love? Please raise your hand."

Even the mothers betrayed me, covering their mouths and wiping away tell-tale signs of laughter before letting their hands drop back in their laps.

I thought about saying something they'd remember for years to come. But before I could, all their little jaws snapped open and began rattling with machine-gun laughter. That's when I realized they weren't laughing at me but at whatever was behind me. What was behind me was Danny Laemon, tongue fished back in his mouth, arm lifted high over his head. He was volunteering to sit beside me.

"That's very kind of you, Danny," crooned Miss Sweet. "It's not everybody who wants to sit by Travis now that his trousers are soaked."

"Traitors," I thought. "Traitors, everyone."

There on the spot I made a mental photograph of where they were sitting. One day I'd work for the FBI and track them down one by one. They wouldn't know why they were being arrested and tortured. It would be a surprise.

"You can choose to sit by Danny or by me," Miss Sweet announced. "Which will it be?"

That was no choice. Didn't she understand that? Either way, I got to sit by the source of my enduring misery.

"I'll sit in the floor."

"State law doesn't permit that," responded Miss Sweet. "Danny or me. That's your choice."

"Fine," I snapped, throwing myself back onto the weather-resistant leather seat I'd earlier occupied.

"And keep your hands to yourself," she ordered.

"As if I'd touch that—hawg."

"Enough!" she snapped.

It wasn't over. She could count on it. I'd get even if it took years. Danny Laemon and Miss Sweet would suffer unspeakable fates. But for now, I just wanted to forget what had happened. I wanted everybody else to forget, too. Soon we'd pass through the entrance to Point Park where doves rested on the arms of a stone sentry standing there. I was sure I was just as brave and stoical as he was—maybe more so. He'd only been shot at by Yankees—not peed on by Danny Laemon. Besides, I consoled myself, Terry and the guys would welcome me back to the fold once I produced the matches needed to fire up the Marlboros Terry managed to conceal on his person with the aplomb of a Houdini.

On arriving, we spilled out of the bus, acting anything like the young ladies and gentlemen we'd been instructed to be. The plan was to move in orderly fashion from one monument to the next, reading dedications and historical information provided for "The Battle Above the Clouds." Actually, it had been more of a skirmish, but the local historical society had made it something more dramatic we could all be proud of as descendants of those snuff munching veterans of the Late Unpleasantness. As with the best laid battle strategies, the plan to keep our attention riveted on the historically significant quickly dissolved. Both Miss Sweet and the mothers retreated to some benches on the edge of the battlefield. Old Miss Sweet's eyes were failing, and the mothers would soon be preoccupied. Our fun could begin.

My friends were following Terry Crutcher in tandem down to the farthest edge of the park. We'd gotten separated due to the unfortunate seating arrangement I'd been forced to endure earlier. Now I was running across open field to catch up. They spotted me and were pointing. With only a hundred yards or so separating us, they responded as if to an alarm, their legs churning into a stampede that led them down a steep declivity and out of sight.

I slowed to a trot. Where were they going? Hadn't they seen me? I owned the matches. Suddenly it hit me with the percussive force of a slap they might be avoiding me. No, I said reassuringly, they wouldn't do that. We were buddies. I was even captain of our Gray-Y football team, the reason being I knew my left from my right on a consistent basis. Probably they'd just found a spot where the smoke couldn't be detected. I ran to catch up.

Sensing something uncertain, even a little dangerous, the instant I reached the high weeds, I paused, sniffing the air cautiously like an animal. Without warning, my friends leaped out of the foliage, bombarding me with persimmons. The assault was furious. Two splattered my shirt even before I could figure out what my so-called buddies were throwing.

"Heifers!" I shouted, not bothering with gender distinctions.

A second volley drove me back a yard or two in retreat. From the opposite direction, another of the small fruits connected, this one exploding on the bare flesh of my forearm. Pulpy amber juice dribbled down my elbow. I was caught in their crossfire. Several more persimmons whizzed by my head, barely missing. Despite my efforts to close ranks by huddling low to the ground, I was a conspicuous target. There was only one thing to do. Fight back.

Persimmons lay on the ground around me. They squished through my fingers as I scooped them up, firing back. It was like heaving the stringy innards of a pumpkin. Suddenly, I knew how Lee and Longstreet had felt, or even Brackston Bragg, worse general in either army.

Vacillating between self-pity and rage, I spewed forth invectives chosen to reinforce features of a lineage I was sure existed.

"Your mothers are collies. That's why you're all sons of bitches."

At least I'd win the verbal volley. There was something in that.

A little titan named David Lauer rose out of the weeds, empty-handed. His face wore a fractured grin.

"Why don't you let Danny Laemon pee on you some more," he suggested.

I clutched at dirt, kudzu, poison ivy, and persimmon guts—anything that would spread the arc of fallout needed to connect with my enemies.

"Oh, no!" shouted David Lauer in alarm. Others began clamoring too.

For a second or two I was confused. Even I knew I was impotent in my rage. Why were they running away from me? The answer was just behind me, mounting an assault with crab apples stuffed in the kangaroo pouch he'd made from his sweatshirt. It was Danny Laemon, charging from the rear, his attack fierce, spastic. The sight almost vanquished me. The last thing I needed was Danny fighting my battles for me. His nostrils flared. The omnipresent tongue found the tip of his nose in the very pose of determination. Danny would help me even if I didn't want him to.

"Oh, Lord!" I said in a wild half-prayer.

But it was too late. Danny had come to my rescue, scattering my one-time friends in all directions. There was nothing for me to do but cuss him good and stalk off. His face blinked, stunned.

At lunch I found myself sitting alone on a fallen log. In the distance, girls switched and shared the contents of sack lunches prepared by the uninspired mothers. Each of us had been forced to fork over twenty-five cents to cover the cost of one peanut butter and jelly sandwich, a bag of potato chips (mostly air), and a Dixie cup of warm lemonade.

The boys sat backed against a giant white oak a hundred yards off, wolfing down lunch and snickering at what could only be the spectacle I offered. Old Miss Sweet was helping Danny Laemon with his lunch and drink, finding him a spot at a picnic table between two mothers. They were helping him unwrap his sandwich. The sight almost gagged me because I knew Danny was anything but helpless. He just put on a good act. That was all.

Maybe it was the glint of sunshine or the precise angle of reflection, but I suddenly noticed Danny's shoes stuffed on his feet under the picnic table. They shone as never before for the simple reason he'd never worn them before. I knew, because my mother had bought them for him, swearing me to secrecy after Old Miss Sweet had telephoned, asking if my mother would contribute toward buying Danny a new pair of shoes. For whatever reason, my mother had bought Danny's footwear outright.

"But why?" I protested. "He's got shoes."

He had shoes all right, but the soles flapped when he walked and were worn so thin he could have stepped on a penny and felt Lincoln's whiskers.

"Because no child should have to be without a decent pair of shoes," my mother had said.

Maybe not. But Danny Laemon didn't have to own a pair of shoes exactly like mine either. My mother had bought him a pair of Buster Brown penny loafers like mine!

The boys were forming a circle in the center of the battlefield, preparing for a game of tag. As I approached the backs of my classmates, I could hear Terry Crutcher declaring bases and asking who wanted to be it first.

"Let Danny be it," I said from the back. "He's got new shoes. They'll help him run fast." Everyone glanced at Danny's feet. If possible, his grin widened.

"Hey," said David Lauer, noticing what I'd counted on him to notice. "Danny's shoes are just like Travis's."

"Not exactly," I rushed to add. "Mine have dimes. See."

I pointed to the pair of Roosevelt dimes slotted in my loafers.

"Danny would have to have dimes in his shoes to be exactly like mine."

I winked at those assembled.

"Hey, I've got two dimes Danny can have," said Terry Crutcher, willing to enter my conspiracy.

"Then Danny, why don't you sit here on the ground so we can put some dimes in your shoes," I urged.

Danny obeyed at once, dropping to the ground and waiting for us to insert the precious coins in the slots of his loafers.

"You'll need to stick your feet up," I said.

The instant Danny lifted his feet, I snatched one loafer off his foot. Terry whisked off the other. We started playing keep away with Danny's shoes.

"Go out for a pass!" I shouted to three of my teammates, who zigzagged as I sailed Danny's shoe over his charging head. He spun, heading in the direction of a loafer, his grin gone, a wild animal-eyed look of fear replacing it. There were just too many of us and he was confused about which shoe to chase. Soon he was panting and grunting after the only pair of new shoes he'd ever owned. Tears streamed down his face and he was licking the salt corners of his mouth with his infamous reptilian tongue.

Then something happened I'd never seen before. In the past, Danny had always been a willing victim, ready to play along with our taunts and tortures of him. Now, he paused in sock-footed stride, chest pounding visibly through his faded T-shirt, and gazed round at us as if seeing us all for the first time. The shock was too much for him. There was nothing left for him to do but let his chin drop to his chest and his eyes squeezed shut as a great, strangling sob rose from his throat. He collapsed onto the ground.

Any other time I would have let loose with a victorious yip. But there was something different about this time, something that made my feet move by themselves toward a spot on the battlefield where Danny sat, hands covering his face, sobbing.

"Hey, Danny, we didn't mean anything," I lied. "Give him his shoes," I ordered my two pass receivers.

I wanted to make it up to him. I wanted to say it was just a joke and he could even have the dimes if he wanted them. I would have said that too if Old Miss Sweet hadn't yanked my collar hard enough to make my eyes bulge.

"What do you think you're doing?" she screeched, whirling me around and clutching my arm with her bony fingers.

It took an instant for my mouth to start working but Old Miss Sweet never let me finish whatever feeble defense I tried to muster. One of the helpful mothers was helping Danny put his shoes back on. Until the loafers were safely back on his feet, the look of fear never left Danny's face. Then his features relaxed, his eyes surrendering to an aura of serenity I'd never seen on his face. That's when I knew that heaven was owning a pair of shoes that were yours and no one else's.

However, my vision of Danny and the beatific didn't last long. Old Miss Sweet had dragged me to a thick edge of the woods, backing me against a tree whose bark I couldn't identify despite my proximity to it.

"What did you think you were doing?" she started.

I wanted to explain, but her rage was overwhelming. She was just waiting to crucify whatever pipsqueak excuse I offered.

"Don't you think I saw?" she demanded. "Don't you think I have eyes?"

She'd caught me in the midst of so many contradictions, so many unidentifiable feelings, I couldn't say a word. The only option I had was to stand there letting my eyes fill up with tears whose source I couldn't identify but only despise.

"Don't you think I have eyes, too?" I finally blurted, recalling Danny and all I'd just witnessed back on the battlefield.

Old Miss Sweet's hand released me at once. Her face searched me hard as I stood at attention before her, determined not to let my lip quiver in the wake of my eyes' betrayal of me. Old Miss Sweet exhaled deeply. Then she lifted her hands to my shoulders.

"Travis, I know you're a good boy and that deep down you've got a good heart."

How did she know that? I didn't know it myself. How could she?

"That's why I'm going to tell you something no one else knows."

Why would she tell me something no one else knew? Why would she do that?

"You see, Travis"—here Old Miss Sweet's ordinarily cloudy eyes became pools of the deepest, most intense blue I'd ever seen—"Danny's got problems no one knows about. His daddy left when he was little, and his mama's got a disease called cancer and can't work right now. Do you know what cancer is, Travis?"

I shivered at the word. It was 1964. Everyone knew what cancer was.

"That's why I called your mother, Travis. She's the milk of kindness and I knew she would help."

Old Miss Sweet smiled at something or someone beyond my remembrance. With a gesture of tenderness I would never have expected of her, Miss Sweet lifted her hand and brushed it against my cheek.

"You've got your mother's eyes, you know," she said.

I had to glance off. Otherwise, my body would fail to listen to anything I told it to do. After a long spell of silence, I asked the question whose answer I had to know.

"Will Danny's mother be all right?"

Miss Sweet shook her head, gazing off too, now.

"I don't know, Travis. I honestly don't."

"What will happen to Danny then?" I queried, sensing I was invading territory whose mysteries might haunt me forever.

"He might have to go to an institution. I can't say. But, Travis, Danny needs a friend. That's why I arranged the seating on the bus the way I did. That's why I seated him beside you. I honestly thought—think—you're the best man for the job. Travis, I'm sorry Danny did what he did to you on the bus. I just didn't know what else to do. Can you forgive me, Travis? Can you forgive Danny and be a friend to him?"

I knew even then Old Miss Sweet was giving me a second chance few people ever got. She was holding out a glimmer of hope for the kind of person I might become in several eons of consistent practice and habitual application of virtues I didn't know yet. Still, it was a start, and I was grateful for the opportunity to do battle another day. Especially since this day was fading.

Back on the bus, there was only one seat left. I took it despite the snickering of Terry and my friends in the back. No longer would I be waylaid by a rearguard assault. I knew my duty now and would do it. Unfortunately, the first thing I noticed on sitting was the odor baked into Danny's clothes. Then I remembered: It was the same odor baked into my own clothes. Danny was rocking gently back and forth. It was a motion calculated to drive me crazy. I reached for his arm and stopped him. With my free hand, I eased two dimes from my trousers' pocket.

"Here. Put these in your shoes," I said.

We rolled toward home, sun having set, darkness causing faces on the bus to grow more indistinct with each mile. Soon even voices began to quieten. Children dozed. So it was with Danny whose new shoes sported dimes like my own. Outside, stars blinked and I could swear I heard the echo of my mother's words reminding me that God loved idiots too.

It was a good thing. There were two of us on the bus that night—one sleeping, one wide awake. Only when Danny drooped over against me did I consider propping him with a sharp elbow to the ribs. But what good would that do? And how much harm would it cause to let him lean on me for what was a short distance anyway? Those were the questions I continued to ponder until my eyes blinked with the heaviness of approaching sleep as unavoidably sweet as the sound of Danny breathing.

40
Writings About Appalachian English

by Delonda Shown Anderson

I AM NOT A LINGUIST. I have studied a minute slice of linguistics (meaning one scant semester), and it was enough to understand less than a smidgen of what I respectfully consider a complex discipline. Thanks to novelist and poet, Edward Francisco, who graciously gifted his professorial library to me (one of my greatest treasures), I own and have read quite the collection of sources on linguistics, words, and language. But I am not a linguist. Who and what I am is 100 percent, unabashedly, a blended assortment of what is Appalachian. And I am a curious soul by nature.

When I was a little girl living in Demory Hollow, my family and I often hiked the hills and mountains all around us, exploring creeks and hills and creatures and all of nature along the way. We doglegged our way up and down the dirt road until we came to a section where one of our way-down neighbors (way down the holler) had cows. I asked my dad about the sharp-edged, twisted, and gnarled metal fencing, and I remember his answer:

"That's bob war."

"Bob war?" I asked.

"Yeah. Don't touch it. Hit'll cutchoo up. People can git stuck in it."

As a matter of fact, everybody around me said it was *bob war*. My parents. My grandparents. Great-grandparents. All the old men who talked to my dad as they congregated outside the local grocer. In the Encyclopedia, I saw pictures of the same fencing when I looked through "W." The metal was rolled up and sat in rows across a wide-open, chaotic landscape of World War I. Men were "stuck" in the rolled fencing, just like my dad said. So, as a seven-year-old, it made sense that they named the fencing after a World War I soldier named Bob. Imagine my surprise when I read the words "barbed wire" one day. There was no Bob. And there was no war.

What was more of a jolt for me was the actual realization that our pronunciation as a people was sometimes *very* different from the written word. It was bewildering, actually. And it took decades for me to embrace my own Appalachian English. Subsequently, I journeyed to find origins of certain words or phrases I would hear all around me. But, as research has a way of doing, I ran down more than one path of Alice's rabbit holes.

The dialect and language of Appalachia *is* unique. Parts of the way we talk hearken back to Middle English. Some of our words are, arguably, even Old English. The word *hit*, for example, is, as Wylene P. Dial writes, "the Old English third person singular neuter pronoun for [the word] *it*…" Much of our speech originated with our ancestors. We keep their word choices, their inflections, and continue to produce an exceptional diction in timbre-like fashion. In other words, our English is an old, beautiful language.

Even so, Appalachians have been ridiculed for centuries over vernacular or pronunciation or accent or take-your-pick. The fact remains that Appalachian English is still heard in these mountains. Yet, its history, beauty, usage, and relevance are waning.

Local folks are often considered "backward," an inference deduced somehow from the way we talk or the way we sometimes do things outside of modernity. But mountain people who were born in Appalachia can trace their ancestors' entry to the 'New World' as far back as 1600 (excepting *Native* Americans). Perhaps even earlier. Yet, they aren't distinguished for lineage or credited with intelligence or noted for ingenuity. And our language isn't seen or respected as something once spoken "by the highest-ranking nobles of the realms of England and Scotland." Instead, the culture and language are ridiculed and maligned.

Some Appalachians are even embarrassed by the way we talk. Why is this? Well, for one thing, Appalachian people have had to work outside our communities due to the dearth of real job opportunities. Small towns have become a beacon for jobs of servitude to wealthy retirees—not factories. We have, therefore, been confronted with what is considered "proper English," and, consequently, we are heavily pressed to "talk right."

We aren't taught about our own language and what makes the way we talk so extraordinary. For example, Appalachian English uses a fair share of double negatives (*You cain't not eat.*), but how many of us acknowledge the times Shakespeare's writings were peppered with these, and even *triple* negatives? Derby demonstrates this in *The Tragedy of Richard the Third* when he says, "I never was nor never shall be." And how about the word *ye* once being the proper way to address someone? So, since we haven't been taught the history of Appalachian English, we change our speech to "fit in" as best we can wherever we are. I know this because I've done the same thing. Ask any Appalachian who has traveled outside the mountains and he or she or they will likely tell the same story.

Appalachian English is actually a mixture of old languages from various countries, and, as such, certain colloquialisms have often been used to illustrate that a distinct saying, a particular phrase, or a specific word derived from a respective motherland. How so? As most of us know, mountain geography keeps people here pretty much isolated. And they have been for ages. Generations of a particular surname have existed in one area for centuries.

Given the remoteness of these mountains, it's easy to pinpoint a particular name and trace an ancestor back to one of the aforementioned European countries. And, since the region is filled with various exemplars of mother tongues, one can also trace the word, phrase, or saying to those countries as well. Take the "complex demonstratives," *this here* and *them there* and *that there* and *those there*. In their journal article, "This Here Town: Evidence for the Development of the English Determiner System from a Vernacular Demonstrative Construction in York English," Laura Rupp and Sali A. Tagliamonte state in the footnotes:

> The envisaged historical origin of the construction is supported by the fact that Appalachian English, spoken in the Appalachian Mountains in the east of the United States, is a conservative variety due to the geographic isolation of the area.

The usage of the word "conservative" here is defined more as "traditional" or "old-fashioned." The authors note the "earliest example cited in the Oxford English Dictionary dates from the late fourteenth century" and that these particular phrases came from Yorkshire. Some usages in Appalachian English can be traced "before Chaucer." A linguist might take an Appalachian's particular phrasing and work backward genealogically to find an origin or first usage.

Several sources indicate that these mountains have a plurality of "Appalachian Englishes." Our English is a mixture of inherited languages from a variety of countries intertwined over hundreds of years up to this Present-Day English. Michael Montgomery says in *Talking Appalachian: Voice, Identity, and Community*:

> Although the English language called Appalachian is often believed to be the most distinctively regional variety in America and is often referred to as if it were a single homogenous entity, the region does not have just a single dialect. The population's ancestry is quite mixed, and in many ways, the English of Appalachia represents a microcosm of American English; its speakers have both preserved forms that are no longer used in most of the rest of the country and innovations of others.

Yet, as already stated, we are not taught to be proud of our language. So, when we are confronted with "proper English," we abandon our dialect. Thus, we acclimate our speaking to accommodate a situation. For example, one day, I'd just hung up the phone after talking with my mother, and my oldest son asked,

"Mom, how come you talk different when you're on the phone with Mamaw?"

"Do I?" I asked, puzzled. My youngest son chimed in,

"Yeah. You do. You talk more country. It's weird."

I have to tell you, I didn't see it at all. I still don't. But I believe and agree that I do. (The irony is on another occasion, my mom told my brother: "She don't talk like us no more.")

But my sons' curiosity made me wonder. Why *do* I speak differently to my mother? In the book *Talking Appalachian: Voice, Identity, and Community*, edited by Amy D. Clark and Nancy M. Hayward, the notion of "voice place" is explored, and a huge difference exists between "home speech" and "away speech."

Talking Appalachian points out that our own conscious efforts to change the way we talk to feel worthier in a situation is damaging. If an Appalachian person was taught "about the origins, linguistic structure, and rich literature associated with 'voiceplace,'" she would better understand herself and her origins.

Mountain people are often labeled as uneducated because they speak Appalachian English. For example, how many times has a comedian used Appalachian or Southern vernacular to make a joke about some ignorant person? According to *Talking Appalachian*, this treatment is, in effect, "linguistic bigotry" or "linguistic prejudice":

> Linguistic bigotry stems from ignorance about how language is constructed, its place in society, and the human tendency to project prejudicial attitudes about a group of people by attacking a cultural trait such as a language. For this reason, perhaps more than any other, many Appalachians have struggled with the concept of an Appalachian identity…

Of course, we shouldn't be surprised about the possibility of linguistic prejudice. Our nation has a history of language denigration. The U.S. government forced Native American children to participate in programs where "their barbarous dialect should be blotted out and the English language substituted." African American vernacular has been mocked for centuries. All one need do is read Modernist literature or watch classic movies to find just a tad of confirmation. No one can forget when the Irish were scorned for their existence and for their language (deemed as the discriminatory "brogue" before they even arrived to the U.S.). Recently, our country has taken issue with Latino dialects (i.e., "speak American," or "talk English"). But this writing will peek at the contributors for Appalachian English vilification.

The way media and literature portray Appalachian dialect often contributes to stereotypes, thereby inhibiting mountain people. In recent decades, many Appalachian people have refused to let that hinder them. We are proud of our dialect. Some states are passing bills recognizing the

Appalachian dialect as a language. Many linguists, I dare to say, would likely disagree with a *single* language in Appalachia.

Appalachian author Silas House says, "The media has taught us that dialect and bad grammar are the same thing." They are not. We, by way of our dialect, are often the comic relief under a bell jar. And we are made to think that no one in the world understands what we are saying, as quoted by this frustrated woman:

> It really upsets me when you have someone from here on the national news, or on a program or something, and they're speaking well, and they [the producers] throw subtitles on it. I mean, it's not like the guy on "Waterboy" that you can't understand, you know?

Depictions of our dialect further exacerbate the oppression and discrimination we encounter. In literature outside Appalachia, "characters are shown to speak more slowly, and exhibit features that are characteristic of the dialect…" which "perpetuates the idea that all Appalachians are uneducated and lazy."

George Washington Harris and John Fox, Jr are two authors who are a bit heavy-handed (in my humble opinion) when it comes to mountain dialect representation. Some have said that John Fox Jr, who wrote *The Little Shepherd of Kingdom Come* and *The Trail of the Lonesome Pine*, "shaped the middle-class perceptions about Southern Appalachia more than any other writer did" by building his "reputations on the presumed mountain people's peculiarities in speech and custom."

Now don't get me wrong, here. As a native Appalachian, I use dialect in my writings. Many, if not all, Appalachian writers do so. And I use a phonetic version of the dialect so readers can "hear" the words on the page. Maybe I'm engaging in a dialogue double standard; I don't know. Since our language is so unique, and since it has been absconded and thrown around like spaghetti noodles on a wall, I figure I have the right to take it back to show the clearer truth.

Not only literature, but television has its own problem with how mountain people are portrayed. When television began, three channels had total broadcasting control: The American Broadcasting Company (ABC), The National Broadcasting Company (NBC), and the Columbia

Broadcasting System (CBS). Through their television shows and news programs, they helped shape public perceptions about places, peoples, America, etc. Sitcoms were a very big part of how mountain people were portrayed. *The Real McCoys*, *The Andy Griffith Show*, and *The Beverly Hillbillies* were massively popular in their day. And they still are. While they may show a moral compass or a quasi-defiance of social stratification, the dialect is often awkward or forced. I mean, who among us has ever heard of a "see-mint" pond? These "shows captured the dialectical relationship between the noble mountaineer and the farcical and base hillbilly at a time when real mountaineers were much in the news." And that is how it seems to have been all along—beginning in newspaper articles as far back as the Hatfield-McCoy feud.

But now, Appalachian opinions about our dialect seem different. A curiosity is afoot about our region and a pride about our language is taking hold. And that's a beautiful thing.

41

On the Lost Art
of the Handwritten Note

by Edward Francisco

W HEN I WAS TEN, MY mother enrolled me in Margaret Howell's
School of Dancing and Etiquette. It was a phase of my male fin-
ishing school education designed to rid the savage within and transform
me into a Southern gentleman, i.e., Chaucer's "verray parfit, gentil
knight." (For the record, all gentlemen do not reside below the Mason-
Dixon line. I'm sure there was a Northern version of Margaret Howell's
School. I just don't know what it was.)

Following on the heels of dancing and etiquette classes, Mother
signed me up for drawing lessons at the Hunter Art Museum perched
on the bluff in North Chattanooga and overlooking the roiling waters of
the Tennessee River below. As it turned out, I was terrible at drawing.
The resident art instructor said as much, telling my mother she'd wasted
her money. Undaunted, and still determined to civilize me, she pressed
on, insisting that I select and learn to play a musical instrument. I chose
drums—mostly out of revenge at having to play anything.

Looking back, I suspect my mother considered her efforts negligible.
What she didn't figure was that I was a work in progress. One thing
she installed in me that *stuck* was the importance of the handwritten
note—especially the thank you note. She even ordered personalized
stationery embossed with my initials. I admit, I was impressed with my
new sense of self-importance. The letterhead sheets begged for deliberate and precise calligraphy in cursive script. Sadly, the instruction we
received in school on "making our letters" is an artifact of the pre-digital

age. For the most part my college students' handwriting is atrocious, if they bother to write by hand at all. Last semester, one young woman in remedial freshman composition complained that she couldn't retain key grammatical concepts.

"Write them out by hand," I said. "If you do, the brain to eye to hand connection will reinforce your ability to remember them. They'll become yours, in effect."

"I'm lazy," she admitted. "I don't like to write. Besides, if you'll write them on the board, I can take a picture of them with the camera on my phone."

Make no mistake. Regarding the thank you note, in particular, technology makes it increasingly convenient not to practice the discipline of gratitude. Gratitude, to my thinking, requires time, focus, and attention to detail. Who of us doesn't recall the thrill of being small and receiving a handwritten note or letter from family or friend on a birthday or Christmas? If the thank you note teaches us anything, it's the value (and joy) of reciprocity. It certainly didn't hurt that I was expected to write great-aunt Matty (who smelled like moth balls), thanking her for the pair of socks identical to the ones she sent last year. (I would be remiss if I didn't interject a stern dictum at this point. If you don't understand why an email thank you is gauche, inappropriate, and tacky—my mother's word—then there's little I can do for you.)

However, I'm happy to report that at least some parents are resurrecting the lost art of the handwritten note and instilling it as an important practice. I know this fact because I recently received an arduously penned thank you note from my six-year-old friend, Theo Trucks, son of friends Heather Schroder and Jesse Trucks. I was also privy to the agonies writing that letter produced. I got my first clue when Heather called one day a few weeks ago. Her words were,

"Can you hear the existential howl in the background? That's my son melting down at having to write you a thank you note."

I almost caved—telling her not to worry—that my birthday gift of two books didn't require a thank you note. But Heather was adamant. She and Jesse are determined to rear a child (Note: One *rears* children; one *raises* pigs.) who is compassionate, thoughtful, respectful, and a pleasure to be around. They are succeeding, but it's not easy work for today's parents, especially when friends of theirs don't hold their own children to the same standard. A few weeks earlier, Heather attended a gathering where those present were stunned that she required her son to write thank you notes.

"How *bourgie* [sic—*bourge*ois]!" one adult scoffed.

Another offered: "I didn't even send thank you notes for my wedding gifts."

Apparently, these speakers were proud to flaunt their disregard of fundamental courtesies that prevent us from inflicting misery on one another. This withering exchange didn't deter Heather, though. She was unmoved, not folding even at the moment Theo wailed, "I love friend Eddie, but he doesn't *neeeed* a thank you note!"

I'm proud to say that Theo's missive arrived in the mail a few days later. The old excitement surged through me as I withdrew the envelope from the mailbox. I couldn't have been more thrilled than if I'd been a six-year-old on the receiving end of a pen pal exchange. Relationships take work, and in my hand was evidence of a tedious, painstaking, and laborious expression of friendship that I happily display on the wall of my office as testament to the lost art of handwritten notes. Another bonus is that Theo graciously consented to let me share my handwritten treasure. To that end, I proudly append the result:

The front and back copy of a letter from
Theo Trucks mailed to the author.

ACKNOWLEDGMENTS

We are tremendously grateful to Tom Anderson, whose patience was immeasurable and whose help was invaluable during this process. We'd like to thank all our family and friends for your encouragement and support.

Thank you, Norbert Elliot, Frances Ward, and the staff at Purple Breeze Press for providing this opportunity and for your gracious patience, kindness, and understanding.

Thank you to all *Appalachia Bare Magazine* contributors, subscribers, submitters, readers, and perusers. Thank you to all our social media followers.

We'd also like to extend a special thank you to the following: Tennessee Mountain Writers, The Authors Guild of Tennessee, Pellissippi State Community College, Appalachian Heritage Project, The Young Creative Writers Workshop, The James Agee Conference, Briar Haus Writes, The Suffrage Coalition, Grant Mincy, Jim Clark, Trent Eades, Mary Ruden, Mark Maguire, Dorrie Pratt, Ruth Anne Hanahan, and especially Carol Luther, who helped light the spark for such a labor of love.

AFTERWORD

I have been a writer as far back as I can remember. I found a piece of paper in my father's belongings after he passed away from the scourge of cancer at the age of sixty-six. The paper was about the size of one's palm and random ballpoint scribbles adorned the page. Then I read my father's handwriting atop the scribbles: *Delonda wrote this when she was six weeks old*. I asked my mother about it, and she told me that one day I just randomly grabbed a pen, bent over, and started "writing" like I knew what I was doing. Many years later, I can attest that a writer's dreams can come true in ways she never expected. And I am forever grateful for a trusted mentor who gave wise and caring counsel along the way.

Writing a book is a wild ride. First, you have your ticket (the contract). Second, you wait in line (the writing process). Third, you take your seat and buckle in (the publisher's turn). And, if you survive the whole ride without throwing up or losing your mind, you're doing great. This book is my first ride, and even though I had more than a few start-stops along the way, the experience has been invaluable.

At the outset, Ed and I thought it wouldn't take much time to put this book together because I had already edited our respective works that were featured in the magazine. My job would be easy, we decided. No problem. But after putting together the manuscript, I realized I had forgotten to consider something crucial. Everything in the online world doesn't transfer perfectly to the paper world (hyperlinks, for example). So, numerous things, including linked sources, had to be wrangled and tossed onto the paper, Chicago Style.

I have learned many things as a writer on this adventure: An understanding publisher is like gold. A writer shouldn't trust her own perception of that "faraway" timeline. Leave room for surprises and disruptions before spouting off a finished-by date. Realize that I am a writer and writers are human (at least for now, we are… mostly).

Delonda Shown Anderson
Chief Editor/ Co-Founder Appalachia Bare

NOTES

SECTION 1: MOUNTAIN FAMILY

3. Potato Soup with a Side of Poverty.

named after James Agee's great grandfather.: Miller McDonald, *Campbell County Tennessee USA* (LaFollette: County Services Syndicate, 1993), 1:108.

renamed Grantsboro. The area was actually first named Grantsbor*ough*, then changed to Agee in honor of James Harris Agee. The area's name was changed a final time to Grantsboro.

James Grant. McDonald, *Campbell County Tennessee USA*, 108.

cornbread and milk. The cornbread and milk are mixed together into a cold gruel. It's considered somewhat of a treat for many people in the mountains. Many people like it with buttermilk.

8. The Ballad of Barbara Allen.

from the Scottish Lowlands: "Mountain Lingo: Where Did 'Ma-maw' and 'Pa-paw' Come From," *Appalachian Magazine*, November 30, 2017. Web. [broken link]

dated January 2, 1665/66: Samuel Pepys, "Tuesday 2 January 1665/66," *The Diary of Samuel Pepys*. Web.

1675 to 1750.: English Broadside Ballad Archive, "Barbara Allen's Cruelty or The Young Man's Tragedy." Web.

as late as 1855.: "Glasgow Broadside Ballads: Cheap Print and Popular Song Culture in Nineteenth-century Scotland," Special Collections Department, Library, University of Glasgow. Web.

cruelty of Barbara Allen.: Oliver Goldsmith, *The Vicar of Wakefield* (London: Adam & Charles Black, 1903), 25.

into tears with… 'The Cruelty of Barbara Allen.': "Barbara Allen / Barbary Allen / Barbary Ellen," *Mainly Norfolk: English Folk and Other Good Music*. Web.

"Sir John Grehme and Barbara Allan.": Thomas Percy, *Reliques of Ancient English Poetry: Consisting of Old Heroic Ballads, Songs, and Other Pieces of Our Earlier Poets* (Ex-classics Project, 2016), 637-638. Web.

study of printed sources,": Ronnie D. Lankford Jr, "Francis Child Biography," *All Music*. Web.

listed as #84: Francis J. Child, *English and Scottish Popular Ballads*, ed. Helen C. Sargent and George L. Kittredge (Boston: Houghton Mifflin Company, 1904), 180-81.

SECTION 2: MOUNTAIN PEOPLE

11. Interview with George Brosi.

child is father of the man.": William Wordsworth, "'My Heart Leaps Up," in *Willaim Wordsworth, Selected Poems*, ed. Walford Davies (London: J. M. Dent & Sons Ltd., 1990), 106.

"Jesus wept.": *King James Bible*, "The Gospel According to Saint John," (Thomas Nelson, 1984), 129.

light within the tribe.": Joseph Parisi, "Langston Hughes," in *Voices & Visions Viewer's Guide*, (Chicago: American Library Association, 1987), 21-24.

dueling banjos, and many other things.": David C. Hsiung, *Two Worlds in the Tennessee Mountains: Exploring the Origins of Appalachian Stereotypes* (Lexington: University Press of Kentucky, 1997).

12. Joyous Freedom: An Interview with Knoxville, Tennessee's Fourth Poet Laureate.

storytellers & songwriters. Poboys & Poets, "Poboys & Poets," Facebook. Web.

to light up as if by fire; to propel. Merriam-Webster Dictionary, s.v. "Fire."

androgynous misogynist. Talib Kweli, "Twice Inna Lifetime," *Mos Def and Kweli Are Black Star*, recorded 1998.

Rhea's term. Rhea Carmon—Knoxville, Tennessee's previous poet laureate.

13. The Brilliant but Troubled Anna Catherine Wiley.

coal-bearing lands.": "In Search of the Big Chestnut," *Coal Creek Watershed Foundation*, May 16, 2014. Web.

New York financiers": As I understand, Knoxville community leaders and New York bankers coerced H. H. Wiley through a series of lawsuits that contested his coal assets. If things continued in this direction, Wiley faced the draining of his fortune, so, he made a deal that gave Knoxville and New York the land, and, in exchange, he ended up gaining money and business contacts.

July 1881 to March 13, 1909.": Revans, "Coal Creek Mining and Mfg Co.," *Anderson County Tennessee Genealogy and History*/ TNGen, August 07, 2011. Web.

new impressionist quality: Betsey B. Creekmore Special Collections and University Archives, "Anna Catherine Wiley Sketches Collection," *The University of Tennessee Knoxville Special Collections*, May 25, 2006. Web.

of Monet's Impressionism.": "Wiley, Catherine (1879- 1958)," *The Johnson Collection*. Web.

one of the best in the South.": Elizabeth H. Moore, "Anna Catherine Wiley (1879-1958)," in Tennessee Encyclopedia, March 1, 2018. Web.

made an entire career of art.": Jack Neely, "A Portrait of the Artist: Lloyd Branson," *Knoxville Mercury*, November 4, 2015. Web.

Southwestern Fair in Atlanta, Georgia.: Moore, "Anna Catherine Wiley," Web.

only then it has meaning.: "Wiley, Catherine (1879- 1958)," The Johnson Collection. Web.

a mental breakdown': Moore, "Anna Catherine Wiley," Web.

hollow-eyed figures.": "Wiley, Catherine (1879- 1958)," The Johnson Collection. Web.

$107,000.: Mike Blackerby, "Tennessee Painting Fetches Record Price," *Knoxville News Sentinel*, January 30, 2012. Web.

sense of personal culture.: Anna Catherine Wiley, "Anna Catherine Wiley Lecture XVIII The Mind in Art; Modern Painting," in *The Woman's Athenaeum: For the Intellectual Industrial and Social Advancement of Women*, (New York: The Woman's Athenaeum, 1912), 176-188.

14. Appalachia's Sons: A Triptych of Talent.

Republicans, and soldiers.": "Jesse Stuart, Poet, Dies at 76; Chronicler of Kentucky Hills," *The New York Times*, February 19, 1984, 48.

"pure hell": George Scarbrough, interview by author, 1990.

singing at the plow.": Jesse Stuart, "Leaves From a Plum Grove Oak," in *Man with a Bull-Tongue Plow* (New York: Dutton, 1959), 7.

"Prayer for My Father": Jesse Stuart, "Prayer for My Father," in *The South in Perspective: An Anthology of Southern Literature*, by Robert Vaughn, Linda Francisco, and Edward Francisco (Upper Saddle River: Prentice-Hall, 2001), 1110.

"Design": Robert Frost, "Design," in *The Poetry of Robert Frost*, ed. R. Frost and E. C. Lathem (London: Jonathan Cape, 1916), 302.

"Pattern for Death": James Still, "Pattern for Death," in *The South in Perspective: An Anthology of Southern Literature*, by Robert Vaughn, Linda Francisco, and Edward Francisco (Upper Saddle River: Prentice-Hall, 2001), 1135.

"Death is a Short Word": George Scarbrough, "Death is a Short Word." in *The South in Perspective: An Anthology of Southern*

Literature, by Robert Vaughn, Linda Francisco, and Edward Francisco (Upper Saddle River: Prentice-Hall, 2001), 1122.

"Tenantry": George Scarbrough, "Tenantry." Web. The poem was used with the author's permission. (Reference interview with author 1990.)

my peculiar ways.": George Scarbrough, interview by author, 1990.

kindness of strangers.": Tennessee Williams, *A Streetcar Named Desire: A Play in Three Acts* (New York: Dramatists Play Service Inc., 1947), 3.1.102-103. Web.

15. On the Other Side of Agee.

fierce races of men.": Edgar Allan Poe, "A Tale of the Ragged Mountains," in *Edgar Allan Poe Stories* (New York: Platt & Munk, 1961), 127-142.

Edict of Nantes: This edict granted religious tolerance, especially to the Huguenots and Calvinists.

road overseer.: Dr. G. L. Ridenour, *Land of the Lake: An Early History of Campbell County* (Jacksboro: Action Printing, Ltd., 1991), 40.

"Musician/U.S. Rifler,": "United States, Registers of Enlistments in the U.S. Army, 1798-1914," database with images, FamilySearch (Washington D.C.: National Archives and Records Administration, n.d.), citing NARA microfilm publication M233. Web.

orderly sergeant, and served guard duty...: Larry and Edie Doepel, "Dr. James Harris Agee Memorial Page," Find a Grave, October 24, 2004. Web.

public spirited man": Paul W. Lemaster, *Campbell County, Tennessee Obituaries, 1822-1959*, copy, n.d.

noble character and high standing,": Manatee Chapter of Anna Maria Daughters of American Revolution, *Agee Family 1670-1936* (Miami: Florida Genealogical Records, 1954), 13.

ability, integrity and justice.": Doepel, "Dr. James Harris Agee," Web.

listed as boot maker.: "United States, Census, 1880," database with images, FamilySearch (Washington, D.C.: National Archives and Records Administration, n.d.) citing NARA microfilm publication T9. Web.

at 'Clinch Street' in Knoxville,: "United States, Panama Canal Zone, Employment Records and Sailing lists, 1905-1937," database with images, FamilySearch (St. Louis, Missouri: National Personnel Records Center), citing NARA record group 185. Web.

1905-1908.: U.S. Postal Service, "United States, Panama." Web.

Laura Whitman Tyler.: "Michigan, Births, 1867-1902," database with images, FamilySearch, citing Secretary of State, Department of Vital Records, Lansing. Web.

16. Faulkner in Knoxville.

postage stamp of native soil,": Stephen B. Oates, *William Faulkner: The Man and the Artist* (New York: Harper & Row, 1987), 62.

milieu for an artist to work in.": Oates, *William Faulkner*, 62.

down to the Gulf of Mexico.": Justin Faircloth, "William Faulkner's Memphis: Architectural Identity, Urban Edge Condition, and Prostitution in 1905 Memphis," *Inquiry: The University of Arkansas Undergraduate Research Journal* 6, no. 4 (2005): 4-13. Web.

17. Richard Marius' *Reading Faulkner*, A Book Review.

Reading Faulkner: Richard Marius, *Reading Faulkner* (Knoxville: University of Tennessee Press, 2005).

not too painful root canal: Marius, 1.

when it seems harmless: Marius, 10.

what he has suffered: Marius, 23.

eliminates the omniscient narrator: Marius, 23.

plane of our consciousness: Marius, 23.

[emerging] ideologies of the world.: Marius, 31.

the hands of Henry Ford.": William Faulkner, *Mosquitoes* (New York: Washington Square Press, 1985), 104-105.

target of jokes and satire: Marius, 31.

postage stamp of native soil,": Stephen B. Oates, *William Faulkner: The Man and the Artist* (New York: Harper & Row, 1987), 62.

condemn the writer as racist.: Marius, 45.

regardless of color.: Marius, 46.

It's not even past.": William Faulkner, *Requiem for a Nun* (New York: Vintage International, 2011), 73.

sound and fury/ signifying nothing.": William Shakespeare, *The Tragedy of Macbeth*, in *The RSC Shakespeare William Shakespeare Complete Works*, ed. Jonathan Bate and Eric Rasmussen (New York: The Modern Library, 2007), 5.5.27-28.

must kill himself.: Marius, 56.

I don't hate it!": William Faulkner, *Absalom, Absalom!* (New York: Vintage Books, Random House, 1972), 378.

carry on the Compson line.": Marius, 55.

impotent against death.: Marius, 64.

pages of Faulkner's *Absalom, Absalom!*.": Teresa Day, Linda Randulfe Marquez, and Craig Cornwell (Executive Producers), Tom Thurman, (Director). (2018). *Robert Penn Warren: A Vision* [Motion Picture]. East Tennessee PBS. Web.

especially sons.: Marius, 120.

permissibly killed.: Marius, 133-134.

like to think is the truth.: Joseph L. Blotner and Frederick L. Gwynn, ed., *Faulkner in the University* (Charlottesville: University Press of Virginia, 1995), 273-74.

18. Cormac McCarthy's *Stella Maris*, A Book Review.

latest novel. Cormac McCarthy, *Stella Maris*, (New York: Alfred A. Knopf, 2022).

see it in color.: McCarthy, 69.

Something like that.: McCarthy, 10.

there's two of them.: McCarthy, 65.

separate species.": McCarthy, 54.

long time coming back.: McCarthy, 137.

fire and language.: McCarthy, 62.

end of something.: McCarthy, 190.

19. Nancy Nanye'hi Ward–Cherokee Warrior for Peace.

one who goes about.". David Ray Smith, "Nancy Ward," Tennessee Encyclopedia, March 1, 2018. Web.

born in Chota: Chota was considered the "mother town" and capital of the Cherokee Nation. The place was also a city of refuge for Cherokee who were in trouble or distress.

Lenni Lenapé Tribe.: The Delaware tribe were dubbed the "Grandfather Indians" because they were believed to be the earliest settlers of the Atlantic Seaboard. A few sources say Nancy Ward was descended from the Cherokee war chief Osconostota. Others, like James Mooney in *Myths of the Cherokee* (G.P.O. 1902), say she was half Cherokee with a white English father. The latter is highly unlikely.

a son, Five Killer (Hi-s-ki-ti-hi).: Five Killer's name has also been spelled Hi-s-*gi*-*d*i-hi, Hiskyteehee, and is registered as "Hisketehe" in the War of 1812. The source for this information was found in "United States, War of 1812 Index to Service Records, 1812-1815," database with images, FamilySearch. (Washington, D.C.: National Archives and Records Administration, n.d.).

more pointed and deadly.": History of American Women, "Native American Women: Nancy Ward," History of American Women: Colonial Women 18th-19th Century Women. Web.

Ghighau (pronounced Gee-gah-ooo): Other spellings of Ghighau: Agi-ga-u-e, Ghi-g*a*-u, Ghi-gu-u.

spoke through the Beloved woman.": History of American Women, "Native American Women," Web.

warrior's "Black Drink,": Smith, "Nancy Ward," Web.

purified themselves for war.": Norma Tucker, "Nancy Ward, Ghighau of the Cherokees," *The Georgia Historical Quarterly* 53, no. 2 (June 1969): 192-200.

the white man's advance...: Museum of the Cherokee People, Cherokee, North Carolina.

newly formed United States": Allyson Schettino and Caroline Klibanoff, "Nanyehi 'Nancy' Ward Helped Lead the Cherokee Nation as a Teenager," *Teen Vogue*, November 30, 2020. Web.

5,000,264 acres of their land.: Tucker, "Nancy Ward, Ghighau,"192-200.

cut the ropes that bound her.": "'But we are your mothers, you are our sons': Gender, Sovereignty, and the Nation in Early Cherokee Women's Writing," in *Indigenous Women and Feminism: Politics, Activism, Culture*, ed. Shari M. Huhndorf, Jeanne Perreault, Jean Barman, and Cheryl Suzak (Vancouver: UBC Press, 2010), 44.

while I am Ghi-ga-u.'": Angela Minor, "Nanyehi—Nancy Ward: Warrior. Peacemaker. Beloved Woman of the Cherokee," *Smoky Mountain Living Magazine*, August 1, 2018. Web.

known to free "Patriot prisoners.": The New York Historical Society, "Life Story: Nanyehi Nancy Ward (1738–1822), Ghigau of the Cherokee," *Women & the American Story*, February 2019. Web.

avoiding further conflicts.: Debra Michals, "Nanyehi (Nancy) Ward," National Women's History Museum. Web.

the same sky covers us all.": Annie Walker Burns, "Quotations from Appleton's Cyclopaedia of American Biography," in *Military and Genealogical Records of the Famous Indian Woman, Nancy Ward* (Washington D.C.: A.W. Burns, 1957), 188.

saved each other's lives.": Minor, "Nanyehi—Nancy Ward," Web.

advocating armed resistance.: The New York Historical Society, "Life Story: Nanyehi," Web.

Let your women hear our words.: Pat Alderman, *Nancy Ward: Cherokee Chieftainess* (Johnson City: Overton Press, 1990), 65.

recognized in the Cherokee Constitution.": Ronald Satz, *Tennessee's Indian Peoples from White Contact to Removal, 1540-1840* (Knoxville: The Tennessee Historical Commission, 1979), 86-87.

disappeared toward Chota.": Alderman, *Nancy Ward: Cherokee Chieftainess*, 83.

a winsome and resourceful woman.": Smith, "Nancy Ward," Web.

an imperious air.": Harold W. Felton, *Nancy Ward, Cherokee* (New York: Dodd, Mead & Company, 1975), 12.

also possessed humility with others.": Minor, "Nanyehi—Nancy Ward," Web.

an antiques dealer in Maine.: Polk County Chamber of Commerce, "Nancy Ward Gravesite," Tennessee River Valley. Web.

transform the government "to a republic.": R. Smith, "The Nancy Ward Page," in The Cherokee History and Culture SiteRing. Web.

20. Danita Dodson's *The Medicine Woods*, A Book Review.

called *The Medicine Woods*.: Danita Dodson, *The Medicine Woods* (Eugene: WIPF and Stock Publishers, 2022).

Bring healing back...: Danita Dodson, "Faces of the Poorest and Weakest," in *The Medicine Woods* (Eugene: WIPF and Stock Publishers, 2022), 76.

SECTION 3: MOUNTAIN REGION

22. Freak Show: Confessions of a Modern Southerner.

I don't hate it!": William Faulkner, *Absalom, Absalom!* (New York: Vintage Books, Random House, 1972), 378.

inexpensive and easy to procure.": A. L. Swan, "America's Dean of Letters," *Newsweek,* August 25, 1980, 66.

"Freedom at the Freak Show: Virginia Mccarley, "Freedom at The Freak Show: Carnivalesque Imagery in the Fiction Of Eudora Welty, Flannery O'Connor and Katherine Anne Porter," Electronic Theses and Dissertations (Master's Thesis, eGrove: University of Mississippi, 2018). Web.

agile Southern furies.": Thomas Merton, "Flannery O'Connor: A Prose Elegy," in *Raids on the Unspeakable* (New York: New Directions, 1966), 37.

God's closing hand. Edward Francisco, Robert Vaughan, and Linda Francisco, *The South in Perspective: An Anthology of Southern Literature* (New Jersey: Prentice Hall, 2001), 707-08.

23. War in Coal Creek.

Rocky Top was once Lake City: The area is also known for Norris Dam, the TVA-FDR project built in the 1930s.

number stamped on it": Hugh Archbald, *The Four Hour Day in Coal: A Study of the Relation Between the Engineering of the Organization of Work and the Discontent Among the Workers in the Coal Mines* (New York: H. W. Wilson Company, 1922), 29.

where the coal was weighed": Joseph Husband, *A Year in a Coal-Mine* (Boston: Houghton Mifflin Co, 1911), 24.

battalion of state militia": Perry C. Cotham, *Toil, Turmoil, & Triumph: A Portrait of the Tennessee Labor Movement* (Franklin: Hillsboro Press, 1995), 62.

demonstration to the stockade.": Cotham, *Toil, Turmoil*, 64.

stockade door with a sledgehammer": Cotham, 70.

"blacklisted": Back in the day, businesses and/or bosses could blacklist an employee, meaning the boss could coordinate with other businessmen and ban 'Joe Coal' from working in a particular industry. So, no one would hire Joe.

scabs and blacklegs.": Cotham, 71.

they began to retreat.": Cotham, 73.

'shoot and be damned': "Coal Creek: Miners at Last Have Been Routed," *Daily Tobacco Leaf-Chronicle*, August 19, 1892, 1.

were killed. E. C. Bruffey, "Lives Were Lost: and Blood Was Spilled to Save Tennessee's Honor," *The Atlanta Constitution*, August 20, 1892, 1.

only a handful": Paul H. Bergeron, *Paths of the Past: Tennessee, 1770-1970* (Knoxville: University of Tennessee Press, 1979), 78.

point of death each time.: E. C. Bruffey, "Lindsay Talks: He Tells the Story of a Day He Will Long Remember," *The Atlanta Constitution*, August 23, 1892, 1.

24. Coal Creek: Fraterville.

"village of Brothers.": Coal Creek Watershed Foundation, "Coal Creek: War and Disasters," Coal Creek Watershed Foundation. Web.

succeeding his father as supervisor.: Andrew Roy, *A History of the Coal Miners in the United States* (Columbus: J L Trauger Printing Company, 1907), 406.

survived for a short time.: "Removal of Bodies from Mine," *The Nashville American*, May 21, 1902, 1.

all died together.: Coal Creek Watershed, "Coal Creek," Web.

—J. L. Powell.: Roy, *History of the Coal Miners*, 376.

Oh, God for one more breath…: Roy, 376-77.

—Powell Harmon.: Roy, 377.

the last bodies recovered.: Roy, 377.

haunted the land for days.: Marshall L. McGhee, *Coal Mining Towns: Stories and Pictures of Anderson and Campbell Counties* (Jacksboro: Action Printing, 1995), 64.

further added to the explosion.: Allen R. Coggins, "Fraterville Mine Disaster," Tennessee Encyclopedia, October 8, 2017. Web.

shortly before the explosion.": James P. Ulery, "Explosion Hazards From Methane Emissions Related to Geologic Features in Coal Mines," Center for Disease Control, April 2008. Web.

Creep: Kentucky Coal and Energy Project, "Glossary of Mining Terms." Kentucky Coal Education. Web.

sixteen-foot fan for aeriation. "Death Snatches 225 Men as They Delve in a Mine," *The Atlanta Constitution*, May 20, 1902, 1.

negligent at the inquest.: "Against Coal Creek Company: So Finds the Coroner's Jury in the Fraterville Horror," *The Atlanta Constitution*, June 25, 1902, 10.

wept bitterly on the stand.: Coal Creek Watershed, "Coal Creek," Web.

25. Coal Creek: Cross Mountain.

"Class B": "Briceville Mine Inspected Twice in Four Months," *Nashville Tennessean and The Nashville American*, December 10, 1911, 1A.

never "had a serious accident.": "Five Entombed Men in the Cross Mountain Mine are Found Alive," *Nashville Tennessean and The Nashville American*, December 12, 1911, 10.

confine the air and force it into: "Chief Inspector Reports on the Briceville Mine," *Nashville Tennessean and The Nashville American*, April 19, 1912, 14.

twelve feet thick and packed tight.": "Chief Inspector Reports," 14.

inspected every two months. "Briceville Mine Inspected," 1A

diggers being carried out. "Hardly One Ray of Hope for 207 Men Entombed in The Tennessee Mine," *The Atlanta Constitution*, December 10, 1911, 1, 2C

would be rescued alive": "Two Hundred Lives Snuffed Out in East Tenn. Mine Disaster," *Nashville Tennessean and The Nashville American*, December 10, 1911, 1A.

search for their husbands and sons.": The Atlanta Constitution, "Women and Children Wailing at Mouth of Ill-Fated Mine; No Hope for Entombed Miners," *The Atlanta Constitution*, December 10, 1911, 2C.

inner most recesses of the mine,": "All Dead," *The Atlanta Constitution*, December 11, 1911, 1.

overcome by the noxious gasses.": "All Dead,"1.

(essentially, an oxygen machine).: Artur W. Page, "'Safety First' Underground," in *The World's Work November, 1911, to April, 1912* (New York: Doubleday, Page & Company, 1912), 551.

twenty-five "oxygen helmets,": Page, "Safety First' Underground,'" 551.

poisonous gas at Cross Mountain.: "Canary Birds in Mine-Rescue Work," *Popular Mechanics*, 1912, 355.

Eighty-two men died: Philip Francis, "Seventy Years in the Coal Mines," RootsWeb. Web.

knocking on the walls of the mine.": "Forty-Nine Men Entombed in Mine Brought Out Dead," *Nashville Tennessean and The Nashville American*, December 14, 1911, 2.

five miners were rescued *alive*: "Thought Dead, Buried Miners Are Found Alive," *The Atlanta Constitution*, December 12,1911, 13.

until discovered tonight.: The Atlanta Constitution, "Thought Dead," 13.

where the men arrived were affecting.": The Atlanta Constitution, "Thought Dead, 13.

175 coffins.: "Eight Bodies Taken from Ill-Fated Mine; No Hope of Rescue," *Nashville Tennessean and The Nashville American*, December 11, 1911, 7.

unidentified by their widows and mothers.": "Forty-Nine Men Entombed," 2.

gas present in the air.": "Chief Inspector Reports," 14.

from one entry to another...": "Chief Inspector Reports," 14.

26. Freeing Free Hills.

means of avoiding scandal: Sonia W. Thomas, "Myths of Southern Women Seen; The Plantation Mistress: Woman's World in the Old South, by Catherine Clinton. New York:

Pantheon Books," The Christian Science Monitor, February 11, 1983. Web.

directed by Booker T. Washington.: Mary S. Hoffschwelle, "Julius Rosenwald Fund," Tennessee Encyclopedia, October 8, 2017. Web.

"cruel radiance of what is": James Agee, *Let Us Now Praise Famous Men*, In *Let Us Now Praise Famous Men, A Death in the Family, Shorter Fiction*, ed. Michael Sragow (New York: The Library of America, 2005), 26.

it's going to be a ghost town.": Joey Garrison, "Tennessee Community Founded by Freed Slaves Fights Extinction," *The Tennessean*, July 9, 2016. Web.

paternal grandfather, Hannaniah: The name has also been spelled Hananiah.

when such initiative is needed most.: Kimberlee Kruesi, "Tennessee Bans Teaching Critical Race Theory in Schools," *Associated Press*, May 25, 2021. Web.

and so dedicated, can long endure.": Steven B. Oates, *With Malice Toward None: The Life of Abraham Lincoln* (New York: Harper & Row, 1977), 366.

27. "Unwomanly Actions" in Appalachia's Labor Movement.

active in "council meetings": "The Power of Cherokee Women," *Indian Country Today Media Network*, Jan 10, 2011. Web.

"heads of Cherokee households,": Women History Blog, "Women's Rights in Cherokee Society," History of American Women, Dec 2008.

aged twenty-one and under.: Jacquelyn Dowd Hall, "Disorderly Women: Gender and Labor Militancy in the Appalachian South," *The Journal of American History* 73, no. 2 (1986), 360-64. Web.

"caustic chemicals"… "petty regulations": Hall, "Disorderly Women," 363-364.

joined them four days later.: Marie Tedesco, "Elizabethton Rayon Plants Strikes, 1929," *The Tennessee Encyclopedia of History and Culture*, Oct 8, 2017. Web.

"rent houses at high rates": Tedesco, "Elizabethton Rayon Plants," Web.

pulled at their machines.": Jacqueline Dowd Hall, Robert Korstad, and James Leloudis, "Cotton Mill People: Work, Community, and Protest in the Textile South, 1880-1940," *The American Historical Review*, 91, no. 2 (April 1986), 255.

where the term *sweatshop* **originated.:** Philip Dray, *There is Power in a Union: The Epic Story of Labor in America* (New York: Doubleday, 2010), 265.

"college-trained supervisors": Hall, "Cotton Mill People," 257.

was dynamited.": Tedesco, Web.

what they had.: Hall, "Cotton Mill People," 273.

hear grievances.: Tedesco, Web.

supposed to be slaves.": Hall, "Disorderly Women," 362.

Women couldn't be supervisors. Edward N. Akin, "Reviewed Work: Like a Family: The Making of a Southern Cotton Mill World" by Jaquelyn Dowd Hall, James Leloudis, Robert Korstad, Mary Murphy, Lu Ann Jones, Christopher Daly," The Florida Historical Quarterly 67, no. 1 (1988): 101-103.

"men's work".: Price V. Fishback, "Operations of 'Unfettered' Labor Markets: Exit and Voice in American Labor Markets at the Turn of the Century," *Journal of Economic Literature* 36, no. 2 (1998): 747.

"cheek to jowl,": Dr. Howard Markel, "How the Triangle Shirtwaist Factory Fire Transformed Labor Laws and Protected Workers' Health," *PBS News*, March 31, 2021. Web.

flammable fabric": Markel, "How the Triangle Shirtwaist," Web.

thirty-three inches wide, dark, and unsafe.: Markel, Web.

only reach the sixth floor.: David von Drehle, "Uncovering the History of the Triangle Shirtwaist Fire," *Smithsonian Magazine*, 2006. Web.

bulk of whom were women. "141 Men and Girls Die in Waist Factory Fire; Trapped High Up in Washington Place Building; Street Strewn with Bodies; Piles of Dead Inside," *New York Times*, March 26,1911, 1.

28. Flooding of Hallowed Ground: TVA and Appalachian People in the 1930s.

William Henry Hawkins: Marshall Wilson, *Norris Reservoir Scrapbook* (LaFollette: LaFollette Press, 1967), 35.

eminent domain: Eminent domain is a policy where the government can condemn private land for the good of citizenry as a whole.

13,449 families from sixteen reservoir areas.": Donald Davidson, *The Tennessee* (Nashville: J.S. Sanders & Company, 1992), 255.

immediate needs of the family.": Daniel Schaffer, "Environment and TVA: Toward a Regional Plan for the Tennessee Valley, 1930s." *Tennessee Historical Quarterly* 43, no. 4 (1984): 333-354.

speculators, land developers, and industrialists.": Ronald D. Eller, *Miners, Millhands, and Mountaineers: Industrialization* *of the Appalachian South, 1880-1930* (Knoxville: University of Tennessee Press, 1995), 44.

due to these tactics.: Eller, *Miners, Millhands*, 56.

company-owned house.": Melissa Walker, "African Americans and TVA Reservoir Property Removal: Race in a New Deal Program," *Agricultural History* 72, no. 2 (1998): 417-428.

toxic coal ash sludge: "EPA Response to Kingston TVA Coal Ash Spill," United States Environmental Protection Agency. Web.

40 feet from the shore.": J. R. Sullivan, "A Lawyer, 40 Dead Americans, and a Billion Gallons of Coal Sludge," *Men's Journal*. May 28, 2021. Web.

God only knows.: William and Wilma Wirt, "Peggy Westerfield Papers," by University of North Carolina Southern Historical Collection, Sept 19, 1938. Web.

29. Redneck Hillbilly.

"Hillbilly Hare.": Robert McKimson, dir. *Merrie Melodies*, "Hillbilly Hare," aired August 12, 1950, performed by Stan Freberg, John T. Smith, Mel Blanc.

"redneck" first occurred: Bethany E. Bultman, *Redneck Heaven: Portrait of a Vanishing Culture* (New York: Bantam Books, 1996), 12.

white laborers of the American South.": Kathleen Drowne and Patrick Huber, "Redneck: A New Discovery," *American Speech* 76, no. 4 (2001): 434.

populist reforms.": Drowne, "Redneck: A New Discovery," 434.

refer to them as 'rednecks.'": Robert Shogan, *The Battle of Blair Mountain: The Story of America's Largest Labor Uprising*, (Boulder: Westview Press, 2004), 169.

esp. of the south-eastern U.S.": Patrick Huber and Kathleen Drowne, "Hill Billy: The Earliest Known African American Usages," *American Speech* 83, no. 2 (Summer 2008): 214.

fires off his revolver as fancy takes him.'": Richard B. Drake, *A History of Appalachia* (Lexington: University Press of Kentucky, 2001), 121.

'Cane Hill billies.' Huber, "Hill Billy: The Earliest," 216.

'hill billies' down in Texas. J. A. Jones, "Southern Sentimentalism: As Seen by a Southerner Through a Flash," *The Freeman*, October 22, 1898, 2.

We don't like it 'a little bit.'": Huber, "Hill Billy: The Earliest," 215.

harebrained stereotypes of hillbillies.": Jeff Biggers, *The United States of Appalachia* (Emeryville: Shoemaker & Hoard, 2006), 5.

faux elegies: Many people in the mountains don't agree with Vance's philosophy in the book. Others may feel like his take on life in Appalachia betrays his heritage. For a true, deep-down-in-the-gut hillbilly, a betrayal is a sting rarely forgotten.

30. What We Don't Do Anymore.

scene in the movie *Deliverance*: *Deliverance*, directed by John Boorman (1972; Warner Bros., Inc.)

with people and light.": James Dickey, *Deliverance* (New York: Dell Publishing, 1994), 240.

and turnip greens and cherry pie.": Dickey, *Deliverance*, 240.

SECTION 4: MOUNTAIN CULTURE

32. J. D. Vance's *Hillbilly Elegy*, A Book Review.

smack your head and ass together.": J. D. Vance, *Hillbilly Elegy* (London: William Collins, 2016), 153. The quote in the book is attributed to J.D. Vance's grandmother.

smartest person I knew: Vance, *Hillbilly Elegy*, 65.

not the same.": Vance, 108.

Bob never was physically abusive.": Vance, 71.

you didn't even notice it.: Vance, 73.

another species.: Dorothy Allison, *Bastard Out of Carolina* (New York: Dutton, 1992), 32-33.

America's elite institutions?": Vance, 207.

regardless of IQ or circumstances.": Psychology Today Staff, "Grit," *Psychology Today*. Web.

permanent American underclass: Vance, 261.

foolproof, inexpensive, and safe: Charles Murray and Richard J. Herrnstein, *The Bell Curve* (New York: The Free Press, 1994), 548-49.

33. Vera and Bill Cleavers' *Where the Lilies Bloom*, A Book Review.

young adult novel: Vera and Bill Cleaver, *Where the Lilies Bloom* (New York: Signet, 1969).

"cloudy headed": Cleaver, *Lilies Bloom*, 10.

We're forgotten people.": Cleaver, 145.

Spring would come—it always did.: Cleaver, 145-46.

all that goes with it.": Cleaver, 17.

gladly pay for.: Cleaver, 39.

We've got work to do.": Cleaver, 91-2.

interest in mountain children.": Goodreads, "Vera Cleaver," goodreads.com. Web.

into a movie: *Where the Lilies Bloom*, directed by William A. Graham (1974; Radnitz/Mattel Productions).

34. You Cain't Whup a Bear.

deck of Hillbilly Tarot cards: Dr. David Brown, "The Hillbilly Tarot & Playing Cards," Sacred Robot Publishing, Jan 1, 2014.

35. Goat Man.

Faulkner was "Count No 'Count,": Stephen B. Oates, *William Faulkner: The Man and the Artist* (New York: Harper & Row, 1987), 62.

proud of our crazy people.: LANEIA, "Top 10 quotes from 'Designing Women'," autostraddle, Aug 26, 2011. Web.

grass skirts of the hula dancers.": R. M. Jr, "Charles McCartney, Known for Traveling With Goats, Dies at 97," *The New York Times*, November 23, 1998.Web.

Prepare to meet thy God.": Mona B. Smith, "Goat Man Leaves the Scent of Legend," *Knox Tn Today*, June 4, 2019. Web.

sometimes numbered up to thirty.: Darryl Patton, *America's Goat Man: Mr. Ches McCartney*. Little River Press, 1994.

more or less sticks to goats.: Cormac McCarthy, *Suttree* (New York: Vintage International, 1979), 197-98.

37. The Strange Case of David Lang.

what had happened to David Lang.: Frank Edwards, *Stranger than Science* (New York: Lyle Stewart,1959), 16.

"intimations of immortality": William Wordsworth, "Ode: Intimations of Immortality from Recollecctions of Early Childhood," in *Library of World Poetry*, (Minneapolis: Amaranth Press, 1970), 622-24.

weak and weary…": Edgar Allan Poe, "The Raven," in *Edgar Allan Poe Stories* (New York: Platt & Munk, 1961), 489.

rapping at my chamber door.": Poe, "The Raven," 489.

39. Danny Laemon.

"revvin' up his mill": Robert Mitchum, vocalist, "Ballad of Thunder Road," by Don Ray and Robert Mitchum, 1958. United Artists released a movie called *Thunder Road* in 1958 starring the same Robert Mitchum.

40. Writings About Appalachian English.

pronoun for [the word] *it*…").: Wylene P. Dial, "The Dialect of the Appalachian People," *West Virginia History Journal* 30, no. 2 (1969): 463-71. Web.

realms of England and Scotland.": Dial, "The Dialect," 463-71. Web.

peppered with these: Dial, 463-71.

nor never shall be,": William Shakespeare, *The Tragedy of Richard the Third*, ed. Jonathan Bate and Eric Rasmussen (New York: The Modern Library, 2007), 4.4.509.

proper way to address someone?: Charles Barber, Joan C. Beal, and Philip A. Shaw, *The English Language: A Historical Introduction* (New York: Cambridge University Press, 2009), 33-34.

in one area for centuries. To be sure, not all Appalachians within a cognomen stay in an area. Some venture out and find their own niche. Others are tired of venturing and come back home. Still others stay in the Appalachian towns where they were born.

complex demonstratives,": Salia A. Tagliamonte and Laura Rupp, "This Here Town: Evidence for the Development of the English Determiner System from a Vernacular Demonstrative Construction in York English," *English Language and Linguistics* 23, no. 1 (2017): 86.

due to the geographic isolation of the area.: Tagliamonte, "This Here Town," 86.

late fourteenth century.": Tagliamonte, 89.

rich literature associated with 'voiceplace': Nancy M. Hayward and Amy D. Clark, ed., "Introduction," *Talking Appalachian: Voice, Identity, and Community* (Lexington: University Press of Kentucky, 2013), ix.

the concept of an Appalachian identity…: Hayward, *Talking Appalachian*, 4.

English language substituted.": Hayward, 3.

before Chaucer,": Walt Wolfram, "Is There an 'Appalachian English'?" Appalachian Journal 11, no. 3 (1984): 215-224.

Appalachian English*es*: Hayward, 8.

innovations of others.: Michael Montgomery, "The Historical Background and Nature of the Englishes in Appalachia," in *Talking Appalachian: Voice, Identity, and Community*, ed. Amy

D. Clark and Nancy M. Hayward (Lexington: University Press of Kentucky, 2013), 29.

dialect and bad grammar are the same thing.": Ivy Jude Elise Brashear, "Rural Reality: How Reality Television Portrayals of Appalachian People Impact Their View of Their Culture" (Master's Thesis, Lexington: University of Kentucky, 2016), 29.

can't understand, you know?: Brashear, "Rural Reality," 52.

uneducated and lazy.": Savanah Alberts, "Hootin' and Hollerin': The Portrayal of Appalachians in Popular Media," Pearl S. Buck Writing Competition (Morgantown: West Virginia University), 2021.

peculiarities in speech and custom.": J. Eagle Shutt and Viviana Andreescu, "Violent Appalachia: The Media's Role in the Creation and Perpetuation of an American Myth," *Journal of the Institute of Justice and International Studies* 36, no. 1 (2009): 62-75.

mountaineers were much in the news.": Anthony Harkins, "The Hillbilly in the Living Room: Television Representations of Southern Mountaineers in Situation Comedies, 1952-1971," *Appalachian Journal* 29, no. 1/2 (2001): 109.

41. On the Lost Art of the Handwritten Note.

verray parfit, gentil knight.": Geoffrey Chaucer, "General Prologue," in *Geoffrey Chaucer, Chaucer's Major Poetry* (Englewood Cliffs: Prentice-Hall, 1963), 239.

PHOTO CREDITS

Mountain Family

3. Potato Soup and a Side of Poverty.

"A mess" of rockfish: The author's father, Benny Franklin Shown, Sr ca. early 1980s at our home in Demory Hollow, LaFollette, Tennessee. From Delonda Shown Anderson's Collection.

Eating 'cornbread & milk' with a side of bread and milk: The author's mother, Pamela Joy *Brooks* Shown, in 1979 in Demory Hollow, LaFollette, Tennessee. My father took this photo on the day of my great-grandmother Goins' funeral. From Delonda Shown Anderson's Collection.

8. The Ballad of Barbara Allen.

Cora Lee *McNeeley* Goins (aka Old Mamaw Goins) ca 1970s at her home in LaFollette, Tennessee. She moved there sometime after leaving Westbourne Coal Camp. The author greatly enjoyed spending time with her there. From Delonda Shown Anderson's Collection, cropped.

Mountain People

12. Joyous Freedom.

Joseph "Black Atticus" Woods: Made for Knoxville series promo.

14. Appalachia's Sons: A Triptych of Talent.

George Scarbrough (sitting) with Edward Francisco on Scarbrough's back porch in Oak Ridge, Tennessee.

19. Nancy Nanye'hi Ward—Cherokee Warrior for Peace.

Nancy Ward likeness: from the Museum of the Cherokee People. Photograph taken by Delonda Shown Anderson.

Nancy Ward statue: from the Museum of Appalachia. Photograph of an image of the statue taken through glass by Delonda Shown Anderson.

Mountain Region

23. War in Coal Creek.

Images of check tags and scrip: The weigh check tag (middle) is from Coal Creek. Scrip 5 is from Blue Diamond Coal Company in Westbourne, Tennessee, the coal camp where the author's maternal family lived; and scrip 10 is from Block Coal and Coke Corporation in Block, Tennessee, where the author's paternal great grandfather, Lawrence Monroe Goodman, worked in the mines. These items were inherited from author's mother. Photo by Delonda Shown Anderson.

Miners Posing: "Coal Creek Miners," 1893, Library Collection, UA464 1st Co.C, 42106, Tennessee State Library and Archives, Tennessee Virtual Archive, https://teva.contentdm.oclc.org/digital/collection/p15138coll18/id/2986.

24. Coal Creek: Fraterville.

"The Most Appalling Mining Accident..." *Journal and Tribune*, May 22, 1902. Newspaper Microfilm; https://sharetngov.tnsosfiles.com/tsla/exhibits/disasters/fraterville.htm

"Coffins Containing Dead Miners: W. R. Queener, a Miner, is shown in Foreground, Wearing Miner's Lamp. He Had Been at Work in Mines Thirty-Six Hours and Was Only Brought Out by Force, so Intense Was His Desire to Recover the Dead" *Knoxville Sentinel*, May 21, 1902, Newspaper, Microfilm. https://sharetngov.tnsosfiles.com/tsla/exhibits/disasters/fraterville.htm

25. Coal Creek: Cross Mountain.

Boys working at Cross Mountain Mine. According to Hine's citation, one boy is James O'Dell. The other boy is unknown. One year later, the Cross Mountain mine disaster occurred, killing at least 84 men. O'Dell is not listed on the names of the deceased.— Hine, Lewis Wickes, photographer. *Hard work and dangerous for such a young boy. James O'Dell, a greaser and coupler on the tipple of the Cross Mountain Mine, Knoxville Iron Co., in the vicinity of Coal Creek, Tenn. James has been there four months. Helps push these heavily loaded cars. Appears to be about 12 or 13 years old. Location: Coal Creek, Tennessee, 1910. December.* Photograph. https://www.loc.gov/item/2018676201/. In 1954, the Library of Congress received Lewis Hine's photographs and negatives from the National Child Labor Committee who stipulated that "There will be no restrictions of any kind on use of the Hine photographic material."

Ready for his shift in the mines at Block: Lawrence Monroe Goodman (right), the author's paternal great grandfather. He eventually became a mine foreman. The author dearly loved him.

28. Flooding of Hallowed Ground.

President Franklin D. Roosevelt signing the TVA Act: The Act, signed in 1933, created the Tennessee Valley Authority https://commons.wikimedia.org/wiki/File:Roosevelt_signing_TVA_Act_(1933).jpg. Image in the public domain

Monument to George Norris: Located at Norris Dam State Park. Photo by Tom Anderson

Mountain Culture

34. You Cain't Whup a Bear.

   A card honoring the author's brave attempt, taken from a deck of
   Hillbilly Tarot cards created by Dr. David Brown.

41. The Lost Art of the Handwritten Note.

   Front and back copy of a letter from Theo Trucks mailed to the
   author.

ABOUT THE AUTHORS

EDWARD FRANCISCO

Edward Francisco is a native Chattanoogan who now lives in Charleston, South Carolina. He was Professor of English and former Writer in Residence at Pellissippi State Community College in Knoxville, Tennessee. His poetry, short stories, and essays have appeared in over seventy-five publications. His most recent play, *Which Side Are You On: The Florence Reece Story*, was very well received. He has authored ten books, including *The Dealmaker* (WP Books), *The Literary Relationships of Robert Coles and Walker Percy* (Edwin Mellen Press) and *The South in Perspective: An Anthology of Southern Literature* (Prentice Hall publishers). His books of poetry include, *Death, Child, and Love* (Walker Publishers), *Alchemy of Words* (Birch Book Press), and *Only the Word Gives us Being* (Birch Book Press). He is the Co-founder and Associate Editor of *Appalachia Bare Online Magazine*.

DELONDA SHOWN ANDERSON

Delonda Shown Anderson is a native of Campbell County, Tennessee, where her family has deep roots dating back centuries. She hails a degree in English literature from the University of Tennessee, Knoxville, and is a former editor of *Imaginary Gardens Literary Magazine* for Pellissippi State Community College. She is a published poet and has received awards for her stories about the region. She is the Co-founder

and Chief Editor of *Appalachia Bare Online Magazine*, Board member and Treasurer for Tennessee Mountain Writers, Inc., a freelance editor, and writing consultant.

www.ingramcontent.com/pod-product-compliance
Lightning Source LLC
Chambersburg PA
CBHW022144170626
46807CB00005B/2074